TO
MY WIFE

SON OF OSCAR WILDE

SON OF
OSCAR WILDE

Vyvyan Holland

FOREWORD AND REVISIONS BY
MERLIN HOLLAND

CARROLL & GRAF PUBLISHERS, INC.
New York

Carroll & Graf Publishers, Inc.
19 West 21st Street
New York
NY 10010-6805

First published in the UK by Rupert Hart-Davis 1954
First published, with Merlin Holland's foreword,
by Oxford University Press 1988

First Carroll & Graf edition 1999

Foreword and revisions © Merlin Holland 1987, 1999

Photographs from the collection of Merlin Holland

ISBN 0–7867–0701–1

Printed and bound in the EC

Acknowledgements

My grateful thanks are due to the Earl of Birkenhead, who encouraged me to write this book, to H. Montgomery Hyde, M.P., who allowed me to take copies of the letters written by Oscar Wilde to Reginald R. Harding and who has helped me in checking references; to the President and Fellows of Magdalen College, Oxford, who gave me access to the letters from Oscar Wilde to William Welsford Ward and allowed me to publish them; to Miss Cecil Ward, daughter of W. W. Ward, to whom I am indebted for "An Oxford Reminiscence" by her father, and who was able to identify many of the persons referred to in Oscar Wilde's undergraduate letters; to the Marquess of Queensberry for permission to use the two letters from Lord Alfred Douglas in Appendix D; and to the Rev. H. Chadwick, S.J., for his patience with regard to the chapter dealing with Stonyhurst College.

I also wish to acknowledge, with many thanks, the permission given to me to quote passages from two books: T. G. Wilson, F.R.C.S.I., Litt.D., author of *Victorian Doctor*, and Ernest Benn, Ltd., publishers of *My Memoirs* by Sir Frank Benson.

VYVYAN HOLLAND

Foreword

By Merlin Holland

I was eight when *Son of Oscar Wilde* was first published in the autumn of 1954. It was not however, until I was fifteen that my father gave me a copy of the book, touchingly inscribed on publication day seven years before 'For Merlin with fondest love from his Daddy'. Until then Wilde, for me, had simply been the author of *The Importance of Being Earnest* and a book of fairy stories, but *Son of Oscar Wilde* led me to read other books about my grandfather and now he appeared in a new light, not wholly flattering but more human, and somehow more approachable as a relation. I began to realise what an emotional strain it must have been for my father to have had to relive those days of childhood as a boy, much the same age as I, but already an orphan. He had, as it were, laid to rest the bitter memory of those early years by the cathartic effect of recording them for posterity. The gradual process by which he came to terms with his past is described by one of his closest friends, Alec Waugh, in *My Brother Evelyn and Other Profiles*:

When I left for the Middle East in September 1941 I felt I knew Vyvyan Holland as well as I have ever known any human being . . . nothing would have surprised me more than to have been told fourteen years later that one of the best selling books of the 1954 autumn season would be *Son of Oscar Wilde*.

I had scarcely heard him mention his father's name and was surprised when going over an old guest book of the Odde Volumes, to have him pause as he turned a page and point without comment to his father's signature . . . It is natural for the son of a highly successful writer to be diffident about following in the same profession and inviting comparisons. But he carried his love of anonymity to an extreme point. His friends carefully avoided mention of his father.

Part of his reluctance was a form of self-defence. No one could be more completely normal and he resented being pestered by homosexuals, foreigners for the most part, who wanted to pay their respects to the sacred memory of 'Oscar, the martyr'. There was another point too. He had adored his mother, he had seen the misery which the case had brought on her. He resented his father's having inflicted this misery on her. Yet loyalty would not allow him to speak a word against his father. Better remain silent . . .

When I returned to London in the summer of 1945 after very nearly four years in the Middle East, I found changes in many of my friends but nothing surprised me more than to find Vyvyan talking freely about his father, without embarrassment, with affection, with wit, treating the sudden vogue in Wilde as a piece of comedy that would have made his father chuckle. During the war he had married Thelma Besant, who had grown up when the scandal of the 'nineties was half forgotten; to her the name of Oscar Wilde was one to be acknowledged proudly. Gradually and with great tact she broke down the barrier. If that barrier had not been broken down, *Son of Oscar Wilde* would not have been written. The Wilde saga would have lacked its coping stone.

On publication the critics were unanimous in their praise of the book. Throughout the reviews the words 'moving', 'sensitive', 'without bitterness', 'dignified' and 'poignant' appear repeatedly, and re-reading them today it is significant how few people had been aware as late as 1954 that Wilde had been married with two sons. My father was quite overwhelmed by the public response. He received several hundred letters from friends, acquaintances and even total strangers, but one letter, quoted by him in his later book *Time Remembered* he found especially moving:

But of all the letters I received I was most affected by one which came from France after the appearance of the translation of my book there. It was written from Issy-les-Moulineaux and this is a translation of it: 'It so happened that I saw your father nearly every day for several months on end. I was ten or eleven years old at the time, a rather small, shy, quiet little boy. My own father did not like his work interrupted by a mid-day meal, and he used to send my mother and me out to lunch 'Chez Béchet', a small restaurant run by Monsieur Béchet and his wife at No 42 rue Jacob. Madame Béchet claimed to have been cook in 'a big house' and, indeed, she cooked efficiently, simply and cleanly. A few days ago I looked through the curtain over the door, to see if the place retained anything of its former character. It seemed to me to be lighter and brighter, but it was still recognisable. The spiral staircase, for instance, in the far right hand corner, which went up to the first floor, was still there.

In those days, the ground floor was frequented by casual visitors, but the first floor was kept for regular clients. All the tables there were reserved and you had to be a friend of Madame Béchet, a charming woman, to be allowed into it. My mother and I went there every day, and the table reserved for us was the one next to 'Monsieur Sébastien*' whose personality attracted my mother very much, as she noticed that there was a certain style about him which was lacking in the other clients, who were mostly minor commercial travellers and clerks. It was a most respectable clientèle; the noisier, more conversational patrons were put by the window and from there they descended in order of quietness, to the table occupied by 'Monsieur Sébastien', who ate with his back to the far wall, silent and alone.

As we occupied neighbouring tables, we used to bow to him on arriving and on leaving, or he would bow to us if we were the first to come or go. My mother held him up to me as a model of deportment, elegance and good breeding, and often used to talk to me about him on our way to the restaurant. What was the sorrow that weighed him down and made him so sad? He must be very unhappy; what happened to him? My mother, who was as tender-hearted as she was pretty, worried about him. She would have liked to have talked to him, but he himself never talked.

Once or twice a thin, rather dark man came to lunch with him: I discovered afterwards that he was Ernest Lajeunesse.‡

I must describe Monsieur Sébastien as he appeared to me. The first thing that struck me was the width of his shoulders, and his height; he was like a man who had been very big but was wasted by illness. His face must have been handsome, indeed it retained traces of this; but his features were extremely tired. He made gentle movements with his hands. I think that his eyes which he seldom raised, must have been a rather dark blue, but I have not a very good eye for colour. An expression of great kindness but of infinite weariness.

He ate what Madame Béchet put before him, and she looked after him like a child. She would prepare special dishes for him and kept coming to see whether he was eating them. If things were not going to

* Monsieur Sébastien was, of course, Sebastian Melmoth, the name assumed by Oscar Wilde when he went into exile and by which he was known until his death.
‡ Ernest Harry Lajeunesse 1874–1917. French littérateur. He published some brief recollections of Oscar Wilde in the *Revue Blanche* of December 15, 1900, and in his book *Cinq Ans Chez les Sauvages*, 1901.

her liking she would say: 'Come, Monsieur Sébastien, you must not give up!'

One autumn evening, while putting on my overcoat after finishing my meal, I clumsily upset something, perhaps a salt-cellar, on Monsieur Sébastien's table. He said nothing but my mother scolded me and told me to apologise, which I did, distressed by my clumsiness. But Monsieur Sébastien turned to my mother and said: 'Be patient with your little boy. One must always be patient with them. If one day you should find yourself separated from him . . .' I did not give him time to finish his sentence, but asked him: 'Have you got a little boy?' 'I've got two,' he said. 'Why don't you bring them here with you?' My mother interrupted, saying: 'You mustn't ask questions, Lucien!' 'It doesn't matter: it doesn't matter at all,' he said with a sad smile. 'They don't come here with me because they are too far away . . .' Then he took my hand, drew me to him and kissed me on both cheeks. I bade him farewell, and then I saw that he was crying. And we left.

While kissing me, he had said a few words which I did not understand. But on the following day a bank employee who used to sit at the table on the other side of us asked us: 'Did you understand what Monsieur Sébastien said last evening?' 'No,' we replied. 'He said in English: "Oh, my poor dear boys!"'

The bank employee went on to say: 'I am almost certain that he is a great English writer who became mixed up in a scandal which rocked England.' My mother replied that she could not imagine such a sympathetic man being mixed up in a scandal, and he replied: 'When a man is too successful, people are envious of him.'

A few weeks later, 'Monsieur Sébastien' ceased to go there. Thanks to the other client who was the only one to witness what had happened, I realise that I had been given those two kisses vicariously—I was just at the age at which you had last seen him. I ask myself whether my clumsiness was not, perhaps, well timed, since it was an opportunity for him to send you an indirect message.'

This letter, written with such sincerity and feeling, gave me a new aspect of my father's last years. In a subsequent letter from the same gentleman, he summed up the whole French attitude towards Oscar Wilde in the following words: 'That your father was destroyed is an inescapable fact. Had he not, within a few hours, lost his social position, his fortune and his freedom? And in family ties, his mother, his wife and his children? And what also counts so much, the hope of being able to regain everything, or even part of it? Who could have fought against it all? And it was at this point that he understood, that he realised, that he had been made the scapegoat of puritan hypocrisy.' (*Time Remembered*, 1966, pp. 9–12.)

Son of Oscar Wilde closes with an end and a beginning. The stray threads of Oscar's last tormented years are woven together; his debts had been paid, his children had been educated, the first collected edition of his works had appeared in 1908, and his earthly remains had been transferred from the simple grave in Bagneux to their final resting place in Père Lachaise. For my father, however, an eventful life lay in front of him. He was called to the Bar in 1912 and practiced briefly as a barrister but when Germany invaded Belgium in 1914 he volunteered almost immediately and served for most of the war in France and Flanders with the Royal Field Artillery. His brother, my uncle Cyril, was killed in action in 1915 but my father survived; he was wounded once, mentioned four times in despatches and awarded the OBE in 1919. Between the wars he travelled extensively in Europe making a modest living and a reputation for himself as a French translator. In 1940, being too old at 54 for active service, he was asked to join the French Service of the BBC where he remained until 1948. From then until his death in 1967 he continued his career as an author and translator. In his last years he found an entirely new outlet for his talents; with his extensive knowledge of the history of costume and antiques he became an historical adviser to the film industry.

August 1961 in London was a long succession of hot days. My father used to rise early to write. One morning he woke me suggesting that we walk in Hyde Park for exercise. The quiet city in pale cool sunlight was a new experience for me; there were no buses and few cars and we could converse with little more than the dawn chorus for background. Our early walks became a daily routine and sometimes for variety we would wander through the empty streets of Chelsea. My father would reminisce about his life between the wars, often prompted by passing a house where he had been a regular guest. He showed me the Wildes' house in Tite Street and the Royal Hospital Gardens, where he and Cyril had played as children, and there was no longer any pain at the memories or a need to conceal them. I was another generation who should know and take pride in them. It was shortly after this that he gave me my own copy of *Son of Oscar Wilde*. With the difference in our ages—he was then 75 and I 15—it might have been difficult for him to relate to a son so much younger; but it was not so. He had a lively sense of humour, a quick wit and a seemingly inexhaustible fund of anecdotes of which I never tired. He was loving and patient and had that very gentleness which he had seen in his own father so many years before but which he had enjoyed for all too short a time. By the time he died at the age of 80, the wounds of early childhood were largely healed and he was able to write in 1966:

> So, given good health, a nice home, plenty of books, a good meal with my family or my friends, with whom would I change? If ever I feel depressed, I count my blessings one by one and say that I am a happy man, that I have no quarrels with fate, which has almost over-whelmed me at times, but which has, in the end, left me, as it were, washed up on the shores of time in the warm sunlight. *(Time Remembered*, p. 191)

A Note for the 1999 Edition

When this book first appeared my father was adamant that he did not want an index. His reason was that he wanted his readers to enjoy it (if that is the right word for such a deeply moving story) as a heartfelt and emotional reminiscence and not as a historical document. In the forty-five years since its original publication, it has been much quoted and has become an integral part of the Wilde tragedy, so I feel that he would not now object to the courtesy of giving today's readers an index.

Without wanting to show any disrespect for my father, I have also taken the liberty of correcting some minor errors of fact in the text. Some of these came to light through readers' letters after publication, but the majority are a result of the detailed research that has gone into the hundreds of books and articles on Wilde published since then, as well as rediscovered family papers. Note numbers refer the reader to a section of addenda and corrigenda at the end of the book.

Preface

SOME TIME AGO I had a dream, in which my mother appeared to me and said: "I want you to tell the story of your childhood and of the loneliness of being Oscar Wilde's son in those far-off days when he was still alive, or only recently dead. Perhaps some people will blame you for it, but many more will approve of your doing so. Besides, you have a young son of your own, and you owe this to him."

I know nothing about spiritualism, nor am I a believer in manifestations from what is known as "the other side," but I was so impressed by this dream that I began mentally to reconstruct my early years. I found that everything seemed to fall into a certain pattern, nebulous at first, but gradually taking shape as my thoughts dwelt upon the past.

The story has no plot and very few highlights, but it may show the bitter cruelty of self-righteous human beings who forget that Christ said "Suffer the little children to come unto me," and base their religion on the Old Testament pronouncement that "the sins of the fathers shall be visited upon the children, even unto the third and fourth generation."

This is not a very amusing or entertaining story. I think, however, that it should be written as part of the whole tragic story of Oscar Wilde. There are always two sides to every question; there are often half a dozen. The Wilde story has been written by those who knew my father, by those who loved him, by those who hated him, and by those who never knew him. So I think it is not altogether inappropriate for the aftermath to be written on behalf of those who, although innocent, suffered in a hurt, uncomprehending way, wondering why they were not treated like other people.

Contents

Illustrations

Prologue

THE story of my ancestry has often been told, but this book may find a reader who, even though he is familiar with Oscar Wilde's books and plays, has no idea of his origin or of his background. Quite a number of people who have read his works do not even know that he was married and had two sons.

When the Chinese Emperors decided to honour a man by ennobling him, they ennobled his ancestors back to a certain number of generations, according to the degree of honour which they wished to confer upon him. But such patent of nobility did not pass to his descendants. The Chinese argued that a distinguished man was the cumulative result of the virtues or eccentricities of his ancestors, who should therefore be given the credit for having engendered him, but that he could not necessarily be expected to hand down these virtues to his progeny.

The name Wilde is Dutch in origin; there are many families of Wildes in the Low Countries to this day.[1] The original Irish Wilde was a certain Colonel de Wilde, the son of Jan de Wilde, a Dutch artist, examples of whose work hang in the Hague Art Gallery. This officer, whose name was presumably pronounced "de Vild*e*," was a soldier of fortune, who offered his services to King William III of England and took a prominent part in the Battle of Drogheda on July 1st, 1690, when Scottish aspirations to the English throne were finally destroyed. For his part in this battle the Colonel was granted lands in Connaught. Subsequently dropping the "de" from his name, he married an Irishwoman and, with his descendants, became more Irish than the Irish. The family estate was subsequently sold, but part of it, at Moytura in Connemara, was reacquired later by my grandfather.

The story that the Wildes originally came from Wolsingham, about twelve miles east of Durham, is due to confusion of thought and names. A certain Ralph Wilde was supposed to have crossed over to Ireland at the beginning of the eighteenth century and to have set up as a builder in Dublin. This is apocryphal. My ancestor's name was unquestionably de Wilde, and its Dutch pronunciation puzzled the simple Irish folk, with the result that "de Vilde" very soon became "the builder." Further evidence in support of this is that the son of the supposed Dublin builder, also named Ralph, became agent to Lord Sandford, at Castlerea in Roscommon; but no one who did not belong to the neighbourhood and who did not know the inhabitants intimately could possibly have occupied this position. The fact is that the Ralph Wilde who became Lord Sandford's agent was the only one of that name, and he was a descendant of the Dutch Colonel who originally settled in Connaught.

The only authority that I have been able to discover for the Wolsingham theory is R. H. Sherard, who claimed that it had come from Lady Wilde herself. No doubt she was quite prepared to accept this story—she may even have invented it—as she would naturally seize any opportunity of drawing a veil over the existence of the Colonel whom, as a soldier in the army of King William, she would regard as an arch-enemy of her country.

In due course Ralph Wilde married a Miss Margaret O'Flynn, of Caher in County Galway. The O'Flynns were a very ancient Roscommon Catholic family and Margaret O'Flynn was something of an heiress. The Wildes were Protestants; I do not know how they adjusted their religious differences, but probably Ralph Wilde embraced the Catho-

lic faith; otherwise he would hardly have been allowed to
marry Miss O'Flynn. This lady bore him three sons, one of
whom won the Berkeley Gold Medal for Greek at Trinity
College, Dublin, which my father won nearly a century later.
Another son went to Jamaica. The third was my
great-grandfather, Thomas Wilde. This brings us back to
the Durham part of the story.

Thomas Wilde was destined to be a doctor. He was
therefore sent to Durham to become a medical student,
Durham having the reputation of providing the best medical training in the British Isles. In those days, largely
owing to religious prejudice connected with the belief in
the resurrection of the body on the Day of Judgment, it
was almost impossible for English medical students to obtain bodies to dissect. So anyone arriving at an English
medical school armed with a dead body was not only
assured of a cordial reception, but was excused his train-
ing-fees as well. My great-grandfather was credited with
travelling from Castlerea to Durham accompanied by a
corpse obtained somehow in Ireland to pay his fees. People
were not so fastidious in those days or so sensitive to unpleasant smells. Embalming was practically a lost art and
any form of preservation was quite unknown; so I hardly
like to think of the condition in which my great-grandfather's offering must have arrived. Anyway, the gift seems
to have been acceptable, and Thomas qualified as a doctor
and returned to Ireland, where he settled down as a country doctor and married a Miss Emily Fynne.

At this juncture the family appears to have become Protestant again. This further improved the status of the
Wildes, as the lady's father, John Fynne of Ballymagibbon
near Cong in County Mayo, belonged to the Irish aristoc-
racy and was connected with some of the more important
families in Connaught, among whom were the Surridges
and the Ouseleys. My father was always particularly proud
of his connection with the Ouseley family, which held a

distinguished diplomatic and military record. The Fynnes themselves were, to say the least of it, eccentric and, as Mr. T. G. Wilson, an eminent Irish surgeon himself, says in his *Victorian Doctor,* which is a life of my grandfather:

> The division between genius and madness is very narrow. The Fynnes were undoubtedly very unstable mentally, and there can be no doubt that much of the later peculiarities of the Wilde family and perhaps much of their genius, can be traced to the Fynne strain in their blood.

My great-grandfather, Dr. Thomas Wilde, was a picturesque character, loved and respected throughout the countryside round Castlerea where he practised. To quote Mr. Wilson again:

> In those days there was but one road running from north to south in County Roscommon, and working conditions for a doctor must have been very difficult . . . Thomas Wilde's practice ranged all over the countryside and included rich and poor, peasant, priest and landlord alike. He practised all his long life, and did his rounds on horseback until the end. He must have been worth seeing, when at nearly eighty years of age he cantered along on his spanking chestnut, encased in his voluminous many-caped riding-coat, broad-brimmed leather hat, buckskin smalls, top-boots, overalls and spatterdashes, with a red culgee coming up to the middle of his nose. Oh, it was a great sight to see that man strip in the hall of a cold night before he went up to the ladies. No representative of Hamlet's gravedigger ever threw off the same amount of covering and no doctor ever will again, we are sure.

Dr. Thomas Wilde had three sons. The two elder became clergymen; the third, born at Castlerea in 1815, was William Robert Wills Wilde, later to become Sir William Wilde, my grandfather.

From the foregoing it will be seen that the Wildes had not been Irish for more than three or four generations at the time of my father's birth. But, as Bernard Shaw pointed out, there is a subtle influence in the Irish climate which rapidly neutralises the characteristics of any other race.

Robert Harborough Sherard was the first biographer to attempt anything like a life of my father. As early as 1902 he produced a privately printed memoir entitled *Oscar Wilde: The Story of an Unhappy Friendship*. This was issued publicly in 1905, and in 1906 appeared his *Life of Oscar Wilde*, the book on which all the subsequent lives of my father have been based.[2] Many years before, Sherard had contemplated writing a life of Sir William Wilde and had painstakingly traced his ancestry, mainly from information supplied and indications given to him by Lady Wilde, of whom he was a close friend. So it may be assumed that, as far as it goes, this record is substantially correct, except in so far as the Wolsingham builder is concerned. Many of my father's biographers have researched, embellished and elaborated, but they have all started with Sherard.

I knew Sherard in his later years and found him a sincere and intelligent man, who felt that he had a mission to protect what was left of my father's good name. But he was trained as a journalist, and a journalist he always remained. A story was a story to him, so long as it was a good story; and if it was a good story, what mattered its accuracy or its source? Sherard's *Life of Oscar Wilde* should be considered from that point of view. It is full of inaccuracies, as, for instance, that my father was born in Merrion Square in Dublin, instead of in Westland Row.

My grandfather, Sir William Wilde, was a most important man in his day. He was the foremost eye-and-ear specialist of his time and a physician of international repute. While still under forty he was appointed Surgeon-Oculist to Queen Victoria. His medical books remained standard works for many years. His *Aural Surgery* was the first of the modern text-books on the subject and was far ahead of any book which had preceded it. But his greatest work in the medical field was the foundation of the Royal

Victoria Eye and Ear Hospital in Dublin.[3] He is credited with having invented the operation for cataract, and has been called "the father of modern otology."

He was also an eminent archaeologist, and wrote about a dozen books on Irish folk-lore, legend and tradition. The best known of these are *Irish Popular Superstitions, Irish Fairy Lore* and *The Ancient Races of Ireland,* all of which are still important sources for the study of Irish archaeology.[4]

At the end of 1851, being then thirty-six years of age, William Wilde married a lady whose fame was far more widespread than his own. Her name was Jane Francesca Elgee. She was the daughter of a Wexford lawyer and grand-daughter of a dignitary of the Irish Church, Arch-deacon John Elgee, Rector of Wexford, a scholar and a man of great personality and popularity. Elgee is an Icelandic name, derived from Alfgeirr, meaning Elf Spear, but my grandmother always declared that her great-grandfather's name was Algiati, and that he came to Ireland from Flor-ence and modified his name to Elgee for convenience. She no doubt had evidence to support this contention, which has been denied by some of her biographers, although they have never produced any evidence to the contrary. She asserted that the name of Francesca was that of her great-grandmother, arguing, with some reason, that it was unlikely that an Irish Protestant would call his daughter by the name of an Italian Roman Catholic saint. Her ap-pearance also supported her theory; like many Florentine women, she was tall, with black hair, blue eyes and a strik-ing figure. A painting of her at the age of thirty-eight by Bernard Mulrenin, R.H.A., clearly shows these character-istics. In later life my grandmother went further and claimed that Algiati was a corruption of Alighieri, and that she was descended from Dante; this was, I am afraid, a figment of her imagination.

Born in 1824,[5] Jane Francesca Elgee at a very early age

embraced the cause of the Irish people in their struggle against English tyranny. When she was twenty-three she was writing political articles and patriotic poems for Charles Gavan Duffy's paper, the *Nation*, signing them first John Fernshaw Ellis and later Speranza, a name which she took from the motto she adopted for herself of *Fidanza, Constanza, Speranza*. She was a fiery champion of nationalism and her writings were wildly inflammatory. She was also a woman of great courage. In 1848 there appeared in the *Nation* an article, about six thousand words in length, entitled *Jacta Alea Est*, and signed Speranza. It was frankly revolutionary and called upon the Irish people to rebel. Gavan Duffy had been arrested some time before on charges of sedition and could not possibly be held responsible for the article. However, at his trial the Irish Attorney-General quoted passages from *Jacta Alea Est* against him. My grandmother, who was in court, immediately rose from her place and cried with disdainful indifference: "I am the criminal who, as author of the article, should be in the dock. I am the culprit, if culprit there be!"

Speranza's connection with Irish politics waned after the conviction and transportation of Gavan Duffy, and they ceased altogether on her marriage to Sir William Wilde. The Wildes had three children, two boys and a girl. The second child was my father, who was christened Oscar Fingal O'Flahertie Wills.[6]

It has been said that my father was named after a son of Ossian, the third-century heroic poet of the Gael. That earlier Oscar was killed in single combat with King Cairbre at the battle of Gabhra. This is a fine romantic attribution, but it does not tally with the story told by my family, which is as follows:

In the year 1854 my grandfather read in a medical journal that King Oscar I of Sweden had been blind for some years. His symptoms were described; although he could not distinguish any forms, he could not only tell the difference between light and dark, but could also distinguish certain colours. This, then, was no disease of the optic nerve and, acting upon impulse, Dr. Wilde, as he then was, wrote to the King and suggested that he might be able to do something for him. The King of Sweden, desperate about his blindness, was naturally interested in anything that held out a hope of recovery. So my grandfather travelled to Stockholm, where he immediately diagnosed cataract and performed his operation.[7]

When the bandages were removed and the King found that he had recovered his sight, he was naturally immensely grateful. Then came the question of what fee should be charged. My grandfather, no doubt reluctantly, refused to take any, on the ground that the whole expedition had been undertaken at his own suggestion. The King was at a loss how to show his gratitude in a practical way, and asked the doctor if there was anything he could do for him; to which my grandfather replied: "I have just learned that my wife has given birth to a son, and I would feel highly honoured if your Majesty would consent to be his godfather." So Dr. Wilde returned to Ireland no richer than by a name to give his son. Three years later King Oscar conferred upon my grandfather the Swedish Order of the Polar Star.

So much for the name Oscar. Fingal was the legendary hero in Ossian's poems, to whom all Erin looked for deliverance from her foreign foes; it is not difficult to see Speranza's hand in this part of my father's christening. O'Flahertie must also have been my grandmother's contribution, derived from some real or imaginary connection with the "ferocious O'Flaherties of Galway." Wills was a family name, shared by Sir William and both his sons.[8]

My father gradually dropped his middle three names, though he still used all of them at Oxford. In the Oxford University Calendar his name as winner of the Newdigate

Prize in 1878 is given as Oscar O'Flahertie Wilde. Later he took an aversion to long strings of names, realising that public figures and famous people are usually known by only two, and sometimes even by one. When my elder brother was born, he received only one Christian name, Cyril; though my father must have changed his mind again, else why should I have been given three?[9]

So far the family history runs with comparative smoothness. My grandfather's reputation as a surgeon grew rapidly; he was knighted for his services to statistical science in 1864, and it was rumoured later that he was about to be made an Irish peer by Queen Victoria for his services to medicine.

About three years after my father's birth, Speranza's dearest wish was fulfilled in the arrival of a daughter, who was given the names of Isola Francesca.[10] Isola was, from the moment of her birth, the pivot around which the family affection of the Wildes revolved. Speranza, with the calm aloofness affected by Victorian parents, may have pretended to be indifferent, but my grandfather and the boys frankly worshipped Isola, and when she died, after a short illness, at the age of ten, the family was inconsolable. My father's *Requiescat*, written in her memory, has become a classic:

> Tread lightly, she is near
>   Under the snow,
> Speak gently, she can hear
>   The daisies grow.
>
> All her bright golden hair
>   Tarnished with rust,
> She that was young and fair
>   Fallen to dust.
>
> Lily-like, white as snow,
>   She hardly knew
> She was a woman, so
>   Sweetly she grew.

Coffin-board, heavy stone,
  Lie on her breast,
I vex my heart alone,
  She is at rest.

Peace, Peace, she cannot hear
  Lyre or sonnet,
All my life's buried here,
  Heap earth upon it.

Sir William Wilde's personal appearance in later life was by no means prepossessing, though a portrait of him by Mulrenin at the age of twenty-eight shows him as quite a pleasant-looking young man. Indeed, his portrait was included in an article in the *Pall Mall Gazette* which inquired into the fact that so many intelligent and eminent men were ugly; he was in good company with, among others, Disraeli, Huxley and Darwin. Yet in spite of this he was popular with women, of whom he was inordinately fond. Speranza was quite aware of this idiosyncrasy, and she soon accustomed herself to it and refused to let it upset her, so long as it did not interfere with her own life. But in the end, largely owing to Speranza's own action, it led to Sir William's downfall. The story of his affair with Miss Mary Josephine Travers has been told in nearly every book written about my father and his parents, and in so many different forms, that I feel I may be excused for giving the version accepted by the family.

Miss Travers, whose father, Dr. Travers, was a professor at Trinity College, Dublin, indulged in an intrigue with Sir William, and was in the habit of visiting him in his consulting-room, ostensibly as a patient. She was a bad-tempered and a very exacting woman: and Sir William eventually tired of her persistence and endeavoured to put an end to his association with her, even going to the extent of trying to send her out to Australia. She, however, would have none of it, and bombarded him with anonymous letters and poems; finally she had printed a

scurrilous pamphlet in which she accused him, under the
name of Dr. Quilp, of having chloroformed and violated
an innocent young lady, easily recognisable as herself. Miss
Travers had this pamphlet—which, as an added irritation,
was signed Speranza—distributed all over Dublin, and sent
copies to Lady Wilde by every post. After some weeks of
this persecution my grandmother lost patience, and on May
6th, 1863, she wrote a furious letter to Dr. Travers, accusing his daughter of immorality and attempted black-
mail. Dr. Travers ignored this letter and did not even show
it to his daughter, who came upon it by accident. She was
overwhelmed with satisfaction, as she now saw her way
clear to revenge. She brought an action for libel against
Lady Wilde.

The case was tried in Dublin in December 1864. Miss
Travers asked for £2,000 damages. Naturally the whole story
emerged to shatter Sir William's already dubious reputation; but it was in effect a little unfair to him. The truth was
that he had not, as Miss Travers alleged, seduced his patient, but that he had given medical treatment to his mistress. Such a delicate differentiation could not possibly carry
any weight in a Victorian court of law, though the award of
one farthing damages showed the jury's opinion of the value
of Miss Travers's virtue. But the case was a *cause célèbre*, not
only in Ireland but throughout the British Isles, and my
grandfather never recovered from the ridicule it brought
upon him. Although at the time of the hearing he was not
yet fifty, he seems thenafter to have lost much of his interest in life. He spent more and more of his time on his country estates in Moytura, near Lough Corrib in Connemara,
and died in Dublin in April 1876, when my father, still at
Oxford, was twenty-one.

My grandfather had never been a very thrifty man: I fear
that thrift is not one of the family failings. He left about
£7,000 to his widow and £4,000 to each of his sons.

My grandmother outlived my grandfather by twenty

years. My own recollection of her, when I was a very small boy, is of a terrifying and very severe old lady seated bolt upright in semi-darkness in her house at 146 (now 87) Oakley Street, in Chelsea, while the sun shone brilliantly outside. She was dressed like a tragedy queen, her bodice covered with brooches and cameos. The curtains all through the house remained permanently drawn, and the drawing-room was lit by guttering candles arranged in the corners of the room, as far away from my grandmother as possible, so that the heavy make-up with which she tried to conceal her age could not be detected. I protested strongly every time I was taken to pay her a duty visit; even when, many years later, I lived in Oakley Street myself, I never passed that part of the street without a sense of foreboding.

My father was devoted to his mother and very proud of her. Even at the height of his success and fame, when he had so many calls upon his time, he never failed to visit her in Oakley Street once or twice a week, and he always made a point of being present on her At Home days. When he was receiving handsome royalties from his plays, he made her life much more comfortable by supplementing her modest income. It was of her more than of his father that he was thinking when he wrote, in the document later to be known as *De Profundis*, "She and my father had bequeathed me a name they had made honoured not merely in literature, art, archaeology and science, but in the public history of my own country and its evolution as a nation." Her death, in February 1896, was a bitter blow to him, and he wrote, again in *De Profundis*: "No one knew how deeply I loved and honoured her. Her death was terrible to me; but I, once a lord of language, have no words in which to express my anguish and my shame." My mother, who knew how much her husband worshipped his own mother, made a special journey from Italy to England to break the news to him in Reading Gaol.

Between 1849 and 1893 Lady Wilde published thirteen books, of which the best known are *Ancient Legends, Mystic Charms and Superstitions of Ireland* and *Ancient Cures, Charms and Usages of Ireland.* Her biography, under the title *Speranza,* was published by Horace Wyndham in 1951.[11]

This book is not a Life of Oscar Wilde, of which there are already quite enough, but, in order to give it continuity, I will touch briefly upon the salient events of his early life.

He was born at 21 Westland Row, Dublin, on October 16th, 1854. When he was ten, and his brother Willie was twelve, they were both sent to Portora Royal School, at Enniskill.[12] In spite of the difference in their ages, the boys seem to have been in the same class. Little is known of the years that my father spent at school, as he seldom referred to them in later years. In the autumn of 1871, however, he won a Royal Scholarship in classics to Trinity College, Dublin, where he remained for three years.

At Trinity he came under the influence of the Reverend John Pentland Mahaffy, who was Professor of Ancient History at the College, and an eminent Greek scholar. My father had known him for some years, as Sir William Wilde and Mahaffy were old friends, having been drawn together by their archaeological interests. My father's keen appreciation of the Greek language and of all things Greek was a further bond between them and, under Mahaffy's guidance, he first won a Foundation scholarship at Trinity College, Dublin, and afterwards the Berkeley Gold Medal for Greek. Finally in 1874 he obtained a demyship, worth £95 a year, at Magdalen College, Oxford.

My father's knowledge of Greek was profound; but it was due more to a prodigious memory than to hard work. Such was his love of the language that he remembered every word he ever read in it, and acquired, in consequence, a vast Greek vocabulary. A story is told of a *viva voce* examination, in which one of the subjects was the New Testament in Greek. My father, being confident that he could pass any *viva voce* examination in Greek without any preparation, had not even troubled to look at it; and the examiner, suspecting this and being anxious to teach my father a lesson, told him to turn to Chapter 27 of the Acts of the Apostles and to start translating. This chapter is probably the most difficult in the whole of the New Testament, being the description of St. Paul's shipwreck on his way to Italy; it contains a number of obscure nautical terms which no one could be expected to know unless they had studied them. My father translated it perfectly, and when the foiled examiner told him that he had done enough, he replied: "Please may I go on? I want to see what happened to St. Paul."

Shortly after his arrival at Oxford, my father met John Ruskin, who was then Slade Professor of Art there. It has frequently been said that Ruskin moulded my father's character at Oxford, but it would be more accurate to say that Ruskin watered the seeds that had been sown by Mahaffy. My father's nascent aestheticism was reflected in his rooms at Magdalen, in which blue-and-white china was the dominant note; this may have been considered eccentric at the time, but it certainly could not have been considered degenerate. His rooms were among the most attractive in the college, overlooking the Cherwell; it is interesting to note that, although after 1895 the name Oscar Wilde was not mentioned at Magdalen for many years, the rooms occupied by him are now used exclusively for purposes of entertainment, and are officially known as the Oscar Wilde Rooms. On one of the windows he scratched his initials O.F.O'F.W.W. where they could still be seen until a few years ago, when the window was accidentally broken. The fragment of glass containing the initials is still preserved in the college.

The man under whose spell my father really did fall was Walter Pater. This obscure Fellow and Tutor of Brasenose College has been accused of being the most baneful influence ever to be at Oxford. His stolid appearance and austere method of life seemed to emphasise the paganism of his writings. He was, in theory at any rate, an out-and-out hedonist. The doctrine he preached was an exaltation of personal experience above all restrictions, "as the ultimate object of life," and he summed it up by declaring that "the theory, or idea, or system, which requires of us the sacrifice of any part of this experience, in consideration of some interest into which we cannot enter, or some abstract morality we have not identified with ourselves, or what is only conventional, has no real claim on us." In other words, he preached that physical sensation is an end in itself, to which it is noble to aspire.

This teaching, coming on top of that of Mahaffy and Ruskin, was exactly what my father required to send him headlong into the paths of aestheticism. Many of his biographers have pointed to his admiration of human beauty, and particularly of male human beauty, as an indication of incipient decadence. This is manifestly unfair. Youth in all its forms has always been an inspiration to the poet and the artist, and my father was only following the lead of Ruskin and Pater, neither of whom could be accused of decadence in admiring beauty for its own sake. Somewhat naturally his fellow-undergraduates did not understand this complicated outlook on life, and many of them even went so far as to chaff him about his exaggerated phraseology in both prose and poetry. To them a poet was a peculiar fellow anyway. Nevertheless, the only attempt to "rag" Oscar Wilde ended in ignominy for the would-be raggers; the story has been admirably told by Sir Frank Benson, a contemporary of his at Oxford, in *My Memoirs*:

At the time Wilde challenged attention by winning the Newdigate he was described by a Balliol don as a brilliantly clever scholar, who had strangely good taste in art and in humanity; a great appreciation of quality in pictures, in horses, in athletics and in ethics: emphatically at that moment a good judge of what is best. He was also possessed of the extraordinary muscular strength that you often find in big, loosely built Irishmen. So far from being a flabby aesthete, there was only one man in the college, and he rowed seven in the Varsity Eight, who had the ghost of a chance in a tussle with Wilde. On one occasion this vigorous athleticism, scarcely to be expected in that lazy, lumbering, long-haired, somewhat sallow-faced individual, with a greeny-brown coat and a yellow tie, came as an unpleasant surprise to the Junior Common Room of Magdalen College.

"Let's go and rag Wilde and break some of that furniture he is so proud of." No sooner said than done. Three or four inebriated intruders burst into their victim's room, the others followed up the stairs as spectators of the game. To the astonishment of the beholders, number one returned into their midst propelled by a hefty boot-thrust down the stairs; the next received a punch in the wind that doubled him up on to the top of his companion below; a third form was lifted up bodily from the floor and hurled on to the heads of the spectators. Then came Wilde triumphant, carrying the biggest of the gang like a baby in his arms. He was about Wilde's size and weight, and hefty at that. His struggles were fruitless, and he was borne by the poet to his own room and solemnly buried by him underneath a pile of his splendid and very expensive furniture— the entombed one was rich but inclined to be parsimonious. When the debris of tables, sofas, chairs and pictures had been raised to the height of a respectable mausoleum Wilde invited the now admiring crowd—crowds are so changeable—to sample the victim's cellar. No second invitation was necessary, and the corpse pinned down beneath the ruin of his rooms was soothed in his dying agonies by the gurgle of expensive liqueurs and choice vintages pouring down the throats of his uninvited guests.

There is no doubt that at Oxford my father lived the life of a normal undergraduate, playing games, drinking a little, cutting lectures and flirting whenever he got the chance. He was even discovered one day with a damsel reclining rather than seated on his knees; unfortunately for him, the discoverer was the young lady's mother, who wrote him a strongly worded letter on the subject. And there is abundant evidence that, towards the end of his Oxford career,

he was contemplating an early marriage with one of his kins-
women.

Oscar Wilde was popular at Magdalen and made a great
many friends. Among them was David Hunter Blair, afterwards Abbot of Dunfermline. Frank Miles, the artist, with
whom he later shared a house in London, was also a great
friend. Another was William Welsford ("Bouncer") Ward,
who, like my father, had won a classical demyship and took
a double first; in later life he was a successful lawyer, and in
1918 he became treasurer of the Merchant Adventurers. And
Reginald Richard ("Kitten") Harding.

I mention these last two because there have recently
come to light two collections of letters which throw a great
deal of light on my father's character during his Oxford days.
These letters are addressed to "Bouncer" Ward and to "Kitten" Harding. Harding got his sobriquet of "Kitten" from a
popular music-hall ditty of the time, which went something
like this:

> Parding, Mrs. Harding,
> Is our Kitting in your garding,
> Eating of a mutting-bone?
> No, he's gone to Londing.
> How many miles to Londing?
> Eleving? I thought it was only seving.
> Heavings! *What* a long way from home!

It was the era of nicknames and everyone had one.
Hunter-Blair was called "Dunskie," while my father was
known as "Hosky," a corruption, presumably, of Oscar. Even
Reginald Harding's brother and sister were known as
"Pussy" and "Miss Puss" respectively, and my father refers
to them all collectively as "the cat family."

These letters were all written in the three years 1876–
1878, when Oscar Wilde was between the ages of twenty-
two and twenty-four. Most of them were written during
vacations, though many of the later ones to William Ward
were addressed from Magdalen, as Ward, being a year senior

to my father at Oxford, took his degree and left the University a year before him.

These letters show my father in a very different light from the one in which some people have tried to put him during his Oxford days, and they serve to dispel the impression that he was a wilting and rather effeminate aesthete at that period. He was certainly intensely interested in the arts and wrote a great deal of poetry, but he seems to have divided his time between literature, art and healthy exercise. He writes enthusiastically about the salmon he has caught, about his shooting prowess and even of how good he is becoming at lawn tennis, a game then in its infancy; and he says that he is "too occupied with rod and gun for the handling of the quill."

A thread of tremendous zest for living runs through the letters, an eagerness to enjoy every moment of life to the full. He finds beauty in everything around him. Even a thunderstorm arouses his enthusiasm; writing to Ward from his uncle's vicarage at West Ashby he says: "I arrived here in an awful storm; it came down as if the angels thought the earth was on fire and were pumping fire-engines on us." The earlier letters, in 1876, are all signed in full, though the later ones are signed "Oscar Wilde" or "Oscar." In one letter to Ward, signed "Oscar F. O'F. Wills Wilde," he adds as a postscript: "I like signing my name as if it was to some document of great importance—as 'Send two bags of gold by bearer' or 'Let the Duke be slain tomorrow and the Duchess await me at the Hostelry.'" He deplores his own laziness in idling away time that he should have devoted to his studies, afterwards showing an almost childish delight and pride in taking a double first. And there is something very refreshing in the way in which from time to time he breaks into undergraduate slang, though it comes as a slight shock after the polished and well-balanced sentences which precede it.

Perhaps the most interesting feature of the letters is the way in which my father continually refers to his leanings, already very pronounced, towards Catholicism. He is fascinated by Cardinal Newman and attracted to him as a moth to a candle. In one letter to Ward he writes:

> I am going to see Newman at Birmingham, to burn my fingers a little more. Do you remember Wise of this place? He is awfully caught up with the wiles of the Scarlet Woman and wrote to Newman about several things; and received the most charming letters back and invitations to come and see him. I am awfully keen for an interview, not of course to argue, but merely to be in the presence of the divine man.

There is little doubt that he would have embraced the Catholic faith during his Oxford days had it not been for family opposition. "My moral obliquity," he is reported to have said during the last months of his life, "was largely due to the fact that my parents would never allow me to become a Catholic."

I have put the more important of these Ward and Harding letters into an appendix to this book, as I think that they are interesting documentary evidence of my father's attitude towards life during his undergraduate days at Oxford.*

In after years William Ward wrote a short memoir of Oscar Wilde at Oxford. It was discovered among his papers after his death by his daughter, Miss Cecil Ward, to whose courtesy I owe its appearance here.‡

In the rooms at Magdalen first occupied by William Ward and later by my father there is a drawing scratched with a diamond on one of the windows;[13] beneath the drawing is written "Little Mr. Bouncer" and it is signed by my father. It represents a somewhat rotund figure, surmounted by a bowler hat; if it is anything like an accurate portrait it may give a clue as to why Ward was named Bouncer.

---

* See Appendix A, p. 209.   ‡ See Appendix B, p. 250.

In 1877 my father and two other young men accompanied Professor Mahaffy on a tour of Greece; he had already travelled with Mahaffy in Italy, two years before. This visit to Greece consolidated his friendship with Mahaffy and confirmed his worship of Greek ideals of beauty.

In 1878 he secured a double first at Oxford by taking a first in Greats; he had taken a first in Moderations two years before. In 1878, too, he won the Newdigate Prize for English verse with his poem *Ravenna*.

Sir David Hunter Blair, in his book *In Victorian Days*, says that, in reply to a question put to him at Oxford as to his real ambition in life, my father replied:

> God knows; I won't be an Oxford don anyhow. I'll be a poet, a writer, a dramatist. Somehow or other I'll be famous, and if not famous, I'll be notorious. Or perhaps I'll lead the βίος ἀπολαυστικός for a time, and then—who knows?—rest and do nothing. What does Plato say is the highest end that man can attain here below? καθεύδειν καὶ ὁρᾶν τὸ ἀγαθόν—to sit down and contemplate the good. Perhaps that will be the end of me too.

But the fact is that he was a little disappointed at not being offered a Fellowship, as, after six years of academic life, first at Trinity, Dublin, and afterwards at Oxford, he had become so used to it that he would have been quite happy to adopt it as his own.

After leaving Oxford my father supported himself for six years by writing articles and poems and by lecturing, in England and in America. In 1884 he married my mother, Constance Mary Lloyd, whom he had met in Dublin in 1883.[14] She was twenty-four.

In its own way, my mother's family was not without importance. Both her father, Horatio Lloyd, and her grandfather, John Lloyd, had eminent careers at the English Bar and both became Queen's Counsel. My mother herself was half-Irish; her father had married a Miss Atkinson, of Dublin, who was connected with the Hemphills, a family of some consequence in County Tyrone. My great-uncle Charles Hemphill, who had been Conservative Member of Parliament for North Tyrone from 1895 to 1906,[15] and had held the position of Solicitor-General for Ireland from 1892 until 1895, was ennobled on his retirement from political life.

My mother's family were opposed to her marriage with my father, considering that he was not good enough for her. They were incurably middle-class and lived their lives by the strictest conventional code, so that my father's notoriety and flamboyance must have offended all their instincts, particularly as my parents were married when the aesthetic period was at its height. I shall have more to say about this aspect of my mother's family later.

That my mother was a very beautiful woman, and that she and my father were a devoted couple, are facts beyond dispute. Frank Harris's description of her as "a lady without particular qualities or beauty" leads me to believe that, as was his custom, he tried to exercise his charm upon her without success. He always disparaged women who did not succumb to his very distasteful advances, persuading himself that they must be very stupid and therefore, by a logical conclusion, ugly. I knew him when I was a young man, and I thought that he was the most sinister and repulsive person that I had ever met. His book about my father has already been exposed as a concatenation of lies, and it should join his other books of reminiscences in the dustbin.[16]

The stories told by my father's biographers about my mother's supposed stupidity are mostly inventions. Particularly the one about her interrupting my father's flow of language with the question: "Oh, Oscar! *Did you* remember to call for Cyril's boots?" This story bears all the hallmarks of untruth. In those days no man of fashion would dream of being seen carrying a parcel, no matter how small, through

the streets of London, and furthermore no lady of the period would have thought of saddling her husband with such
a domestic detail, when every middle-class household
boasted at least two servants to fetch and carry. Had my
father been seen carrying a parcel containing boots, whether
Cyril's or not, he would have been the laughing-stock of his
friends. It is quite possible that, as is the habit of women,
she interrupted a diatribe of which she did not wholly grasp
the import, but it was certainly not *à propos de bottes*. My
mother was not stupid by any standard; she was a woman of
considerable culture. She spoke French and Italian fluently,
and much of her reading was done in those languages. She
may not have had much sense of humour, but then she did
not have very much to laugh about.

To a certain extent my mother felt strange in the bohe-
mian, unconventional atmosphere of Chelsea, in spite of
the fact that all the most famous artists and authors of the
day were constant visitors at her house. It has often been
said that all her clothes were specially designed and chosen
for her by my father. This is not quite correct, for my mother
would never have submitted to such dictatorship. In the
eighties, when my parents were married, women's fashions
had reached the lowest depths to which they had ever
plunged until that time. The prevailing colours were mauves
and nondescript browns; the prevailing materials heavy silk
reps, corded silks and bombazines. Wasp-waists, bustles and
tight-fitting leg-of-mutton sleeves combined to make even
the most graceful woman look clumsy, and to deprive the
most beautiful of her attraction. It was even worse out of
doors, where women wore heavy fringed shawls, often
weighed down with jet beads, and bonnets which rose from
the back of the head straight into the air and gave the wearer
a peculiar lobster-like appearance. My father implored my
mother not to do herself the injustice of following this terrible fashion, but to look to a more classical period for her
inspiration. My mother, who was a great admirer of the Pre-

Raphaelites, was only too willing to comply with my father's wishes, and all the photographs of her taken at that period show her in loose, flowing, wide-sleeved garments which were admirably suited to her type of Irish beauty, and which she designed herself.

Throughout my early years there was one person who always made me happy, and that was my mother, whom I adored. I knew that she loved me too, but I was always conscious of the fact that both my father and my mother really preferred my brother to myself; it seems to be an instinct in parents to prefer their first-born. In *De Profundis* my father mentions my brother Cyril by name, but there is no mention of myself except collectively as "my children."[17] I was not as strong as my brother, and I had more than my fair share of childish complaints, which probably offended my father's aesthetic sense. I was more sensitive than Cyril, who was a tough little animal with higher spirits than I possessed. And, most of all, both my parents had hoped for a girl as their second child, just as my grandmother had hoped for a girl when my father was born.

CHAPTER I

The Happy Years

I WAS born in my parents' house in Tite Street in November 1886. Many years later, the doctor who attended my mother told me that it was a bleak, cheerless day, with a heavy fog, and that, summoned in haste, he had some difficulty in getting to Chelsea from his own house in Grosvenor Street. The doctor's name was Charles de Lacy Lacy; he was not only the family doctor, but his family and my own were close friends; he died in 1932, at the age of eighty-four; he was the kindest and gentlest of men, with an extraordinary influence over children and animals.

The Wildes already had one son, my brother Cyril, born seventeen months before myself, on June 5th, 1885. My arrival was a disappointment to my father, who wanted a daughter to remind him of his sister Isola, for whom he had always retained such a deep affection. If he had had a daughter, he would have named her Isola Deirdre. However, like other fathers before and after him, he had to take what was given him, and I was named Vyvyan Oscar Beresford. The name Vyvyan was, no doubt, a fantasy, in the same way that I named my own son Merlin; Oscar clearly needs no explanation; but where the Beresford came from has always puzzled me, as I cannot trace any connection between either my father's or my mother's families and the Waterfords. Nor do I think it was because my parents thought the name attractive.

In my birth certificate, my father's profession is given as "author." The declaration was made by my mother; my birth was not registered for some weeks after I was born, as my father and my mother each thought that the other had seen to the matter. When the time came, no one could remember the exact date on which I had been born, though everyone was sure that it was during the first five days of November; so eventually the 3rd was selected, as being the mean date. My mother's brother once told me that the real reason for the apparent confusion was that I was actually born on November 5th, but that this fact was suppressed, in order to avoid any possible connection between the Aesthetic Movement and Guy Fawkes Day. Be that as it may, one great advantage that I derive from this uncertainty is that I am completely immune from the importunities of astrologers as, far from being able to tell them the exact hour of my birth, I cannot be certain of even the exact day.

My parents had no more children. I had only one god-father; if I had a godmother I was never told who she was. My mother, who was a close friend of John Ruskin, asked him to be my godfather, but he refused, in a letter which I have, on the grounds that he was too old. My godfather was Mortimer Menpes, an artist of some repute in the eighties; I still possess some of his etchings which he bestowed upon me in lieu of a christening mug; the etchings are not very good, and there was always some element of doubt as to whether Mortimer Menpes did them himself. He was a man of private means, something of a dandy, and a friend of Whistler and all the Pre-Raphaelites. Many years later, when I was twenty-one, Sir William Richmond, R.A., told me that at one time Mortimer Menpes's name had been put forward for membership of the Royal Academy. Doubts were cast upon his being able to produce, unaided, any work of art at all, and at the beginning of this century a small committee of Academicians, including Richmond himself, was deputed to visit his studio and to ask him to paint or draw or etch something in their presence. Menpes stood upon his dignity, refused to comply and ushered the committee off the premises. He was not elected to the Royal Academy, and the significant fact is that after this incident he retired from the artistic world and never produced another work of art, though he continued to write about art until he died in 1938.

My brother also had only a godfather—the explorer Walter Harris, who spent his life travelling in obscure African and South Pacific countries, and once told my brother and myself, when we were very small boys, that he had unwittingly attended a cannibal feast and had partaken of the fare, which he described as being "rather like sucking-pig, but more delicate in flavour." But he admitted that when he discovered what he had eaten, he was unable to eat anything more for days. Walter Harris was a great friend of R. B. Cunninghame Graham. They shared a house in Tangier, where they lived as Moors; they both wore beards, and long sojourn in Morocco had deepened the tone of their skins; they also talked Arabic so well that they could pass as Moors. They had both made the pilgrimage to Mecca, and had entered the Kaaba. To have been discovered doing this as an infidel would have meant almost certain death, and Walter Harris told us that he very nearly betrayed himself by the way in which he washed his hands, which he did as a European and not as a Mahommedan, who would have performed his ablutions according to a certain ceremonial rite. Cunninghame Graham eventually embraced the Moslem faith and so, I believe, did Walter Harris.

It is difficult to be accurate in recalling one's earliest impressions and memories. In his early years there is so little change in a child's daily routine that what he thinks he remembers at the age of two or three may well have happened at the age of five or six; this applies particularly to children brought up in the country, in ancestral homes in which life has remained more or less unchanged for generations. Indeed, a child's so-called memories are often stories of his early childhood which have been so much repeated in his presence by relatives that he is convinced he remembers incidents which occurred almost at the time of his birth.

My brother and I were town-bred children. Many such, who spend all their lives in the same district or the same street, obviously suffer from the same disabilities as country-bred children, so far as memory is concerned; but we ourselves did pay a lot of visits and my recollections of these excursions into the outer world are quite clear.

The first time that I can definitely remember was when I was nearly three; it was summer-time, and my brother and I were staying at Frognal, near Sunninghill, with the Walter Palmers, who were great friends of my mother. They were connected with the firm of Huntley & Palmer, and I even remember being taken to the biscuit factory in Reading and eating biscuits straight out of the oven.

We often stayed with the Palmers, and I have happy memories of our visits, to which we always looked forward eagerly. I remember sitting on a grown-up person's knee and having my hand held while "writing" letters to my mother about the Shetland ponies, and the poppies in the garden, and goldfish in the artificial lake at the back of the house, which I tried to lure into my clutches with soft words—or was it soft worms? And the nursery tucked away in one wing of the house, in which the Palmer children, older than ourselves, held undisputed sway. Both my brother and I went rather in awe of the elder daughter, Gladys,[18] who ruled the nursery with all the power of her eleven years. When I was twelve or thirteen I claimed to remember these things, only to be told that I was inventing them. But years later the letters I "wrote" to my mother from Frognal came to light, together with her replies, thus proving my memory not to have been at fault.

The Palmers had very strict ideas about the sanctity of

the English Sunday, but this was manifested in a peculiar way. Dressed in their Sunday best, the adult members of the household went to church, while the younger ones had to idle the time away. No games of any sort were allowed, nor any running about. Most of the time was spent sitting on uncomfortable chairs in the nursery; apart from the Bible, the only book allowed was, for some reason which I have never been able to fathom, *Gulliver's Travels*, which I should have thought eminently unsuitable for the Sunday reading of small children, even in an expurgated edition.

My early childhood was as happy as that of most children of the period, considering the discomforts which they had to endure. Their clothes and boots were hot and uncomfortable; all children, both boys and girls, wore tight-fitting stays until they were about seven years old. These were supposed to prevent them from slouching and to keep their backs straight. All medicines were horrible; they were supposed not to do you any good unless they almost made you sick.

The number of our house in Tite Street was 16. The street continued over Royal Hospital Road into Upper Tite Street, but this was separately numbered; since those days the two streets have been merged into one, and all the houses numbered consecutively, so that 16 has now become 34. Built in the late fifties or early sixties of the nineteenth century,[19] they were more spacious inside than their frontage led one to expect. At that time it was considered more important to have an imposing entrance hall and staircase than to have spacious rooms. This was carried to absurdity in some contemporary houses, in which half the available space was taken up by sweeping staircases presumably intended to impress the casual visitor with a sense of lavishness and grandeur. The architect of our house had not gone to those lengths, but a great deal of the ground floor did indeed consist of hall and staircase, or so it seemed to me at the time.

To the right of the front door, as one entered the house, was my father's study, in which most of his work was done, at a table that had once belonged to Carlyle.[20] The motif of this room was red and yellow, the walls being painted pale yellow and the woodwork enamelled red; on a red column in one corner stood a cast of the Hermes of Praxiteles. A few small pictures hung upon the walls: a Simeon Solomon, a Monticelli, and Beardsley's exquisite drawing of Mrs. Patrick Campbell. But most of the wall-space was occupied by bookshelves, filled with copies of the Greek and Latin classics, French literature and presentation copies of the works of contemporary authors. It was a place of awe, and it was sacrosanct; a place in the vicinity of which no noise was to be made, and which must only be passed on tiptoe. When my father was there we were not allowed into it except by special invitation; and even when he was not in the house it had a sort of "A" certificate attached to it, in that we were forbidden to enter it unless accompanied by an adult. Whenever my brother and I did manage to penetrate into this Holy of Holies, we always made straight for the waste-paper basket in search of treasure-trove. The basket was often half full of discarded manuscript for which collectors would probably fight one another today; and there were gaily-coloured boxes that had once held cigarettes and had a lovely grown-up smell. Waste-paper baskets seem to have a fascination for all children; my own small son always goes to my basket in order to retrieve empty boxes, foreign stamps, sale catalogues, pieces of coloured string, and similar treasures.

It was from my father's study that the hooligans stole everything that they could lay hands upon when he lay in prison and we were in exile, and the brokers were in and were completely indifferent to what happened to the treasures there. Manuscripts and presentation copies of books which could only have come from that room still turn up from time to time at auction sales in England and America; even some of my mother's letters to my father were stolen and have been dragged in the mire of the public auction rooms.

Beyond this room was the staircase and, facing the front door, the dining-room, looking over the back garden. How spacious it all seemed to me then. The whole house, indeed, was vast to the eyes of a child. Doors the handles of which could only be reached at arm's length, inaccessible sideboards with their loads of fruit and other dainties, windows so high that one could not look out of them and which could only be reached from chairs clambered upon with prodigious effort, and a magic hatchway through which came ominous rumbling sounds as the service lift came up from the kitchen.

The prevailing note in the dining-room was white blending with pale blue and yellow. The walls were white; the Chippendale chairs were painted white and upholstered in white plush, and the carpet, concerning the cleanliness of which we were constantly being admonished, was also white. At the left, as one entered, a long glass-fronted case hung on the wall, just beyond child's reach; in this were displayed various items of family silver, including my father's and my brother's christening mugs, a pair of very ornate repoussé silver claret-jugs presented to Sir William Wilde and inscribed, one in Erse and one in English, silver tankards and other miscellaneous objects. The house was visited twice by burglars; it is a peculiar fact, and one for which I do not attempt to advance any explanation, that on each occasion the ancestral silver from my father's side of the family was left untouched. Bow-windows looked out over the garden at the back of the house, and the right side of the room, where the sideboard stood, was raised above the floor-level by a step. Nursery meals were served in the dining-room, unless my mother was giving a luncheon party, because the nursery itself was so far away from the kitchen.

It has often been asserted that the decoration of the house had been carried out by E. W. Godwin, with help from Whistler, but this was true only of the ground and first floors. On the first floor Pre-Raphaelitism was given free rein, though a certain amount of Japonaiserie had crept in. I particularly remember black-and-white bamboo chairs, and bulrushes in tall Japanese vases. The walls were buttercup yellow, and a large part of the room was, or so it seemed to us children, occupied by a painted grand piano upon which I do not remember anyone playing. Etchings, several of them by Whistler, who had given them to my father, lined a great part of the walls. Opposite the fireplace hung a full-length portrait of my father by the American artist Harper Pennington. It was a bad painting, out of keeping with the rest of the room; it has now returned to its country of origin. As a concession to Whistler, who conceived the idea, two large, many-hued Japanese feathers were let into the ceiling. Small chairs, oriental vases, and occasional tables covered with bric-à-brac and bygones stood about the room in too great a quantity for our liking, as they were so easily knocked over. So, although we were not forbidden to enter the drawing-room, my brother and I never did so unless we were sent for to be exhibited to guests; a ceremonious procedure which, in common with most healthy small boys, we viewed with disfavour and avoided whenever possible.

One day our parents were holding a reception in Tite Street. Cyril and I were going to a particularly grand children's fancy-dress party in a few days' time and, at my father's suggestion, Cyril was to be dressed as Millais's "Bubbles," while I was to masquerade as Little Lord Fauntleroy.[21] And this was in face of our demand to be given sailor suits to wear. Papa had not yet seen us in our finery, which had arrived only that morning, and asked that we should be sent down from the nursery all dressed up, to give him and his guests a pre-view. This was more than childish flesh and blood could stand; so on our way down we crept into Papa's smoking-room, opposite the drawing-room, removed every stitch of our clothing, and pranced into the drawing-room in the nude; we must have been about six and seven at the time, but our youth did not save us from the disapproval of the Victorian visitors. We were hustled upstairs again, but my father took the hint, the offending garments were returned, and shortly afterwards we were given the sailor suits for which we longed. Not the ordinary children's sailor suits either, but suits made of real naval cloth by a naval tailor, complete with black silk scarves and knives at the end of lanyards. We went to our fancy-dress party in these and were the envy of all the poor little creatures made to go as cupids and Little Boy Blues and Little Lord Fauntleroys. We were inordinately proud of these suits; one of the severest punishments that could be inflicted upon us was not to be allowed to wear them.

My father's smoking-room was, apart from the study, the most awe-inspiring room in the house. It seemed very dark and gloomy to us, but I suppose that it was only dark by contrast to the brightness of the other rooms in the house. The walls were covered with the peculiar wallpaper of that era known as Lincrusta-Walton and had a William Morris pattern of dark red and dull gold; when you poked it with your finger, it popped and split, and your finger might even go through, so this was not much encouraged. The decor was North African. Divans, ottomans, Moorish hangings and lanterns filled the room. Glass bead-curtains hung before the windows; these were naturally a never-ending source of delight to Cyril and myself. I am quite sure that the room had been designed by Walter Harris. My father used to sit in this room for

hours, smoking and talking to his friends, since, true to
Victorian traditions, no one could ever smoke in the
drawing-room. My father did actually smoke in the dining-
room, but this was considered to be very daring and *fin de
siècle*. Twilight and mystery were the dominant notes in the
smoking-room, which smelled exquisitely of tobacco-
smoke.

The second floor contained my mother's bedroom at
the front and my father's dressing-room at the back. This
dressing-room was also pressed into service as a spare room
if necessary, particularly when relatives came over from
Ireland.

My mother's bedroom contrasted strangely with the
drawing-room on the first floor. She had a Victorian love
of draperies, lace curtains and needlework chair-covers,
which she made herself. A great deal of the wall-space
was occupied by Chippendale bookcases containing her
favourite books. When she needed calm or solace she always turned to the poets. I still have the copy of Keats's
poems which she had as a girl of nineteen; it accompanied
her wherever she went and was with her when she died.
By her bedside she had a carved book-rest which held her
favourite books; this took to pieces for convenience of
packing and went with her on all her travels. After the
English poets, her favourite reading was Italian poetry; she
knew a great deal of Dante by heart, and she was also
something of an authority on Petrarch and Tasso.

The top floor belonged to us children, and the usual
wicket-gate prevented us from toppling downstairs. There
were two rooms on this floor, the night-nursery on the left
and the day-nursery on the right; and between the two was
the bathroom, which was lit by a skylight through which
the burglars were supposed to have got into the house.

The day-nursery contained two large, built-in platforms, about a foot from the ground and four foot deep,
stretching round two sides of the room. The larger one,

on the right as you went in, belonged to Cyril, and the smaller, beneath the window, was mine; on these we erected our forts, placed our cannons and marshalled our armies of lead soldiers; it was always a sore point with me that I had to clear part of mine away every evening to enable the curtains to be drawn, whereas Cyril could leave his as they were. We devastated each other's troops with peas shot out of the cannons, and there was an obscure system of taking prisoners, invented by my brother, in which I always seemed to get the worst of it and to lose all my soldiers, until my shouts of protest brought Higher Authority upon the scene to restore peace and my soldiers.

I suppose my brother and I got on together as well as any brothers can be expected to do. Brotherly love is one of the rarest phenomena in family life. In *The Importance of Being Earnest* Gwendolen says to Cecily: "Now that I come to think of it, I have never heard any man mention his brother. The subject seems distasteful to most men." I think my brother was jealous of me, though he had no cause to be, and I was really far more jealous of him. Cyril had curly hair and was the favourite of both my father and my mother. He was stronger and healthier than I; he excelled at games, even as a small boy, whereas I took little interest in them. It may be that the natural antipathy between brothers is largely due to impatience and intolerance on the part of the elder for the comparative weakness of the younger, who becomes acutely conscious of this but eventually accepts it as being inevitable.

In the nursery my brother always had, or so it seemed to me, the best toys, and even if a toy was meant to be shared, I was usually deprived of my rights in it. There were no electric torches in those days, but on one occasion we were given a bull's-eye lantern lit by a small oil lamp. By turning the top the beam could be made clear or green or red; this top was, however, almost impossible to manipulate because as soon as the lamp was lit it became far too hot to touch, and if we used our handkerchiefs they got burnt. The lamp was enamelled all over, and the heat made the enamel burn with a pleasant aromatic smell. It was a thoroughly unpractical toy and a very dangerous one, and I do not know why we were allowed to have it; but it was Heaven and Romance to us because it enabled us to play real trains, in the dark, complete with signals.

The train game, in its simplest form, consisted of one of us trotting round the nursery table as the train, making puffing and hissing noises to represent the engine, while the other doubled the parts of guard and signalman. The drawback to this arrangement, from my point of view, was that when my brother was guard and signalman he naturally had to have the lamp with which to signal to the engine-driver; when, however, he was the train, who ever heard of a train travelling at night without a head-light? So my own share in the lamp was confined to the daytime. Some years later, in Italy, my maternal uncle gave me a similar lamp as a Christmas present, for my own personal and exclusive use. But my triumph was short-lived. My brother cajoled and pleaded and practically black-mailed me into selling the lamp to him for about a third of what it had cost, and the same thing started all over again.

Another smarting injustice, for which I could blame no one, not even myself, was that my brother liked liquorice, whereas it made me sick. The injustice lay in the fact that for the sum of one penny my brother could buy a sheet of liquorice, looking rather like a five-inch square of black plastic, which would last him the whole morning. The best that I could do for a penny was to buy four brandy-balls which, even with the utmost restraint and care, could not be made to last for more than an hour.

I have described all the house in Tite Street except the basement. This contained a large kitchen at the back, the servants' bedroom at the front, and the cellars under the pavement. As for most children of that generation, the kitchen was the most friendly room in the house. The cook was our very special friend, to be relied upon in any emergency; she and my nurse had different ideas of how to bring up children; the cook believed in spoiling them, so naturally she was our ally. There was a series of housemaids and finally Arthur, the general factotum, footman and butler. I do not know where he slept, but I believe that he had an alcove tucked away somewhere between the second and top floors. We spent a good deal of our time in the kitchen, sampling anything that was being cooked and making bread. All our bread was made at home in cottage loaves; we were allowed to make tiny ones for miniature tea-parties with our toys in the nursery, which took place with great frequency and were regularly attended by both our parents.

We played mostly in the Royal Hospital Gardens, which were only a stone's throw away—or during summer in Battersea Park and sometimes in Hyde Park. Hyde Park could be reached only by walking to Sloane Square and then taking a bus to Knightsbridge. This was rather an adventure; the bus was an enclosed one-horse affair, which plied up and down Sloane Street all day; it had no conductor, only a driver who stopped for would-be passengers and at the pulling of a bell-cord by those inside; the fare was one halfpenny, which you placed in a box at the far end of the bus; there was no one to see that you paid your fare except your fellow-passengers, to whose advantage it was to see that you did pay it; otherwise the bus would have stopped running.

Our games in the gardens were of the simplest kind. We had bows and arrows and pop-guns, but none of the complicated toys that children have nowadays. We had to rely largely upon our own resources, and play touch-wood and cross-fig and hide-and-seek among the bushes with other boys; the girls kept much to themselves and played their own feminine games, mostly based upon hopscotch and skipping. In the Royal Hospital Gardens the Chelsea Pensioners were all our friends; we dug in their gardens and listened to their stories of bygone campaigns which they were never tired of telling to anyone who would listen. And there were great days when we were invited to their rooms to have tea with them and to drink out of great thick mugs and eat slabs of bread-and-butter and cake. There was one whom I particularly remember because he was nearly a hundred years old, had been a drummer-boy at Waterloo and had returned to England after the battle in the same ship as the Duke of Wellington.

When it rained, and after dark in winter, we played in the house, without very much supervision. We played in the nursery, up and down the stairs, in the hall and in the dining-room, and usually managed to get into some sort of mischief. Once, when our nurse was out, we discovered a sword-stick belonging to my father and we had a duel with it, my brother having the sword and I the stick, which made it rather an unequal contest. We cannot have been more than eight and seven at the time, and it is a wonder that the bout did not end in tragedy. As it was, seriously handicapped by the inadequacy of my weapon, I soon turned tail and fled, closely pursued by my brother, who succeeded in driving the point of the sword into my behind, which bled profusely. Bellowing with pain and fear, I rushed down into the kitchen, where I was debagged by the cook and had my wound dressed. My brother was also in a panic and yelling loudly. The wound was quite deep and the scar still remains.

The house was often filled with the literary, theatrical and artistic celebrities of the day, which was probably one reason that Cyril and I avoided the drawing-room for our games. Grown-up people of that generation were apt to take themselves too seriously. There were exceptions, of course, notable among them being my father. The Irish people who came to the house were also gay, but there were a lot of Scottish relations-by-marriage of my mother's, who neither understood nor approved of my father or his circle; I think that my brother and I felt this disapproval overflowing on to ourselves; I suppose they thought that there was something not quite respectable in being Irish, particularly as Irish as we were. To my mother's receptions came people of such widely different interests as Henry Irving, Sir William Richmond, R.A., Sarah Bernhardt, John Sargent, John Ruskin, Lily Langtry, Mark Twain, Herbert Beerbohm Tree, Robert Browning, Algernon Swinburne, John Bright, Lady de Grey, Ellen Terry and Arthur Balfour. All the Pre-Raphaelite brotherhood were constantly in attendance, and my brother and I used to go to children's parties given by them at their houses and in their studios.

My father was beginning to reach the pinnacle of his fame and success, and we were invited everywhere, particularly at Christmas and Easter. And it was at a party at Sir Edward Burne-Jones's house, The Grange, in Kensington, that I first fell deeply in love, at the age of seven. It was an Easter party at which coloured eggs were hidden all over the garden. Anyone who found an egg handed it in and received a small prize in exchange. So it was that I found myself hunting for these treasures with a little girl of about my own age named Rosemary, who wore a blue silk accordion-pleated dress and was the most exquisite thing that I had ever seen. No lily could have been more graceful, no kitten more lively. And after tea she did a little dance, holding out the hem of her skirt. And when she left the party she kissed me and said "You're nice." So of course I fell violently in love with her. For months afterwards I would lie awake at night and see myself rescuing her from mortal peril. I would brush lions from her path with my unaided hands, rescue her from precipices and shipwrecks, and fight all-comers for her. I never saw her again, and I never knew what her other name was.

Tite Street was a peculiar social mixture in those days. Both Whistler and Sargent had their studios there. The artist G. P. Jacomb Hood[22] also lived in the street and, by an ironical coincidence, at No. 46 lived Mr. Justice Wills, who was to pronounce sentence on my father at the Old Bailey in 1895.

On the other hand, the west side of the street backed on to Paradise Walk at that time, one of the most forbidding of Chelsea slums. It was a row of small tenement houses with wretched, filthy back-yards, from which the sounds of brawling rose nightly. And when anything more serious happened a procession would form and walk up Paradise Walk, along Cheyne Place and down Tite Street to the Casualty Ward of the Victoria Hospital for Children, which was on the other side of the street from us. We had an excellent view of these processions from the night-nursery, which boasted a small balcony, and I particularly remember one in which the central figure was a tall, pale-faced woman, her head enveloped in a shawl, whose husband had stabbed her in a drunken rage.

There was no such thing as child psychology in those days; children were either clever or stupid, forward or backward, good or naughty. My brother and I were terrified of Paradise Walk, and in the course of time we peopled it with dreadful creatures that crawled up the wall of our house at night and tapped or scratched at the nursery windows to get in. I can see some of these creatures now. They were greyish and had huge horns and phosphorescent eyes; very often only their horns appeared above the window ledge. What our nurse ought to have done was to have taken us along Paradise Walk on some quiet, sunny morning, when everything was calm, to show us that it was just an ordinary street and not the boiling inferno which we had pictured in our minds. As it was, the only glimpses that we caught of it at ground-level were when we were hurried past the end of the street, lest we should be contaminated, and we had an impression of blowsy women with shawls over their shoulders and men's caps on their heads, and dirty barefoot children in rags.

Nowadays the relative characters of Tite Street and Paradise Walk have changed. Paradise Walk is one of the most colourful streets in Chelsea. All the little houses are painted in different shades of blues and reds and greens and yellows; window-boxes in nearly all the windows are alight with flowers: even the dwellers in the houses are clad in brilliant colours. From being a slum it has become the home of a colony of students and artists who are justly proud of the gaiety of their street. Tite Street has also changed in character. Many of the houses were abandoned by their occupants during the 1940 Blitz, and were taken over by the Chelsea Borough Council, which let them out in flats. No. 16, having changed its number to 34, is now occupied by several families.[23]

It was only during these early years that I knew my father; after 1895 I never saw him again. Most small boys adore their fathers, and we adored ours; and as all good fathers are, he was a hero to us both. He was so tall and distinguished and, to our uncritical eyes, so handsome. There was nothing about him of the monster that some people who never knew him and never even saw him have tried to make him out to be. He was a real companion to us, and we always looked forward eagerly to his frequent visits to our nursery. Most parents in those days were far too solemn and pompous with their children, insisting on a vast amount of usually undeserved respect. My own father was quite different; he had so much of the child in his own nature that he delighted in playing our games. He would go down on all fours on the nursery floor, being in turn a lion, a wolf, a horse, caring nothing for his usually immaculate appearance. And there was nothing half-hearted in his methods of play. One day he arrived with a toy milk-cart drawn by a horse with real hair on it. All the harness undid and took off, and the churns with which the cart was filled could be removed and opened. When my father discovered this he immediately went downstairs and came back with a jug of milk with which he proceeded to fill the churns. We then all tore round the nursery table, slopping milk all over the place, until the arrival of our nurse put an end to that game.

Like other fathers, he mended our toys; he spent most of one afternoon repairing a wooden fort that had come to pieces in the course of various wars, and when he had finished he insisted upon everyone in the house coming to see how well he had done it and to give him a little praise. He also played with us a great deal in the dining-room, which was in some ways more suited to romping than the nursery, as there were more chairs and tables and side-boards to dodge through, and more room to clamber over Papa as well.

When he grew tired of playing he would keep us quiet by telling us fairy stories, or tales of adventure, of which he had a never-ending supply. He was a great admirer of Jules Verne and Stevenson, and of Kipling in his more imaginative vein. The last present he gave me was *The Jungle Book;* he had already given me *Treasure Island* and Jules Verne's *Five Weeks in a Balloon,* which were the first books I read through entirely by myself. He told us all his own written fairy stories suitably adapted for our young minds, and a great many others as well. There was one about the fairies who lived in the great bottles of coloured water that chemists used to put in their windows, with lights behind them that made them take on all kinds of different shapes. The fairies came down from their bottles at night and played and danced and made pills in the empty shop. Cyril once asked him why he had tears in his eyes when he told us the story of *The Selfish Giant*, and he replied that really beautiful things always made him cry.

He told us about the family house at Moytura, where he was going to take us one day, and of the "great melancholy carp" in Lough Corrib, that never moved from the bottom of the lough unless he called them with the Irish songs learnt from his father; and he would sing these songs to us. I do not think he sang very well, but to us he had the most beautiful voice in the world; there was one particular song, called *Athá mé in mu codladh, agus ná dúishe mé*,[24] meaning *I am asleep, and do not wake me*, which I came across again when I was grown up and was trying to learn the Irish language myself. And he invented poems in prose for us which, though we may not always have understood their inner meaning, always held us spellbound. Many of these were never published, but he was constantly weaving them. When I came of age, I met a lady whom my father had known as a girl; she who had gone straight home after he had been fascinating her and some of her friends with his stories, and had written them down exactly as he had told them, so far as she could from memory. She gave me a copy of what she had written, and I have put the stories at the end of this book, so that they shall not be lost.*

My father lived in a world of his own; an artificial world, perhaps, but a world in which the only things that really mattered were art and beauty in all their forms. This gave him that horror of conventionality which destroyed him in the end.

Perhaps my father was at his best with us at the seaside. He was a powerful swimmer; he also thoroughly enjoyed sailing and fishing and would take us out with him when it was not too breezy. I do not think we took to it very much; personally I was much too concerned for the plight of the fish flapping about on the floor-boards. I preferred

* See Appendix C, p. 257.

helping my father to build sand-castles, an art in which he excelled; long, rambling castles they were, with moats and tunnels and towers and battlements, and when they were finished he would usually pull a few lead soldiers out of his pocket to man the castle walls. I remember him so well, in a Norfolk jacket and knickerbockers, no shoes or stockings and a large grey hat which he had probably brought back with him from the United States. We ourselves were dressed in much the same fashion. It never struck parents in those days that the most sensible costume for children on the beach in the hot weather was a pair of bathing-trunks; they were much too afraid of their catching cold or getting sunstroke.

In London my father always carried a gold-headed malacca cane, about three foot six inches long, as was the fashion among the dandies of the day. This fascinated me and I would rush to take it from him when he came home. I asked him to let me have it when I grew up, and he said he would give it to me as soon as I had reached its height. So the next time he came in I greeted him with books tied to the soles of my feet, so that I was taller than the stick. This pleased my father immensely, but he refused to hand over the cane; he compromised for a half-sovereign, which was promptly banished to our money-box. This was a constant source of frustration to us until we discovered that no money-box was proof against a table-knife and a little ingenuity.

This malacca cane incident was one of the last of my memories of my father. It must have been in January 1895 during the Christmas holidays.

One of my vivid recollections was being taken by my father to see a children's play at the Haymarket Theatre in April 1894. It was called *Once upon a Time* and was a medley of stories for children, including *The Pied Piper of Hamelin* and *The Emperor's New Clothes*. The chief rôles were taken by Herbert Beerbohm Tree, and in the interval my father took me round to see him. I am told that Tree asked me, for want, presumably, of something better to say, whether I had seen *A Woman of No Importance*, and that I replied (I hope this isn't true) that I had not because "my mother tells me that the play contains certain epigrams which are not right for children to hear." To this day I wonder where I got this from.

During this part of our childhood we spent a great deal of time at Babbacombe, near Torquay, with Lady Mount Temple, who was a great friend of all the Pre-Raphaelites and of my father. Her house, Babbacombe Cliff, was designed for her by Ruskin and decorated largely by William Morris and Burne-Jones. In all the living-rooms hung pictures by Burne-Jones and Rossetti; these are now in the Tate Gallery, to which they were bequeathed by Lady Mount Temple. The Cliff, as it was called, was a large, rambling building, following no particular style of architecture. Lady Mount Temple had her own apartments, quite separate from the rest of the house, and shut off from it by what really amounted to her own front door; there she lived most of the time, and no one ever went into this part of the house uninvited. The principal room in it was a very large drawing-room, part of which was built over an archway in the carriage-drive. It lay at the end of the house and was entered by a short flight of stairs; there were windows in three of the four walls, so that when the sun was out it always shone into the room. This room was called "Wonderland" because, we were told, it had originally been decorated with scenes from *Alice in Wonderland*. All the other rooms in the house bore the names of flowers, according to the pattern of their wall-paper: Daisy, Lily, Primrose, Poppy, Marigold, and so on. And each room had its name painted on the door. They were happy times at Babbacombe, and when we went to our preparatory schools we spent a large part of our holidays there. A rambling garden ran from the top of the cliff down a steep

declivity almost half-way to the sea. Not much grew in this
garden, except ivy and saxifrage and woodland flowers. It
was, in fact, more a small wood than a garden; but it made
a perfect playground for children, as it was full of
hiding-places and there was nothing in it to spoil.

Lady Mount Temple was a sister of the first Lord
Tollemache and a distant cousin of my mother's. She was
a very tall and stately lady, well advanced in years when I
knew her, but with shrewdness, wit and a prodigious
memory. When I went down to Babbacombe again, some
ten years later, shortly before she died, she seemed not to
have changed in any way, except that she had become im-
mobilised in her armchair in Wonderland, in an alcove,
from which she could see the rise and fall of the tides in
Babbacombe Bay and the setting of the sun. When she
died, a memorial fountain was put up to her on Babbacombe Cliff itself, not by the Borough Council but by sub-
scription among the cottagers and fisher-folk. The house
is now a luxury hotel; just before the last war I drove
through Babbacombe and paused at the top of the hill; but
I went no further for I wanted to remember it always as I
had known it in the old days.

Babbacombe Cliff was the first house in the West of
England to have central heating installed. This was confined to the corridors and landings, where it was really
needed in the cold weather; everyone was frightened of it,
as well they might be. It was a very primitive affair, with
no safety devices of any kind, and it was always either
freezing or blowing up.

When my brother was nine and I was seven and a half
we were sent to separate preparatory schools. This was in
May 1894. My brother's school was principally a preparatory school for the Navy,[25] and as such was apparently
rather a Spartan place with no indoor staff at all, except,
presumably, in the kitchen. The boys themselves had to
make their own beds, empty the slops (there was no such

thing as running water in schools in those days), and keep the place clean and tidy generally. From what my brother told me, I gathered that he rather liked his school, though he never entered into much detail. I was sent to Broadstairs to Hildersham House, the headmaster of which was the Rev. H. C. V. Snowden. The school is still flourishing. Mr. Snowden was succeeded by his son, who was at the school with me, and it is now being conducted by his grandson. It has, therefore, been going for sixty-three years with only three headmasters, all of the same family.

Mr. Snowden was a benevolent gentleman, who believed in fairly strict discipline. There were about fifty boys at the school, aged up to fourteen. I was the youngest, the next oldest being over eight; consequently it was a continual struggle to keep up with the curriculum. I particularly suffered in dictation, as until then my education had taken the form of reading more than of writing; and in my desperate efforts to keep up I would smear far more ink over my hands, face and clothes than on the paper. However, after I had got over my initial homesickness, I was quite happy there. I was too young to enter into rough children's games with boys so much older than myself, for I was always being knocked down and trodden upon; yet I wrote to my father, after I had been there a short time, to say that I was well and happy and that the boys were very "koind" to me. I am sure I did not mean it; a small boy is rarely kind to another small boy.

At the beginning of 1895 the storm-clouds were gathering and the relentless forces of fate were being arrayed against the House of Wilde. In March my father applied for a warrant for the arrest of the Marquess of Queensberry for publishing a criminal libel against him. The case came up at the Old Bailey on April 3rd and resulted in Queensberry's acquittal on April 5th. On the evening of the same day my father was arrested.

Easter Day fell on April 14th that year, so the Easter holidays had not started when the storm broke; but it became obvious to our mother that we could no longer remain at our schools, so we were immediately removed and returned to London. And that, for the time being, was the end of our scholastic careers in England. Curiously enough, I never at any time heard any mention of the public school or schools to which we were at one time undoubtedly destined to be sent. It would be interesting to know what my father's ideas were on the subject; I am rather afraid that they would have inclined towards Eton.

My father was refused bail and was lodged in Holloway Prison. Nowadays magistrates will usually release accused persons on bail unless there are very cogent reasons against doing so, but in Victorian times bail was granted very charily; thus my father had to labour under a heavy handicap in preparing his defence. Even after the jury had disagreed at his first trial at the end of April, his bail was fixed at the huge sum of £5,000, and it was three days before any of his former friends could be found to go bail for him, as they feared that such an act of kindness and mercy would incriminate them.[26] Many of his more intimate friends, such as Robert Ross, were not at that time persons of sufficient substance to be acceptable to the Court.

Such was the outcry against my father that even before his trial, when he had two plays running simultaneously in London, *An Ideal Husband* and *The Importance of Being Earnest*, his name on the programmes and placards was covered by strips of paper pasted over it. New York, where *An Ideal Husband* was running on Broadway, followed suit and the name of the author was obscured as in London. The two plays running in London lingered on, but they were eventually withdrawn on April 27th and May 8th respectively. All books by Oscar Wilde were removed from booksellers' shelves and he, who had been making an income of some thousands of pounds a year, suddenly found himself penniless. Had it not been for the generosity of a few friends he would have been unable to pay for his defence.

At his second trial, at the end of May 1895, he was found guilty and sentenced to two years imprisonment with hard labour.

Before I proceed with my narrative, I want to emphasise two things. One is that, although by the age of eleven I knew my father had been in trouble, I was quite unaware of the nature of the offences with which he was charged until I was eighteen. The other is that after reading R. H. Sherard's *The Story of an Unhappy Friendship* I was so depressed that I decided to read no more books about my father, no matter who wrote them; and to that resolution I adhered for many years. Even now I have read very few. People have often blamed me for this attitude, but it was simply a form of self-protection. I have so often been approached by well-meaning people intending to write about my father and been asked to give them information, and I have always given the perfectly genuine answer that I was far too young at the time of my father's trial to know anything about what happened, and that in any case I probably knew less about it than anyone else in the world. So much so that when, at the age of twenty, I was asked by Sir Coleridge Kennard to meet Robert Ross, the name meant nothing to me. I was very much embarrassed at his emotion when I met him, because at the time I had no idea of where he came into the story, or of how much he had done and was still doing for my father's memory.

My brother was not so lucky as I was. Shortly before he was killed by a German sniper in the first war he wrote to me: "I was nine years old when I saw the first placard. You were there too, but you did not see it. It was in Baker Street. I asked what it meant and I received an evasive answer. I never rested until I found out." His opportunity for doing so soon arose. He went to stay with cousins of my mother's in Ireland, where it was intended that I should follow him later. While he was there he read newspapers left lying about and realised that something was desperately wrong. He was terribly distressed, and the hackneyed expression "he never smiled again" was for him almost true.

On my return from school I remained in London for the time being, and my main recollection is of my mother, in tears, poring over masses of press-cuttings, mostly from Continental newspapers. I was of course not allowed to see them, though I could not help seeing the name OSCAR WILDE in large headlines; but I had no inkling of the true state of affairs.

The hue and cry after the Wilde family was just as bad, if not worse, in Ireland, the land of my father's birth; so our plans were changed. It was thought better, after all, that we should go and hide ourselves abroad. There at least we could live unmolested, and there we had many real friends.

The Carlos Blackers lived in Baden, my mother's brother, Otho Holland Lloyd was with his family in Switzerland, and my mother's great friend Lady (Margaret) Brooke, wife of Sir Charles Brooke, the English Rajah of Sarawak, had a villa in Northern Italy. Abroad we could lose our identity and forget the past. Unfortunately, so far as Cyril was concerned, the damage was already done, and it was a very solemn-faced little boy, puzzled and unhappy, that set off with me for the Continent one cold and cheerless April day, in charge of a hurriedly engaged French governess, who was a complete stranger to us. And so started an exile that was to last for more than three years.

My mother remained behind, to be of what assistance she could to my father, until she too was driven from her home by the entrance of the bailiff's men, and the subsequent sale of all the contents of the house.[27] That sale was a scandalous piece of barefaced robbery. Even before it took place, the house was full of riff-raff, souvenir-hunting and stealing anything they could lay hands upon. I have seen a priced catalogue of the sale. Books, of inestimable value for their association interest, were sold in bundles of twenty or thirty for two or three pounds a bundle. Among them were first editions of all my father's books with inscriptions to my mother, to my brother and to myself, which were kept in my mother's bedroom, in a special bookcase to the right of the door. They have never reappeared,[28] and it can only be supposed that the pages with the inscriptions were torn out, to avoid their being identified; copies of these books are frequently offered for sale, even today, thus mutilated.

For months afterwards, my brother and I kept asking for our soldiers, our trains and other toys, and we could not understand why it upset our mother, since of course we knew nothing about the sale. It was only when I saw the catalogue, many years later, that I realised why my mother had been upset. The sale consisted of 246 lots; number 237 was "A large quantity of toys"; they realised thirty shillings.

CHAPTER II

Exile

The flight of my brother and myself in charge of the French governess took place without my mother, who was to join us later. Our ultimate destination was the little Swiss village of Glion, at the top of the funicular railway from Territet, near Montreux. It was a nightmare journey for both of us, but particularly for Cyril, in view of what he had discovered in Ireland. He wanted to shield me and to keep me in ignorance of the truth, so that I should not suffer as he did. The only person with whom he ever discussed my father was my mother. This self-enforced reticence turned him, while yet a child, into a taciturn pessimist.

Neither my brother nor I had ever been abroad before, and we were deeply conscious of going out into the unknown, and aware of the fact that every moment was taking us further away from the life we knew and from our familiar surroundings and possessions. Our departure was so hurried that only necessities were packed for us.

The journey down to Dover seemed interminable, and the noise and bustle of the port confused and frightened us. There was a strong gale blowing, which added to our depression, and the French governess, who knew very little English, started lamenting and talking about *mal-de-mer* even before we crossed the gangway. Once on board, however, I had a stroke of luck. Profiting by the governess's attention being momentarily distracted by a ticket-collector, I escaped from her and wandered about the boat by myself, finding my way into the neighbourhood of the engine-room, where I spent most of the voyage talking to the engineers and watching the huge crankshafts turning the paddle-wheels; eventually I got down into the engine-room itself. I did not rejoin the governess until we reached Calais and the wheels ceased to revolve. I suppose I was lucky to find her, as she herself was far too ill to bother about what had happened to me. She had collapsed at the first tremor of the engines and, for aught that she knew or cared, I might have fallen overboard and been drowned. She had, nevertheless, managed to keep a firm hold on my poor brother, who, seeing Mademoiselle in such a miserable state, naturally concluded that to be sea-sick was the correct procedure for experienced travellers, and followed suit. It was a very forlorn couple that I followed on shore at Calais.

I suppose we had to pass through the customs, though this must have been a very simple formality compared with the ordeal of today, particularly as the only dutiable articles were wines, spirits and tobacco, none of which we could be suspected of having in our possession. Then into the train for Paris. Everything about the French railways was strange and forbidding to two already tired and homesick children. The porters in their blue blouses, shouting at one another and at everyone else in a way which their more soberly-clad English counterparts would have considered to be beneath their dignity. The platforms at ground level, and everyone, passengers as well as railway staff, strolling unconcernedly and unchallenged about the permanent way. The huge carriages into which one had to climb up a steep flight of steps. The billows of black, cindery smoke rolling from the engine's inferior French coal. But most disturbing of all were the telegraph poles. Being used to the straight, orderly ones in England, the crooked French variety filled me with terror; I saw them as live creatures, snakes writhing out of the ground and swaying to and fro, seeking something to devour.

The journey from Calais to Paris seemed as endless as

the one from London to Dover. Mademoiselle had bought
a pile of French newspapers and magazines at Calais and
sat absorbed in them. Cyril and I had nothing to read or
to play with, and nothing to do but to gaze through the
carriage-windows at the distorted telegraph poles and the
almost continuous advertisement hoardings that defaced
and obscured the landscape; then night began to fall and
even those distractions were taken from us. Besides, we
were both very hungry. We had left London after breakfast and had been supposed to lunch on the steamer.

It was quite dark when we reached Paris, and we drove
to a small hotel on the left bank of the Seine. Here we
were shown into a bedroom containing, among other
items of furniture, two beds. The regulation two candles
on the mantelshelf were already lit. In those days that was
the only illumination ever supplied in any small French
hotel bedroom unless one liked to go to a great deal of
trouble and expense; it was really a monstrous imposition,
and one which it was almost impossible to avoid; the cost
of the candles to the proprietor was ten centimes each, and
they appeared on the bill as *Bougies, 2fr.* Since rooms in
small hotels cost only three or four francs a night, this procedure added about fifty per cent to one's bill.

Our luggage was brought up, but Mademoiselle was in
a hurry and did not even trouble to unstrap our bags, saying that we were continuing our journey next day and did
not really need anything for the night. We were now
taken to the hotel restaurant and regaled with coffee,
which nauseated us, and rolls and butter—scarcely an English boy's idea of an evening meal after a luncheonless day.
However, that was all we got, and when we had finished
we were taken upstairs again and sent to one of the beds
in our underclothing. The governess, who had no doubt
made her arrangements in advance, then blew out the candles and went out on some assignation of her own, leaving us by ourselves in the dubious light of a flickering

street-lamp which cast eerie shadows on the ceiling through the uncurtained window. The room was hot and stuffy and we tried to open the window; but either we did not understand the French window-catches, or we were not strong enough to deal with them; anyway, we did not succeed and so went back to bed, eventually to fall asleep.

Early next morning Mademoiselle roused us and made us rinse our faces and hands in cold water and put on the remainder of our clothes. Then we were given more coffee and rolls and butter. We were beginning to wonder if we were ever going to get a square meal again; this was a feeling that we had for some time afterwards, while we were becoming acclimatised to the Continental food that we ate during the next few weeks until our mother arrived and took matters in hand.

After this so-called breakfast, our governess took us to the small, dark, hotel writing-room, exhorted us to be good, told us that we were on no account to leave the hotel and then went out again herself. I imagine that she was probably a Parisienne and was snatching every moment she could to see her friends and relations before going into the wilds of Switzerland. When she went out that morning, we naturally supposed that she was going on some errand and would be back shortly; but, as the hours passed and she did not return, we began to feel more and more forlorn and to think that perhaps she had abandoned us for ever. It was long past our usual lunch-time when she came back and took us to a restaurant; she herself ate nothing, saying that she had a headache, but I have no doubt the real reason was that she had already had a *recherché* luncheon with her friends.

That afternoon we drove to the Gare de l'Est and resumed our long journey to Switzerland. By this time both my brother and I had taken a violent dislike to the Continent of Europe and to Mademoiselle. She was a deeply religious Catholic, spent much of her time in prayer and looked on us as little pagans; she tried to make us say the Lord's Prayer in French, which rather shocked us in a vague way; we had always thought of it as being an essentially English prayer. She was a grim and rather hysterical woman who was frankly bored by children and avoided our company as much as possible. She was preoccupied with her devotions and with perpetual letter-writing.

We now entered upon the last stage of our journey, which seemed to us to be even more drawn-out than the earlier ones. The journey from Paris to Geneva took about sixteen hours, including a change of trains at the Franco-Swiss frontier. There was no restaurant-car on our train, and the passengers had to snatch what they could at the station buffets and eat it as best they might; and the fear that we were never again going to eat properly increased. We still had nothing to read or to play with and were told not to fidget; so we were bored as only children can be bored when they have nothing to do and are forbidden to invent any occupation for themselves. At nightfall my brother and I tried to sleep head to foot on one of the carriage seats, covered by one of the rugs that were an essential part of the equipment of every Englishman travelling abroad; these were rolled round a bundle of umbrellas, parasols and walking sticks, the whole being secured with a "rug-strap." We were travelling second class, where sleeping-cars were unknown.

The remainder of the night is a little vague. I suppose we were too tired to care very much what happened, and the next thing that I remember is our arrival at Geneva in the middle of the morning. Here we changed trains once more and trundled slowly, in a small local train, all along the north shore of the Lake of Geneva as far as Montreux. During this part of our journey our spirits rose considerably, as there was something reassuring about the calm waters of the lake in the midday sun and the calm massive uplands of French Savoy beyond it. Besides, we were nearing the end of our journey; there remained only the drive from Montreux to Territet, which was fun, and the funicular railway from Territet to Glion, which was a hair-raising adventure. And with our arrival at Glion our new life began.

We were booked in at the Hôtel du Righi-Vaudois under our own names, Cyril and Vyvyan Wilde; I do not think we ever knew the name of the governess, whom we always called Mademoiselle to her face, whatever we may have called her behind her back. It was springtime, and my brother and I ran quite wild. Whether Mademoiselle was supposed to give us lessons I do not know, but she certainly did nothing of the kind, beyond giving us a little half-hearted instruction in French. Even that was only oral; we were never called upon to write anything down. The weather was wonderful and we spent most of our time wandering among the undulating fields and woods in the neighbourhood. The beautiful Gorges du Chaudron, to the west of Glion, were one of our favourite playgrounds; a little later they were filled with such masses of narcissi that we could not walk there without treading on them, and they seemed to form one huge bouquet. Byron makes special mention of these narcissi in his *Prisoner of Chillon*.

Our greatest friends at Glion were two old sisters, who took a liking to us and spoiled us. They were Russian Countesses and they lived in two rooms, a bedroom and a sitting-room, at one end of the hotel. They had occupied these rooms for years and had filled them with gewgaws and knick-knacks, Russian icons and oriental hangings. The old ladies smoked perpetually, pushing Russian tobacco into tubes of brown cigarette-paper ornamented with the Imperial Russian arms. They used little sticks for this purpose, and a great treat was to be allowed to do this ourselves, though we probably ruined more tubes than we filled. Sun was anathema to our friends, who, so far as my brother and I could discover, never left their rooms, even to have a bath. They always had a fire burning and were swathed in layers of shawls; they must have been very dirty, but they were extremely kind and gave us sweets and Russian stamps, thus starting us on the path of philately.

One day these ladies were in a great state of excitement because they had had a letter from a nephew who was passing through Switzerland and was going to pay them a visit. They spent the next few days tidying up the sitting-room and re-arranging everything, and when the great day arrived they even went to the length of drawing back the curtains. At last the nephew arrived, a magnificent figure, enormously tall, with a massive red beard and moustache. He wore a grey frock-coat and top-hat and talked to the old ladies in French. Also, which was much more to the point, he gave my brother and myself each a set of Russian coins, from one kopeck to one rouble. He was a General in the Imperial Russian Army and a close friend of the Tsar.

Whatever other qualifications Mademoiselle may have possessed, as a governess she was a failure. She did not often leave the hotel except to repair to her devotions; indeed, she passed most of the day in her bedroom, where she had erected a little shrine, before which at least two candles burned for hours at a time; the number would increase whenever the occasion seemed to warrant it, in accordance with its importance. Late in May, a day or two after the end of my father's trial at the Old Bailey, she hired a rowing-boat to take us over to St. Gingolph, a place of pilgrimage at the opposite side of the lake. On our way back a storm got up. Storms can be very unpleasant on the Lake of Geneva, but this one did not seem to me to be particularly fierce, nor do I suppose it was. The governess and Cyril were duly seasick, and the governess was nearly bereft of her wits with terror, but I rather enjoyed the wind and the rain and the rolling of the boat. The boatman was perfectly calm and there was obviously nothing to fear, but very shortly after we got back to Glion Mademoiselle's room became a blaze of lighted candles.

Unfortunately for her, this was the very evening on which my mother arrived to join us. Mademoiselle did not long survive as our governess. My mother cross-examined us about her activities, concerning which we eagerly supplied details, and the last straw was the presentation of the bill with an item of hundreds of francs for candles offered up in devotion or thanksgiving; the governess tried to explain that it was all quite necessary as insurance for our safety, but this made no impression upon my mother, who, in spite of the mental agony which she had been through, had not lost her sense of indignation. So Mademoiselle was told that she was a useless expense and a source of irritation and must go. She was furious and accused my brother and myself of, to put it mildly, exaggeration; there were "words," and we were hustled out of the room while the argument continued. But Mademoiselle left in a huff early next morning, without even saying good-bye. This suited us very well, since we could usually make rings round our mother, so far as discipline was concerned, and contrived to be left more to our own devices than ever. My mother soon made friends with our Russian Countesses, and we had tea with them nearly every day, out of a samovar, with cakes which my mother brought in from the local *pâtisserie*.

Shortly after my mother's arrival, I found a ten-franc gold piece in the street, just outside the hotel. Such wealth had never come my way before. One franc a week each was all that we were allowed as pocket money, and this was really enough, as very few things that we required in our daily lives cost more than five or ten centimes each. But these ten francs enabled Cyril and myself to satisfy a month-long ambition, which was to take the rack-and-pinion railway from Glion right up to the Rochers de

Naye, a celebrated beauty-spot high above the lake. The climb up to this place was too much for our young legs, but we reckoned that we could climb down again quite easily. The fare by the railway was five francs each way. When I found the ten-franc piece I told my mother, and for one horrid moment I thought I was going to lose it, for she said that it must belong to someone and we must try to find the owner; however, wiser counsels prevailed and the more just principle of "finding's keeping" was applied to my treasure-trove.

So we set off on our journey. Unfortunately we omitted to take any of the ordinary precautions adopted by travellers. We omitted to tell our mother what we were going to do; this was understandable, as Mademoiselle would never have noticed our absence, at any rate until nightfall, since we frequently asked for sandwiches to take out in the middle of the day when we went to the Gorges du Chaudron. We also did not trouble to find out how long the journey took, and though we were returning on foot we had not really planned our route, except that we had decided to avoid the long, winding path and to attempt to come back more or less in a straight line. But the line we took lay mostly through vineyards and young standing crops, and we spent much of the return journey dodging irate farmers and viticultors who pursued us with shouts and sticks. And when we did reach home, quite exhausted and very hungry, we were too late for dinner and were given a mere apology for a meal and packed off straight to bed in disgrace.

It was a brief happy time for us children. Bad news, even if it travels slowly, is inexorable in its progress, and when my mother had been at Glion for a short time, the manager of the Hôtel du Righi-Vaudois realised who we were and, fearing for the good name of his house, politely informed my mother that we were no longer *personae gratae*. Cyril was nearly eleven and I was only nine, but we were pariahs and undesirables in the eyes of a Swiss hotel manager.

Margaret Brooke, the Ranee of Sarawak, had for some time been urging my mother to come to Italy, to be near her. She had a charming house, the Villa Raffo, on the sea-front, just outside the little village of Bogliasco, on the Ligurian coast; it lay about eight miles east of Genoa and less than a mile from Nervi, a market town of local importance. My mother had been contemplating this move for some time, and the hostile attitude of the hotel manager decided her; so we proceeded to Nervi, where the Ranee had booked rooms for us at the main hotel.

The tram journey from Switzerland to Italy took us through the St Gothard tunnel, which was then the longest in the world. We had been warned that it would be an awe-inspiring experience, so we were prepared for something peculiar. Electric trains had not yet made their appearance and, as there was no ventilation along the whole twelve miles of the tunnel, extraordinary precautions had to be taken to prevent people being suffocated by fumes from the engine. The engine-driver and the fireman wore gas-masks, and before the train entered the tunnel the guard went right through the train to make sure that all windows and ventilators were properly shut. An open window or ventilator would almost certainly have had a disastrous effect on the passengers in that particular compartment.

The train took half an hour to pass through the tunnel. The smoke gradually filtered through the edges of the windows into our compartment until we could hardly see across it; the solitary oil-lamp in the roof grew dimmer and dimmer, and the temperature kept on rising. To add to our discomfort, the noise of puffing and clanking was deafening. Presently, above all the din, some small children in the next compartment got into a panic and started screaming. And just as we thought that we could stand it no longer and wanted to open the carriage door and throw ourselves out, the blessed daylight reappeared; we were out of the tunnel and the train stopped. The carriage windows were so blackened by smoke that we could see nothing at all through them; so we got out on to the line and walked about while the carriage aired and men sluiced the windows down with mops. We felt thankful to be alive; and a little surprised too. Nowadays, a spotlessly clean electric train does the journey in twenty minutes and in comparative silence.

We arrived in due course at Nervi, where we were met by the Ranee in a landau and driven to the hotel. Everyone, including the hotel proprietor, was most courteous and kind. The Ranee was a lady of great strength of character and people were probably a little scared of her. She came of a very forceful family, the de Windts; her brother, Harry de Windt, was a famous explorer at the end of the last century, his most remarkable feat being to travel from Pekin to Paris overland in 1887.

Here again we ran wild. My mother looked after us herself, as best she could, having had enough of governesses for the time being, but she was preoccupied with her sorrow and her health, which was steadily growing worse. Some months before leaving England, she tripped on a loose stair-carpet and fell down a whole flight of stairs, injuring her spine and her right hand, and she never recovered from this accident. But she was happier than she had been for some time, in the companionship of the Ranee, who was a comfort and a consolation to her until the time of her death three years later.

So Cyril and I lived an almost unfettered existence. Some desultory attempts were made to continue our education, and we paid periodical visits to a mysterious gentleman in Nervi, who gave us instruction in the three Rs and also in Latin and French. But during most of the day we roamed, either along the rocky sea-front, watching the longshoremen fishing for squid and octopus with a rag of red flannel at the end of a pole in one hand and a trident in the other, or into the lovely country behind, which was full of thrills. There were newts and tadpoles to be caught in the streams and brought back to the hotel in glass jars and fed on breadcrumbs until they succumbed to this diet; and hundreds of lizards sunned themselves on the rocks and were not to be caught at all, though we spent hours trying to do so. Masses of flowers, too, many of them quite new to us, which we used to gather and bring back to adorn our mother's room. And this gave us an idea of how we could enrich ourselves.

We noticed that the flower-shops in Nervi were selling violets to tourists at the price of one lira a bunch. Now one lira was the equivalent of tenpence, which was the equivalent of at least half-a-crown today. So we spent a lot of time picking violets, which we would sell to foreign visitors for half a lira a bunch, thus ruthlessly undercutting the legitimate market, and pretending not to understand English or French if addressed in either of those languages. This enabled us to buy all sorts of things, mostly of an edible nature. No doubt our appetites suffered, but not sufficiently to arouse suspicion. This might have gone on for a long time, had we not suddenly decided to be devils and to invest some of our earnings in a very small flask of Chianti. We smuggled this into the hotel and one day, when Mother was away at the Ranee's villa, we bought some food and with it and our flask we retired to the hills behind Nervi to hold a feast.

We had discovered an ideal hide-out, a little open hut, mounted on stilts and accessible only by a rickety ladder. It had been built as a look-out post from which shepherds could keep watch over their flocks, but had long been disused. So we climbed into our hide-out and ate our food and drank our wine and immediately fell into a sort of alcoholic stupor, from which we did not wake until after nightfall. We were cold and very scared and did not know what to do, as it was pitch dark, and we did not dare leave our eyrie. However, we started shouting and after a time attracted the attention of a search party that had been sent out to look for us. We were taken back to the hotel, where our rescuers were no doubt handsomely rewarded; then under a severe grilling we broke down and confessed all. And that was the end of our first large-scale financial enterprise.

We did not stay very long at Nervi, because my mother had to return to England to settle up some of her affairs.[29] She did not want to take us to England with her and she could not very well leave us alone at Nervi, particularly as she knew what pranks we got up to when left to our own devices. The Ranee had no room for us in her villa, as she had two grown-up sons who were constantly coming and going. So, en route for England, my mother took us to her brother, Otho Lloyd, at Bevaix, a little village about nine miles south-west of Neuchâtel, in Switzerland, where he had been living for some time on the top floor of a two-storey châlet. This was in the early summer of 1895, and our second experience of the St Gothard tunnel.

The châlet was called La Maison Benguerel, after the proprietress Mademoiselle Benguerel, who occupied the ground floor, where she made gruyère cheese. There was also a cellar which contained wine in all stages of maturing, in cask as well as in bottle. My uncle's part of the châlet was reached by a flight of wooden steps outside the house, leading to the dining-room from the large garden, of which we had the use. He lived there with his second wife and their two children. He was a scholarly man who devoted his whole life to the study of the Greek classics. He had been at Oxford at the same time as my father, though they never met there, and he resumed our education, which had been almost entirely neglected during the previous three months.

My mother did not go on to England immediately, and one day, shortly after our arrival at Bevaix, my brother and I were called into the dining-room, which also served my uncle as a study. We were told to sit down and were then informed that in future our names would no longer be Wilde, but would be changed to Holland. And we were told to practise writing our new names, and were given some sort of document to sign. In my own case the name Oscar was dropped and, as a further disguise, my first name was respelt Vivian (later I reverted to the original spelling of Vyvyan). At the same time we were told to forget that we had ever borne the name of Wilde and never to mention it to anyone. All our possessions were gone through to make certain that the name Wilde did not appear on any of them, and all our clothes were re-marked. I think that my young cousins were present at this conference; indeed, they must have been, otherwise they might have been curious at our change of name and have discussed the matter outside.

My mother and my uncle were so solemn about it all that I realised something was wrong, but the feeling was a vague one. It was different for Cyril; he had already discovered too much in Ireland. It is significant that I do not remember my brother ever mentioning our father's name to me from that day onwards. Be that as it may, my brother retired to a summer-house in the garden and refused to speak to anyone or to eat until my mother's tears and entreaties drew him out of his lethargy of despair.

Holland was an old family name on my mother's side. Her family did not want her to take her maiden name of Lloyd because, I suppose, they thought it might lead to complications and misinterpretation. My uncle, who took a great interest in ancestry of all kinds, possessed a family tree of the Hollands of Lancashire, going back to Sir Stephen Holland, Lord of Skevington in the time of Edward the Confessor. This family tree is an imposing document on parchment, measuring about five foot by two; it was prepared at the beginning of the nineteenth century and contains many interesting names, including that of Sir Otho Holland, one of the original Knights of the Garter.

Our own connection with the family was rather remote, one Molly Watson, whose mother was a Holland, having married John Lloyd, my great-great-grandfather, at the end of the eighteenth century. However, as a name had to be chosen, they might just as well choose one that had once belonged to some member of the family. I still possess the imposing Royal Warrant, by which our names were officially changed. It is a mass of Whereases and seals and is enclosed in a red morocco case richly gilt. There was even a new grant of arms, of which, I need hardly say, I have never taken any advantage.

My mother went to London soon after this ceremony, and the main joy of our lives became fishing in the Lake of Neuchâtel. The lake was less than half a mile from the village, and we spent hours trying to catch fish in it, not with the idea of feeding the family, but with the object of stocking a large artificial pond in the middle of our garden. The day's catch may not have weighed or measured very much, but size is not everything, and the pride of bringing fish home alive was immense. Our tackle consisted of ordinary twine to which a hook was attached, baited with bread pellets. Why any fish was ever deceived by it remains a mystery; no rod or reel or catgut marred the purity of the sport. The only distasteful part was the removing of the fish from the hook, which made me feel like a cold-blooded torturer. Anything we caught was carried back to the châlet in a tin full of water and transferred to the pond, where it promptly disappeared among the thick weeds until the time, not long afterwards, when it died and came up to the surface again to float.

One day we all made an excursion into Neuchâtel by

lake-steamer, driving in a pony-trap through two miles of vineyards to Cortaillod, which was the nearest embarking place. While waiting on the pier for the steamer to arrive, my fascinated eyes lit upon a shoal of fish in the water round the pierhead. I had never seen so many fish in my life before, and in my imagination I saw the pond in the Bevaix garden teeming with them. That night I hardly slept at all, counting the fish gobbling up my bait, and the next morning I rose at daybreak, gathered up my fishing-tackle, some bread and a large tin, and made my way on foot to Cortaillod. I arrived there in a state of bubbling excitement, only to be met with a blank refusal of admittance to the pier without the production of a ticket or a small coin. Alas! In my eagerness I had not considered details of this kind, but eventually my bitter disappointment proved to be a suitable substitute for an oblation, and the pier-master let me crawl, with my equipment, under the turnstile.

This adventure had been undertaken with the full approval of my uncle and aunt, who had provided me with luncheon. So I remained at Cortaillod nearly all day. The results were hardly up to anticipation. As the gambler at Deauville dreams of the day when the croupier calls for *"Un panier!"* in which to remove his vast winnings, so I had dreamed of someone arriving with a wash-tub with which to help me home with my catch. But the fish round Cortaillod pier were not so naive as those nearer Bevaix; they had probably already been fished for by small boys, and all I caught were about ten tiddlers, which I carried home rather shamefacedly and emptied into the pond.

Life went on peacefully at Bevaix all that summer. Then came September and the vintage, which put every other thought out of our minds. Bevaix is in the heart of the country in which some of the best red wine of Neuchâtel, and indeed of Switzerland, is made—Cortaillod, not unlike a Beaujolais in character. It is made from the purple

Pinot grapes which cluster thickly on the vines before the vintage, offering a wonderful contrast of colour against the vivid green of the leaves.

From the first day of the vintage, my brother and I and our cousins were in the vineyards from morning until night, gathering the grapes, eating a good many, and packing the rest into miniature *caques*, small imitations of the larger ones used by the grown-ups; these *caques* were like tapering casks and were provided with two leather straps, enabling them to be carried on the back like knap-sacks. The smaller *caques* were easy enough to borrow, in all sizes, because the vintage, which took several days, occupied the whole time of every man, woman and child in the village. It was beautiful September weather, and we foreigners worked as hard as anyone—though probably not so effectively as the local children, who had been doing it since they were able to walk.

When our *caques* were full, we hoisted them on to each others' backs and carried them to the roadside; there they were lifted down and their contents emptied into barrel-shaped carts, which bore them to the basement of the Maison Benguerel, where they were transferred to the wine-press. As soon as the press was full, a cover was put on and forced down by means of a huge wooden screw turned by men leaning on poles; the grape-juice then flowed out through holes in the bottom of the press into large jugs. These were in their turn poured into open vats.

The aroma rising from the grape-juice was delicious and permeated the whole house. When the last load of grapes was emptied and pressed, and the bustle and activity had died down, the grapes were allowed to ferment in peace. Every evening we would go and look at the seething vats and watch the scum being removed, and the *vignerons* would give us small glasses of *moût*, or must, to taste. Naturally, this *moût* grew stronger day by day, until at length we came back to the house in a state bordering upon the hilarious and were forbidden to drink any more.

While this was going on, another kind of fermentation had been taking place upstairs. My aunt had been experimenting, some time before, with fruit-bottling, about which she knew nothing at all, and suddenly the bottles began to burst, one by one, like bombs. No one dared go near the cupboard where they were stored, for fear of being blown to bits. Eventually, during a lull in the bombardment, my uncle (heavily armoured) transported the bottles into the garden, where he bravely cut the string with which the corks were secured. As each cork was released, it shot into the air like a rocket, followed by a foaming mass of fruit and liquid. The experiment, so far as bottling was concerned, resulted in a total loss; but the juice remaining in the bottles was salvaged and, after a suitable interval, re-bottled, and an excellent home-made brew resulted, sweet, heavy and extremely potent.

After the vintage, the weather began to break up. Heavy rain fell at frequent intervals, and the nights began to be very cold. My mother wanted to go south again to Italy, to be in the sun and near the Ranee; and in any case Bevaix, which was sixteen hundred feet above sea-level, was no place in which to spend the winter. My mother, however, did not wish to be left alone, even with her own children; so the Ranee found her a very pleasant apartment, large enough to accommodate both her own family and that of her brother, on the upper floor of a villa on the outskirts of Sori, a little village about two miles from Bogliasco. So we packed up and set off on our travels again.

The expense of this continuous travelling would be prohibitive today, but it was relatively cheap on the Continent in those days, if one was content to take slow trains and to travel second class.

There was the St Gothard tunnel to be faced again. This was the third time for my brother and myself in less than six months, so we took it quite calmly and felt very superior to my uncle's family, who had never been through it before. We were becoming, in fact, hardened and experienced travellers.

I have never revisited Sori, though I have passed through it often, but my recollection of it is as vivid as though I had left it yesterday. It was then a quiet little fishing village, huddled in a deep valley round the piers of a huge viaduct which carried the coastal railway from Genoa to Spezia and then on to Rome. Our own villa was just beyond the east end of the viaduct, high above the village. It had a steep garden, full of rocks and heliotrope and lizards, stretching down to a low cliff, from which a rickety flight of wooden steps led to the beach. There were snakes in the garden, the cliff was crumbling, the steps were about to collapse, and the shore was notorious for its quicksands. However, the garden was only accessible through a room on the ground floor, whose tenants promised that they would not let the children through unless they were accompanied by a grown-up; so we managed to avoid these perils.

The apartment itself consisted of a large living-room with two bedrooms, between which ran a short corridor. Beyond the bedrooms, at one end lay the kitchen and the "usual offices," and at the other a covered terrace which made an admirable playground in wet weather, of which there is a great deal on that coast. It also enabled us not to get too much in one another's way. We children were discouraged from being in the living-room during the day, except at meal-times—and in the mornings, when our uncle continued his efforts to instil knowledge into us.

On fine afternoons we would either go down the winding road into the village of Sori to watch the fishing fleet coming in, or along the road east, to Recco, where there was a firework factory. We were only allowed to look at this from a distance, for fear it might blow up at any moment and take us with it: it had already blown up several times before. And twice a week my brother and I used to go into Nervi, three miles away, to buy bread for our mother. There was a heavy tax on salt in Italy at the time, and the Italian peasant could not afford to buy it; consequently bread baked in country districts seldom contained any salt. This was all right for us, but my mother was unable to digest it, and the nearest place where bread baked with salt could be obtained was Nervi. The three-mile walk each way was too long for us, so we took the train into Nervi and walked back.

Unfortunately for our poor mother, the smell of the new bread was irresistible, and about half-way home we would start picking corners off it and eating them, so that by the time we reached Sori the loaf was usually rather dilapidated. One day we ate nearly the whole loaf and felt so guilty that we threw what was left away and said that we had lost it, which was, in a way, the truth. After that, the procedure was reversed; we would walk into Nervi and take the train back, being considered fairly trustworthy over such a short journey.

Constantly walking along the same road soon began to pall and it occurred to us that we might be able to avoid it by reviving our flower-selling business in Nervi, now that we were free from supervision there. This, in order not to arouse suspicion by over-long absence, entailed taking the train both ways; we could well afford it because, since it was winter time, there were more foreign tourists in Nervi than ever.

In our second financial venture we carefully avoided the pitfalls of Chianti and even of over-eating. Most of our takings we changed, in Sori, into coins of very small denomination. The villagers were poor, and most of their daily domestic shopping was done in centesimi. Consequently there were in circulation coins of one, two, three, four and five centesimi, many originating from before the

Unification, and similar coins from every country in Europe, some of them well over a hundred years old. The villagers were mostly illiterate and went by the size of the coins, not by their superscriptions; they would accept anything that was circular and had a device upon it; I even got a couple of Victorian English half-farthings. We amassed a remarkable collection of these small coins and practically denuded the village of them.

In these ways we managed to occupy ourselves in the afternoons, and that enabled our uncle Otho to pursue his Greek studies undisturbed.

One really frightening pleasure was watching the midday express train from Rome to Genoa pass by. It was the essence of excitement and a refinement of torture. The railway that runs along the Ligurian coast is a remarkable piece of engineering. There is very little foreshore, and the line passes through dozens of tunnels, often with deep open archways leading from sides of the tunnels to the open sea; and the tunnels themselves are connected by stretches of open line and viaducts. Just below our villa there was one of these stretches of open line, about twenty yards in length; it was in fact nothing more than a gap in the tunnel between Recco and Sori. My brother and I would go to this gap just before luncheon and wait for the express. We could hear the engine whistle as it left Recco station, two miles away. Shortly afterwards the first rumblings would be heard; they would grow louder and louder and gradually resolve themselves into the puffing of the engine and the metallic sound of the wheels passing over the rails. The noise grew and grew, but it was impossible to judge how near the train was. The air pushed before it by the advancing engine began to form a wind which whistled out of the tunnel and caught up loose twigs and leaves, whirling them about and adding to the general sense of foreboding. We longed to take to our heels, but would stand there fascinated, with our eyes fixed on the

mouth of the tunnel. Suddenly the engine hurled itself
into view with a roar, exuding smoke and sparks and steam
and, as it seemed to us, maledictions, only to plunge, twenty
yards further on, into the short section of tunnel which led
to Sori viaduct. We were quite overcome by this train and,
like people who gaze from a height and want to throw
themselves down, I used to feel like casting myself in front
of the advancing monster, a willing and even an eager
sacrifice to Juggernaut.

The covered terrace at one end of the Sori apartment
was more or less given over to Cyril and myself. We each
had a space on it partitioned off; but my brother, who
always went on the principle that what was mine was his
and what was his was his own, freely entered and left my
territory, although I was always forcibly prevented from
entering his. We had acquired very few new toys during
our wanderings and were inclined to rely on our imagination for amusements. But we now became enthusiastic
carpenters, and the chief desiderata in life were putty,
planks of wood, saws, hammers, sawdust and nails with
which to play on the terrace in wet weather.

Cyril and I had many friends among the local inhabitants, prominent among whom was Pacifico, the village carpenter, who had a workshop half-way down the hill into
Sori. He was a huge man with a black cavalry moustache,
and he always wore a black hat and a leather apron; if ever
a man's appearance belied his name it was his, though
he was really a remarkably good-natured person. He gave
us most of the raw materials we wanted, such as pieces of
wood, sawdust and putty; the tools we bought with the
flower-money. No one seemed to think it strange that
saws, hammers and nails should materialise out of nothing.
In those days I looked upon putty as being a gift of the
gods, a mysterious, esoteric substance almost endowed
with animation. It was so malleable and could be used for
so many purposes. If constantly cared for it would retain

its texture, but if neglected it would grow hard and unresponsive and, as it were, suffer death. I shall never forget the disillusionment of discovering that putty consisted of a mixture of french chalk and linseed oil, two substances which held no hidden meaning for me. The child of today has its plasticine, which is an enormous improvement on the putty of my own childhood. Putty could be got only by cajoling carpenters and builders; and even then it was only available in small quantities.

But the real home of mystery in the village was the *pasta* factory, where all the macaroni, spaghetti, caneloni, alphabeti, etc., were made. We were allowed to go in and watch the machines cutting the *pasta* into all the numerous shapes in which it is manufactured, and we even learnt the closely-guarded secret which has puzzled other people for generations, namely, how the hole is put into macaroni. The *pasta* factory fed all the surrounding hamlets. The peasants in this part of Italy lived entirely on fish, *pasta*, *polenta*, bread, olive oil, and of course a little wine. Most of them had never eaten meat in their lives, but they did not seem to be any the worse for it. They were a sturdy race.

On February 3rd, 1896, my father's mother, Speranza, Lady Wilde, died in London. A few days later, my brother came out of my mother's room in Sori with a set look on his face and said to me: "Go in to Mother; she wants to talk to you." I went in, and my mother told me the news. Death is always distressing to the young, even when the person who dies is someone whom one has not known very well; it is a crumbling of part of the citadel of life which one has built round oneself. Then my mother said: "I am going back to England to tell your father." "Where is Father?" I asked. "Why don't we ever see him now?" I suppose this was the question my mother had been dreading for months. She replied: "He has not been very well. He has had a great deal of trouble." I was afraid to ask any more; but the vague misgivings with which I had been assailed at Bevaix when our names were changed seemed to take a firmer hold upon me. I was conscious only of the heavy load of despair that was weighing upon my mother, and I wished that I could bear part of it for her.

I do not know what passed between my mother and my brother, but it is significant that she broke the news to us separately. I suppose she was afraid that he might say something that she did not want me to hear. After all, he *knew*.

My mother went to England and was away for about three weeks, during which she saw my father and told him that his mother was dead; she never saw my father again.[30] Then she returned and our normal life was resumed.

On Easter Monday there was a grand Battle of Flowers at Nervi; it was the most important event of its kind on the Ligurian coast, and people would come from as far away as Spezia to attend it. The Ranee took a suite of rooms on the first floor of the Hôtel Nervi and invited the three of us to come and see the fun.

We arrived at the Nervi hotel by barouche, early in the morning to avoid the rush, and were enthusiastically welcomed by the hotel manager, who insisted upon addressing my mother as Mrs. Wilde, repeating the name every time he spoke to her. Many years later the Ranee told me that my brother put up with this for a time, but finally expostulated, telling the manager that my mother was no longer Mrs. Wilde but Mrs. Holland; whereupon the manager, knowing nothing of the true state of affairs, came to the conclusion that she must be a widow who had married again, and started congratulating her, until the Ranee hurriedly changed the subject.

The suite taken by the Ranee was filled with flowers, tied up in small bunches, convenient for throwing at the girls in the flower-decked carriages as they paraded along the street. The people lining the street also threw bouquets, and the Battle of Flowers was on.

The Ranee had with her her eldest son, Charles Vyner Brooke, who afterwards succeeded his father as Rajah of Sarawak and ruled that country until it was annexed by the British Government at the end of the last war. He was something of a god to us small boys, for he was very handsome, a good athlete and an undergraduate at Cambridge. When the Battle had been raging for a short time, Charles caught the eye of a lady of outstanding charms in a window across the street exactly opposite to us. So, ignoring the ladies in the carriages, he spent his time making the small bunches of flowers into larger ones and trying to hurl them into the window opposite. The lady did her best to catch them, but he never succeeded in scoring a bull's-eye, though he was all round the target. So after a while he gave it up and left the room; and the next we saw of him was in the window opposite, brazenly chatting with the lady of the outstanding charms. And that was the last seen of Mr. Charles Vyner Brooke on that occasion.

Our mother, on her return from England, decided that we must now have a more formal education. It was quite obvious that the existing arrangements could not go on for ever. She had consulted Carlos Blacker, and on his advice she decided to send us to a German school. My father's works, totally banned in England, were already being used as textbooks of English in Germany, and it seemed to her that there, even if our identity were discovered, we would be safe from further persecution. So we packed up once more and resumed our travels, our destination this time being Freiburg-im-Breisgau.

CHAPTER III

Germany

FREIBURG-IM-BREISGAU, where Charles Blacker and his wife Caroline and their three children had been living for some time, is the chief city of the upper Rhenish province of Baden, and the seat of a famous university, established in 1456. Like university cities all over the world, it also harboured a number of schools. To one of these my brother and I were sent as boarders, while our mother exercised remote control and watched over us from the Blacker residence.

Even in those days the German people were sheep, herded and bullied by their overlords, who, like sheep-dogs, marshalled them and kept them in order. We, however, as free-born Irishmen, resented this regimentation and dug in our toes against it. So the experiment was not a great success. On the second or third day after our arrival the master of our class started beating me about the head with a ruler for some trivial breach of discipline. My brother, always fiercely protective of me as being more delicate than himself, retaliated by kicking the master violently on the shins and driving already powerful fists into his stomach, while I attacked him from the rear. So we were expelled and sent to another German school, with admonitions as to the attitude we were to adopt towards the masters.

This also turned out a failure because, although our behaviour to the masters was exemplary, we took exception to certain anti-British sentiments expressed by the other boys. My recollection of what actually happened is a little hazy, but, according to the evidence of my mother's letters to my uncle, it appears that we challenged the rest of the school, consisting of about twelve boys, to a fight, defeated them and put them to ignominious flight. In telling the story, my brother always claimed that we had killed three of them; I doubt whether that is true, and I am afraid it was only poetic licence on his part. Anyhow, we were once more expelled.

Our sojourn at both these establishments did not occupy more than a fortnight altogether, and today I have no recollection of what the schools were called. After the second débâcle my mother abandoned the idea of giving us a Teutonic education, and discovered an English school, run on English lines, at Neuenheim, a suburb of Heidelberg, where she had friends.

Heidelberg possessed a large English community, an English Chapel, an English Club and even English restaurants. This community was periodically swollen by the arrival of English and American tourists; so my mother, who liked to remain more or less within call in case of any disaster befalling us, spent a good deal of time between Heidelberg and Freiburg.

The school was called Neuenheim College; we went there at the end of April 1896, at the beginning of the summer term. There was another English school there, in the heart of Heidelberg itself and called Heidelberg College. This used to cause the Germans some amusement. Heidelberg is the oldest university in Germany, having been established in 1386; so it was as though someone were to start a German school in the middle of Oxford and call it Oxford Kollegium.

There was no love lost between the two schools, members of which were apt to attack one another whenever they met. The chief reason for this dislike was that almost half the boys and masters at Heidelberg College were German, whereas at Neuenheim College nearly all the boys and all the masters except the language teachers (who in any case had no authority over the boys) were English. We at Neuenheim had all the traditional contempt for foreigners of the English boy of the period, and we honestly believed that any English boy could take on two foreign boys in a fight and beat them with the greatest ease. Besides, to the bewilderment of the local inhabitants, we wore Eton jackets on Sundays; the others did not, so we did not consider them to be gentlemen. The two schools played against each other at Rugby football and cricket and rowed against each other on the River Neckar. Neuenheim habitually won all these contests.

The school consisted of three rather gaunt houses just outside the village of Neuenheim, which was separated from Heidelberg by the river. The centre one, the largest of the three, contained the school dining-room and the headmaster's quarters, on a floor slightly above ground-level. The floor above held the other masters' rooms and the boys' dormitories. The east building housed the class-rooms and the playroom, which was lined all round by the boys' lockers. In winter, when it was really cold, we spent a large part of our free time in the playroom, trying to keep warm by playing boisterous games, involving penalties and humiliations for the losers.

The third building, to the west, was called the Army House, and was a cramming establishment for the Army, the Navy and the Civil Service. It was presided over by Mr. Alan Armitage, the son of a former headmaster of the school. The older boys lived there, with private studies of their own; an aloof existence from which they emerged only for field games, in which they joined the younger boys. These games consisted of cricket in the summer, Rugby football in the winter, and rowing all the year round; and when the river was frozen and the snow lay thick upon the ground, so that it was impossible either to row or to play football, paper-chases were organised by the master in charge of games. No form of exercise is quite so utterly pointless and boring as a paper-chase, and we used to try to slink off and get lost and find our way home by ourselves; though this, if discovered, was apt to lead to a painful interview with the games-master.

I was very unhappy at Neuenheim College. The school was run on austere lines, and a lot of bullying went on as well. Many of the boys suffered, like ourselves, from some kind of disadvantage; some of them had been expelled, or at any rate withdrawn, from English schools; others were the sons of marriages between Englishmen and German women and had, therefore, a semi-Prussian outlook on life. I myself was confused by the events of the previous year. I was also once more the youngest boy in the school, and this seemed to make me automatically the object of attack. My brother did his best to shield me from unnecessary cruelty, but he could not be with me the whole time. Once, shortly after I arrived, I was shut in an empty locker in the playroom; it was just large enough to hold me in a crouching position, and I was kept there, in a state of abject terror, until my screams began to daunt even my tormentors, who, instead of letting me out, ran away. Then one boy with more sense than the others told a master that he had heard noises coming from the playroom and the master came and let me out, in a state of hysteria. I have suffered from claustrophobia ever since.

There were several prefects among the bigger boys in the lower school, and these wielded summary jurisdiction over the smaller boys. It was my only experience of the prefect system recognised in so many English schools, where an unpopular boy may well be driven to suicide by the brutality of his fellows, while the masters adopt the callous attitude that it is no concern of theirs.

The bigger boys were nearly all armed with catapults, which they used with the most deadly accuracy. The standard ammunition was ordinary buckshot, and the favourite target the calf of a small boy's leg. One might be peacefully reading at a desk, when suddenly one felt as though one had been stung by an outsize hornet. It was an agonising pain and there was nothing one could do to relieve it. I think I must have been very different from other boys, since never in the whole of my childhood did I feel a desire to inflict pain or suffering on anyone who had done me no harm, or to kill birds or little furry creatures. I have a very deep respect for life, and I am sure that people who go about slaughtering anything that moves do so out of motives of jealousy, because they know they cannot create life themselves.

The headmaster of Neuenheim College, whose name was Girdlestone, was a scholar who devoted most of his time to the supervision of the Army Class and only very seldom interfered with the lower school. His wife was a kindly woman who presided over the kitchens and the dining-room; she kept a motherly eye on the very small boys and noticed if they looked scared or unhappy. Unfortunately, however, no boy would have dreamt of admitting that he was unhappy or scared. The so-called schoolboy code of honour is an amazing thing. It is really a set of unwritten principles laid down by the older boys of a school, to enable them to do exactly what they like to the smaller boys.

The masters varied. Some of them were quite human, but others were fiends, who relied upon the cane and mass floggings to maintain discipline. Once the whole school was caned because a din was set up in one of the dormitories and the master on duty, not being able to locate the exact place from which it came, decided to punish everyone, so that in any event the culprits should not escape. I felt the injustice of this keenly, as my own dormitory was very quiet and well-behaved on that occasion, and I was actually roused out of a deep sleep to take my quota of punishment.

One master in particular, who was a very dour Scot,

used as a punishment to make us write lines holding the paper against the wall at eye-level. The result of this was that the ink ran down the penholder on to our hands and wrists. This meant that the whole of the next break had to be passed in the washing-place, scrubbing our hands with pumice-stone to remove the inkstains. Inkstained fingers were a grievous crime, to be punished with smart rappings on the knuckles at the next lesson, by the same master, whose eyes would light up with pleasure as he wielded his cane. Sometimes I made my hands bleed rubbing them with pumice-stone trying to get them clean. I have often wondered whether the master was himself an exile, and whether this made him bitter and a hater of mankind.

On Sundays the whole school was supposed to attend the morning service at the English Chapel, but there was no supervision, and the masters themselves did not often go. That was the only occasion on which we were allowed to go into the town of Heidelberg, since the other side of the Neckar, and even the bridges across it, were out of bounds. Mr. Girdlestone used to give us each fifty pfennig for the offertory, and we usually spent the morning (and the fifty pfennig, which amounted to the equivalent of an English sixpence) in a cake-shop. It was a rather hazardous thing to do, since if we were found out it meant a beating; and Mr. Girdlestone had an embarrassing habit of asking us to tell him the text of the sermon. This was circumvented by interrogating the boys, of whom there were quite a number, who went to church voluntarily. When our mother was in Heidelberg, my brother and I had to go with her; but this had its compensation, as we were allowed to lunch with her afterwards.

The religious instruction accorded to Cyril and myself had been much the same as that of most English boys of the period and, even though we had both attended preparatory schools run by clergymen, our ideas on Christian theology were vague. The English Chapel at Heidelberg was a bare, barn-like building, in the severest tradition of the Reformed Church. There was no pulpit, but a gallery ran above the altar, and from it the sermon was delivered. The incumbent was an elderly, bald and rather irascible clergyman with a long flowing white beard. And once, when he was in particularly good form, he raised his fist to the heavens and thundered forth: "I am the Lord thy God, which have brought thee out of the land of Egypt, out of the house of bondage!" I believed that he was telling the truth and was deeply impressed, even though I was rather puzzled as to why the Almighty should have chosen Heidelberg as His earthly residence.

In spite of all the drawbacks of Neuenheim College, there were many pleasant interludes, particularly during the summer term. A good deal of our leisure time was spent playing cricket. The master in charge of games, Mr. Kent, was, I believe, a cricket blue and, as such, was very much looked up to by the boys, to whom he used to give individual coaching. He was a nice man; he caned me once, but I remember regarding the punishment as just, and I bore him no ill-will for it.

My brother and I had fled from England with all our summer and winter clothing, but until this time we had had no occasion to wear our cricket flannels, which had been carefully wrapped up in brown paper and stowed away from moths. When the first half-holiday arrived and we went to our dormitory to change for cricket, we were aghast to find that, in the general Wilde-Holland change-over, these garments had apparently been overlooked and all bore the names Cyril Wilde and Vyvyan Wilde prominently displayed upon them. Luckily they were all written with marking-ink on tapes and sewn on to the garments, and I can see my brother now, in the comparative seclusion of the washing-place, frantically hacking away at the tapes with his pocket-knife. The most difficult name to remove was mine from my cricket-belt, as the stitching had gone deep into the webbing. Eventually, Cyril cut out the centre of the tape, leaving the edges adhering to the belt.

This incident seemed to bring back my sense of disaster in a great wave. I realised that we had had a narrow escape from imminent danger. I wonder how many people understand what it is like to be in such a position. To be an illegitimate child is a simple condition compared to the one in which we found ourselves—there are, after all, so many thousands of illegitimate children in all walks of life. But we had known what it was to have our father fêted and admired, and now to have to deny him and to lock up all knowledge of him in our hearts was a terrible burden for children to bear. The thought that at any moment an indiscreet remark or a chance encounter with someone from our former lives might betray us was a sword of Damocles constantly hanging above our heads. From that summer day in Bevaix a year before, when we were called into the dining-room to sign our new names, we had been supposed to leave behind us everything even remotely connected with our former lives. All the friends, places and objects with which we had been familiar had to be obliterated from and torn out of our minds, as Cyril tore our names from our cricket flannels. My mother's advisers were, of course, foolish, since it was clearly impossible that the secret could be kept for ever. All my mother's numerous family knew that we had taken the name of Holland, and some of them were bound to talk. I think that their immediate concern was to protect themselves; the problems of the future were for our own solution when the time came. If there was ever a secret that was bound to develop into a *secret de polichinelle*, it was that one.

At Neuenheim, when we played cricket matches against outside teams, there was serious work to be done. These out-matches were fairly frequent, as there were several other English schools in Germany within fairly easy reach; the English colonies of Heidelberg, Frankfurt and

other near-by towns could also be relied upon to scratch up
a cricket team on occasion. The masters played for our
team and Mr. Kent, at least, could always be expected to
put up a good performance.

I said that at these times there was serious work to be
done. I must elaborate this point. There were numerous
itinerant Italian ice-cream vendors in Neuenheim, but we
were forbidden to buy from them, as their wares were suspected of harbouring typhoid germs. There was, however, one exception, in the person of a gentleman named
Della Bona; I suppose that his place of business had been
inspected and pronounced to be run on fairly sanitary
lines. So Signor Della Bona drove a prosperous trade, particularly on out-match days. Large ices, consisting of four
spoonfuls of ice-cream dug out of the wheeled ice-box
and tastefully arranged in a papier-mache container, cost
twenty pfennig, or one could buy one spoonful for five
pfennig. So far, so good. But Signor Della Bona was a
good psychologist. He knew that a boy with one mark in
his pocket might easily lose his yearning for ices after eating two large ones, and that he would then spend the remaining sixty pfennig on something else. So he put
temptation in our way by issuing books of tickets for the
sum of one mark, which were available for six ices instead
of five. Many boys fell into this trap and Della Bona's business must have prospered; but I evolved an idea by which
I, too, could profit by this scheme.

Signor Della Bona was not allowed inside the school
gates but had to take up a position in the roadway outside;
he was therefore some distance from the cricket field. So
during out-matches, instead of watching the cricket I
would buy a book of one-mark tickets and wander around
among the older boys and spectators, offering to fetch ices
for them. I was paid cash in advance and was usually given
five pfennig for doing it, so that my profit was at least forty
per cent on every six ices fetched. It was arduous work on

a hot afternoon, but it was well worth it. I might easily make two or three marks profit and that, with pocket money at one mark fifty pfennig (including the offertory money) per week, was a godsend.

These cricket matches took place on whole holidays, of which there was one a week during the summer term. A whole holiday was called a *Frei*; we had a school language, like any other English school, with the difference that it was largely based on German words. Sulphur-impregnated matches, for instance, which gave out a pungent and unpleasant smell when lit, were called *Stinkerei*. We bought them for one pfennig a box, which was reasonable, and we used them for lighting tubes of blotting-paper, which we smoked and which made us sick. On *Freis* on which there was no cricket match we would walk along the banks of the Neckar or wander about in the hilly country to the west of Neuenheim. There lay the Philosophenweg, the Philosophers' Walk, along which, hundreds of years before, students of philosophy at Heidelberg University used to stroll while discussing the profundity of their knowledge. It was a beautiful walk, extending for two miles along the slope of the Heiligenberg, chiefly through vineyards. From there we would make our way to the top of the Heiligenberg, through woods full of bilberries and wild strawberries with which we stuffed ourselves. At the summit there was a ruined castle, a church and a café where we could buy cakes or lemonade or beer if we had any money. We usually came back through the valley of the Hirschgasse, but when we did that we formed ourselves into parties of six or more, as we were afraid of meeting bands of hilarious students from the University, who frequented a famous tavern in this valley where they used to fight their duels. They were inclined to be very rough in their cups. And on Midsummer Day, which was also a *Frei*, the ruins of the famous Heidelberg Castle were floodlit by the University students by means of red and green bengal lights; the students also gave a firework display on that evening, and we were allowed out for that.

In due course the term came to an end. I do not think I learnt anything during the term except a smattering of German and a certain amount of French and arithmetic. I do not remember any other lessons.

My mother had discovered a delightful little hotel, called the Schloss Hotel, just behind the Castle, on the heights behind Heidelberg. It stood about six hundred feet above sea-level, among trees and in extensive grounds of its own; an atmosphere of coolness and shade seemed to pervade it. It was on the way to nowhere, so no passing traffic disturbed its peace; yet it was conveniently placed in relation to the town, as a funicular railway ran from the market-place almost to the door of the Castle. In this hotel we spent our summer holidays.

It was a joyful time, in spite of certain obvious drawbacks; in England we would have spent our time playing cricket and swimming, but there was none of that here. Nevertheless we thoroughly enjoyed ourselves, resuming our comparatively unfettered existence of Switzerland and Italy. There was nothing to do but to wander in the woods, pick fruit and flowers, sleep in soft, deep-sided German beds, and rise in the warm dawn refreshed and eager for the adventures of another day. And adventures there were, too, in plenty; falling into streams and out of trees (especially at cherry-picking time) and getting lost in the woods.

Once when Cyril and I were exploring the wild slopes leading down to the river my brother uttered a cry and disappeared from view. When I called out to him there was no answer, so I scrambled home in a panic and the hotel staff organised a search party. After a short time we found him, bruised and scratched and rather dazed, but with nothing seriously wrong with him. He had slipped through the top branches of a tree rooted in a ravine; other branches had broken his fall until he landed at the end on his bottom; he had been only slightly stunned and had not heard me calling.

On another occasion we were playing castles, with the help of some railings near the front door of the hotel, when I sat down sharply on an iron spike. My cries of pain and fear soon brought help, and I was lifted off and hustled upstairs. Unfortunately, my mother was down in Heidelberg at the time, so all the people staying in the hotel took it on themselves to render first aid. I was laid face down on my bed, minus my trousers, and it seemed to me that most of the population of the town came in parties to examine my injury and to advise as to what should be done. Eventually Frau Köhler, the hotel proprietor's wife, came along and ordered everyone out of the room; then she washed and bandaged my wound, which, though quite deep, was by no means mortal. I was more frightened than anything else, and I think Cyril was considerably alarmed too, as he felt that he was responsible, and he remembered the incident of the swordstick in Tite Street. It was some time before I could sit squarely on a hard chair and the game of castles was banned.

But life during these holidays was not all play. Our financial position was not at all good, so we formed ourselves into a Committee of Ways and Means, to solve the problem of poverty. The main attraction of Heidelberg is the Schloss, which, though largely in ruins, still contains a great many interesting objects, including the famous Heidelberg Tun, a monster cask which holds 49,000 gallons of wine. Entrance to the Schloss cost one mark, half-price for children. So we would loiter near the funicular station and grin at Americans and Englishmen as they stepped out of the train. They usually grinned back and it only needed the discovery that we were English for a friendship to be struck up.

The way to the Schloss from the funicular railway lay through a beer-garden, and it was a foregone conclusion that our new friends would want a glass of beer and would invite us to have a large (Della Bona size) ice with them. The rest was easy. After explaining our presence there, we would lead the conversation round, quite naturally, to the Schloss; we knew a great deal about this, as we had made it the object of special study. Almost inevitably the next question would be: did they have guides to show you round? Yes, they did. Did the guides speak English? Ah! That was a very difficult question to answer. Some of the guides spoke English, when they were taking round large parties of English-speaking people, but there was no guarantee that they would do so, particularly if the English-speaking people in their party were in the minority. The truth was that all the guides spoke fluent French and English and always delivered their harangues in both these languages as well as in German.

We were next asked whether we could spare the time to go round the Schloss with them, to explain and interpret. We could and did. And at the end of the long conducted tour, involving a lot of climbing about the ruins, we were surprised if we did not get another large ice-cream apiece, and a small gift of money, usually one mark each. We had grown older and wiser since the Nervi days, and this activity of ours was never discovered, even though the enemy, in this case our own beloved mother, was so near at hand.

The proprietor of the Schloss Hotel and his wife, Herr and Frau Köhler, were a most sympathetic couple. They immediately took a great fancy to all three of us. Frau Köhler and my mother would sit sewing and talking for hours together, improving each other's English and German respectively. Herr Köhler was a large man with a big black beard, whose main interest in life, apart from conducting his hotel, was philately. He was reputed to possess the finest collection of German stamps in the world. He collected nothing after 1890. Between 1849 and that date twenty different German States and Post Offices had issued their own stamps, the number issued, with minor varieties, being just over one thousand. But, including errors, blocks of stamps, and in some cases whole sheets, Herr Köhler had accumulated over fourteen thousand. My brother and I were occasionally allowed to look at parts of this collection, so long as we did not touch anything; it filled us with an almost reverential awe, though we were unable to appreciate its finer points. And naturally Herr Köhler gave us a great many stamps for our own embryo collections.

He was a Roman Catholic and a very religious man, and he refused to work on Sunday. He would not even look at his stamps on that day. But in the afternoon, having spent the morning at his devotions, he and a friend of his would walk down to Schlierbach through the woods, invariably taking us with them. Schlierbach is a little village on the bank of the Neckar, upstream; it was about two miles from the Schloss Hotel as the crow flies; but as a man walks, and particularly as a boy wanders, it was more like twice that distance. We looked forward to these Sunday walks all the week. Herr Köhler walked with a slow and very dignified step, and Cyril and I would dash about, hither and thither, looking for mushrooms to take back to our mother. We followed a winding path, shaded by trees, but every now and then it would cross a clearing full of rank green grass and wildflowers and sun.

The reason for choosing Schlierbach as the object of this walk was that the railway to Heidelberg ran through it, so that once we reached the village our labours were over for the day. We all adjourned to the local beer-garden, where we refreshed ourselves with Löwenbräu beer; Cyril and I were given a small glass each, while Herr Köhler and his Companion consumed several large Steins. It was delicious after our hot walk, and though it made us sleepy it never did us any harm. When we had rested, we took the train back to Heidelberg and the funicular up to the Schloss.

Herr Köhler always paid for us on these jaunts, and would not hear of our mother paying our fares. I do not think she knew about the beer, and I doubt whether she would have approved, so we pretended to take it as a matter of course and never said anything about it.

During part of August that year my mother paid a visit to England; she used to go back from time to time, usually while we were at school, to look after her affairs, to see her friends and relations and to discuss with them how she could reconstruct her life and ours. It was too early to come to any definite decision, but she must have felt that our exile could not last for ever, and that sooner or later some *modus vivendi* would have to be found for us in England.

When she went, she left us in charge of Frau Köhler, who was very kind to us, but made us behave properly and be in time for meals and go to church on Sunday mornings, when she took us down to the Heiliggeistkirche in Heidelberg. This church must have been unique, since both Roman Catholic and Protestant services were held in it at the same time. In 1705 the nave was separated from the choir by a wall, the nave being reserved for Catholics and the choir for Protestants. Frau Köhler took us into the Catholic part. I doubt whether this had much effect on my brother, but I was deeply impressed by the solemnity of the ritual. This was my first introduction to the Catholic Church, and when my mother returned I told her about it and how much more I liked it than the English Chapel, "because it was so beautiful."

Towards the end of the holidays we were taken down into the town to be photographed in our Eton suits: two self-conscious little boys, my brother solemn as usual, I restless and a little sentimental. My mother sent copies of these to my father and they were in his possession when he died. In a letter to Robert Ross from Berneval, he wrote: "I have heard from my wife—she sends me photographs of the boys—such lovely little fellows in Eton collars—but she makes no promise to allow me to see them: she says she will see me, twice a year, but I want my boys." I do not think that my brother was ever again taken by a professional photographer in a studio, though I have snapshots of him and photographs taken in groups. I myself was not photographed again for twelve years, except in groups.[31] I suppose that none of the people we were allowed to know were sufficiently interested in us to want our photographs.

The summer holidays passed all too quickly, and we went back to Neuenheim College. And so one of the happiest times in my early life was succeeded by one of the most miserable. My brother, who with his superior physique and knowledge was a hero to me, began to lose interest in me and, I thought, actively to dislike me. I felt this very keenly. I had no friends in the school, and I felt that the hand of every man and boy was against me. I often wonder how I managed to survive that term; I suppose that, although the sorrows of childhood are in some ways much more poignant than those of adult life when one has acquired a certain amount of philosophy, the power of resistance to sorrow in a child is greater too.

The term started badly enough, with an injustice and a disillusionment. My mother had given me five marks to take back to school with me. Apart from a few pence, this was all the money I had; but it was quite enough, since all the necessities of life, such as sweets, lemonade, cakes and matches, were very cheap. I was not yet ten years old, and to have five marks all at once was wealth. The day after my return, one of the bigger boys, aged about sixteen, found out that I had this money and asked me to lend it to him until the following day, as his allowance had not yet arrived from England. I did so without any misgivings, and that was the last I ever saw of my money. He never paid me back; I asked him for it two or three times; at first he put me off with an evasive answer, but in the end he aimed a kick at me and said: "To hell with you and your five marks!" So I just had to bear my loss with a heavy heart and brood over the dishonesty of the human race.

Twenty years later I met this boy again. He did not recognise me, as my name meant nothing to him and he had been blinded in an accident some years before. And for a terrible moment I wondered if I had cast a spell upon him and whether, if he repaid me my five marks, even at that distant date, he would recover the use of his eyes.

As soon as we were safely back in school, our mother went to see her friends in Italy and we were left without her moral support. Frontiers seem to separate people far more than mere distances; so long as our mother was in the same country as ourselves we felt that she was near us, but as soon as she went to another country she seemed very far away indeed.

Cricket was over and Rugby football started. I cannot say that I enjoyed it. Like all games played at English schools in those days, it was delightful if you were good at it but sheer purgatory if you were not. There was one sadistic master, whose name I have deliberately forgotten, who delighted, on cold afternoons, in taking the smaller boys out to the football field for what he called "scrum practice." This was the most dreaded of all the forms of recreation provided by the school. It consisted in getting the boys to form serums, while he circled round them, slashing at their buttocks with a cane in order, he said, to make them push harder. Eventually one of the small boys complained to his bigger brother, who complained to the headmaster, and our tormentor left shortly afterwards; not, however, before he had tried to justify himself, in the presence of the elder brother, by saying that it was good for the boys because it made them tough. It did not make me tough; day after day I came back from the football field with my behind covered with weals and crept exhausted into a corner until the pain wore off.

Middle-class Germans were only just learning to play games, so they were taking them very seriously. The only sports still indulged in by the Junker class were hunting, duelling and beer-swilling; they looked down on any form of athletics and team-games as fit pastimes only for boors and peasants. We were constantly regaled by the sight of swaggering students from the University parading about the town, either in open landaus or arm-in-arm, occupying, with their inevitable Great Dane dogs, the whole of the pavement and much of the road. Their faces would be swathed in bandages as the result of their duels. Nearly all the students belonged to one or other of the numerous student clubs or *Korps*, each of which had its distinctive cap. Duels between the members of the different *Korps* were of daily occurrence and were fought for the most trivial reasons, merely as an excuse for fighting. When a student had fought three duels he wore the *Korps* colours on a ribbon worn diagonally across his chest. And he wore an extra ribbon for each further three duels: some of the students wore almost a dozen of them.

But some of the more progressive German schools were already becoming keenly interested in football, and one day we received a challenge from Frankfurt-am-Main, about fifty miles north of Heidelberg. Rather foolishly, as it turned out, we accepted this challenge. The Frankfurt team came down to Neuenheim, and a crowd of about two thousand of the local inhabitants turned out to see the match. Neuenheim College won by some fantastic margin like 60-nil; this so humiliated the Germans that they accused us of cheating by playing masters, which was quite true. The indignant German crowd stoned the school and broke some of the windows. They began to be more and more hostile and were eventually dispersed by the appearance of the local fire brigade, which threatened to play the hose on them. That was the only time we attempted to play any games against the Germans while I was there.

I will not enlarge upon the misery of that term; the cold, and the efforts to efface myself in order to avoid being bullied. To distinguish between us, we were not called major and minor, as in schools in England, but Holland *einz* and Holland *zwei*, and I was constantly in dread of hearing someone call out "Holland *zwei!*" which usually boded no good for me. The schoolboy code of honour forbade me to complain to the masters; it was a time when I really needed a father to whom to appeal; but when the Christmas holidays came round I poured out my heart to my mother and she realised that things could not possibly go on like this.

We spent the Christmas holidays in Freiburg with the Blackers.[32] They were one of the few families whom we still knew and who had been friends with both sides of our own family. We had a quiet time, as the ground was nearly always under snow in the winter. We skated and tobogganed and went for slithery walks in the neighbourhood of the town. Carlos Blacker took Cyril and myself to the Cathedral, which is one of the finest Gothic buildings in Germany, with its 380-foot tower, nearly thirty feet more than the length of the Cathedral itself, giving it an almost overpowering majesty. He taught us the elementary differences between the simplest styles of architecture, showing us from books how the Gothic developed from the Norman and the Early English Perpendicular. And he entertained us in the evenings with conjuring tricks, of which he had a seemingly inexhaustible repertoire.

Freiburg is one of the most beautiful towns in Germany, but it was spoiled in those days by the students from the University, who filled the streets, vying with the young army officers in crowding civilians—particularly women and children—off the pavements into the roadway. Here too, as in Heidelberg, the really smart student was almost improperly dressed for the street unless he was accompanied by a Great Dane, which occupied more space than the student himself.

During these holidays my mother sounded me about the Catholic Church, to which I had been so attracted when left in the hands of Frau Köhler in Heidelberg. She asked me whether I would like to go to an Italian Catholic school and I, having reached the point at which I would rather have gone anywhere than back to Neuenheim, was delighted at the prospect. So once more Cyril and I went to different schools. Indeed, we never attended the same school again.

Quite apart from my unhappiness at Neuenheim College, I think that another factor entered into the decision. My mother was always afraid that, with our two rather unusual names of Cyril and Vyvyan, our identity might be discovered, particularly as my father's works were still widely read in literary circles, and our names appeared as the speakers in one of the dialogues of *Intentions*.[33]

In any case Neuenheim College was too rough for me at the age of ten. My brother did not seem to mind this roughness; he had already started on his determined mission in life to rehabilitate the family name by sheer force of character and by overcoming all weaknesses and obstacles. After I had left Neuenheim I received a letter from him saying: "I am writing this in prep. We have been having a lovely fight and the master is going to cane everyone. This letter is awful tripe. Your loving brother, Cyril." I could picture the situation; it was from exactly this that I had wanted to escape.

My brother remained at Neuenheim College until the summer of 1898, when we both returned to England. After the second world war, I tried to discover what had happened to the school, but met with no success. A school magazine, the *Neuenheimer*, was published periodically, but there is no copy in the British Museum. I have convincing evidence that the school was in existence as late as 1939, when a great many German families sent their sons there to acquire a little English culture. It was not to be expected that an English school in Germany would survive two world wars. Recently I addressed a letter to "The Headmaster, Neuenheim College," enclosing an International Reply Coupon. My letter was returned to me, coupon and all, endorsed in German: "Return to Sender. College occupied by U.S. Army."

So Cyril went back to Neuenheim College and I, at the beginning of 1897, was taken by my mother to Monaco and handed over to the Jesuits at the Collegio della Visitazione, once more to enter upon a new and entirely different system of life.

CHAPTER IV

Monaco

IT may seem odd that Monaco should have been chosen
for my further education. The choice was mainly due to
the fact that one of the people who had remained loyal to
my father was Princess Alice of Monaco. She had always
protested against the inhumanity of his treatment. She was
a devout Catholic and it was she who suggested that
I should go to this Jesuit school, promising my mother that
she would keep an eye on me, see that I was reasonably
happy, and let me come and play with her family on Sundays and holidays, whenever I wished to do so. For some
time, also, my mother had had strong leanings towards the
Catholic Church, though she was never actually received
into it. My father, too, was always attracted to Catholicism;
in a letter to my mother—which, together with other
letters from my father to my mother, was subsequently
destroyed by members of my mother's family—my father
said that he thought it would be a wonderful thing if his
sons could be brought up as Catholics. And finally,
Monaco, being close to the Italian frontier, was only a
short distance from Nervi.

My mother suggested to my brother and myself that
we should both go to this school; but Cyril was comparatively happy at Neuenheim, where he was making good
progress in work and games, and he said he did not want
to leave. Afterwards he told me that he was not so much
happy as untormented, since he felt sure that in that remote
backwater of English education his identity would never
be discovered. I, on the other hand, having been unhappy
at Neuenheim, eagerly seized on the opportunity for a

change. So one day in January 1897, after my brother had returned to Neuenheim, my mother took me to Monte Carlo. After two days at the Hôtel Bristol, to give us an opportunity of calling at the Palace and of paying our respects to the Princess, my mother handed me over to the authorities of the Collegio della Visitazione, who received me, Protestant and therefore infidel that I was, with all the eagerness of a boa-constrictor welcoming a rabbit. My mother remained in Monte Carlo for a few days, during which I spent part of each day with her, so that I might become gradually acclimatised to my new and strange surroundings; then she bade me farewell and returned to Nervi, so as to be once more near the Ranee of Sarawak.

The outlook was not, to say the least of it, very bright for me. All the masters in the school were Italian Jesuits, and most of the boys were Italian also, with a sprinkling of Monegasques. My French was not bad and I could scrape along with German, but my Italian was rudimentary—simply what I had picked up from the inhabitants of Nervi and Sori. Fortunately a good many of the Jesuits spoke French.

The school had been built between 1665 and 1675 as a convent, and had had a varied career. During the French Revolution it had become a military hospital, but in 1816 the nuns were ejected and the place was turned into a barracks. In 1860 it became a Jesuit seminary, and in 1870, when the Society of Jesus was banned in Italy as a Teaching Order, it became a school for the education of Italian boys of good family whose parents wanted them to have a Jesuit education. The Italians remained until 1900, when the ban was lifted and they returned to Italy, their place being taken by French Jesuits. Since 1910 it has been a lay school with French government-appointed masters.

It was a large, irregularly shaped building with a frontage on the Place de la Visitation, from which it took its

name. At one side of it was the school chapel, built at the
same time as the convent and showing considerable
baroque influence. This chapel, named La Chapelle de la
Visitation, was open to the public, who had access to it
through the main entrance on the Place; the school had
its own entrance into a side-aisle, from the main ground-
floor corridor of the school. Beyond this corridor there
was an inner courtyard, which must originally have been
a cloister in the convent days. The sun never seemed to
penetrate into this courtyard, which was lined with widely-
spaced and heavily barred windows, giving the place a
prison-like appearance. I do not know which of the rooms
had windows overlooking the Place, but none of these
was accessible to the boys; and, as the back of the building looked out over the sea, no one inside ever caught a
glimpse of the outside world. The boys were never
allowed out by themselves, and this was very irksome to
my sense of freedom, which had been highly developed
during the previous eighteen months. The impression left
on me by the school is of dimly-lit rooms and corridors
and perpetual supervision.

All the floors of the building were paved with red tiles.
The only carpet, the only upholstered chairs, indeed
the only signs of any comfort I ever saw, were in the
reception room. In this room parents interviewed their
children.

The overpowering sense of gloom with which the
school filled me was enhanced by the fact that only in the
study-places and in the playground was conversation
allowed. Silence had to be observed in the corridors, along
which we walked in single file, hugging the walls. Even in
the refectory conversation was not allowed except on Sundays and important feast-days. On ordinary days passages
from the Lives of the Saints would be read by one of the
senior boys. Of course whispered conversation was carried
on but as all the Jesuits dined with us and had eyes

like hawks and ears like bats, this was very hard to achieve undetected and was avoided by the prudent, since, if it was discovered, swift retribution would follow.

The chapel and the refectory were the only places where all the boys met on common ground. In every other department of scholastic life the boys were grouped into four different watertight divisions, according to their ages. This was part of the Jesuit system of education all over the world. We naturally spent a great deal of our time in the chapel, where we all had our allotted places in four division blocks. But the refectory was the most cheerful place in the school. The building stood on the edge of the steep southern slope of the rock of Monaco, just above the spot where the Musée Océanographique now stands, so that the ground floor was, as it were, on two separate levels. The refectory was on the lower level, facing the sea over the bigger boys' playground, and it was the only room lit by large windows through which the sun used to pour on fine days, which are not nearly so frequent as inhabitants of the Riviera would have us believe.

The refectory contained five long tables and a pulpit reading-desk. The top table was occupied by the masters, and the other four by the boys, who sat on benches on either side of their table with their division Prefect at the end. This division Prefect was one of the masters, whose job it was to supervise the boys under his care, to keep discipline and to see that no rules were broken. Each boy had a small carafe of watered wine at dinner-time, and it was forbidden to trade one's wine with another boy for marbles. The possession of real money was not allowed, so there were various other forms of currency in circulation, chief among which were marbles. Dire were the penalties if one was caught disposing of one's wine ration.

On the whole the food was very good, particularly on Sundays and Saints' Days, when we had chocolate instead of coffee for breakfast and chicken for dinner. This was a very good way of impressing upon us the importance of religious festivals. In the summer one of the masters would stand at the door of the refectory as we filed into breakfast and give each of us a dessertspoonful of some form of brimstone and treacle. It tasted quite pleasant and no one tried to avoid it; we all had it from the same spoon, and it did not seem to do us much harm.

Each division had its own classroom, its own study-place and its own dormitory, and no boy from one division was allowed to speak to a boy in another one unless he was his brother or near relation. Even when the school went bathing from the La Condamine beach, the four divisions went at different times. The result of this was that there could be no system of boy prefects, nor was any bullying possible.

The study-place was also our playroom when it rained and after sunset. When I first arrived, I was in the lowest division, consisting of about twenty-five boys, and the room struck me with instant fear. It was a large square room with desks and rush-bottomed chairs placed all round the walls, sideways to the centre of the room. Each desk had a drawer and a raised back on which was a shelf for books and further possessions. This arrangement prevented one from seeing or having any communication with the boys on either side of one, but it did not prevent the Prefect, who sat on a rostrum between the two windows through which very little light ever penetrated, from seeing everyone. The lighting in the study-places consisted of one lamp hanging from the centre of the ceiling. Many years later I read Julian Green's *Minuit*,[34] which almost exactly reproduces the atmosphere of that room. We all complained that we could not see to prepare our lessons, but nothing was ever done about it. I know that it ruined my own eyesight, for in that light we had to trace maps and copy drawings, and I remember raising my head from my desk and looking round and finding that everything was in a haze. My sight had been very good until then, but when I returned to England I had to wear glasses.

In recreation-time in the study-place there was not much to do. We read, played marbles, talked and got very bored. There was not enough room for any active game, but we played draughts and I learnt to play chess.

The sanitary arrangements were elementary. There was one small closet, leading out of the study-place, and I am sure that it dated from the foundation of the convent. There was no running water either there or in the dormitory. If we wanted a drink, there was a large earthenware filter in one corner of the study-place; this was periodically filled up from a watering-can by one of the servants.

The dormitory also led out of the study-place; it was furnished with open-fronted cubicles with wooden partitions. In each cubicle were a bed and an iron washstand holding a china basin containing water. Cleanliness was not encouraged and was certainly in no way linked with godliness. I think they went on the same principle as the one in Victorian England that a woman who took more than one bath a week was suspected of leading an immoral life.

There was only one bath in the school and that was in the infirmary. I discovered this because I was always allowed a bath on the day before my mother was due to arrive at Monte Carlo. And in the sacred cause of modesty I was always given a bathing costume to have it in! On Thursdays of alternate weeks hot water was supplied either for a footbath or for washing one's head, which was always kept convict-cropped. That was considered to be enough ablution for us: of course, we did not take violent exercise, like small English boys, so I do not suppose we were much dirtier than they were.

We all wore uniforms, even down to our underwear and night attire. My own pyjamas were taken away and I was given a long cotton nightgown to wear, with red cot-

ton stitching down the front and on the wrists. And a
night-cap! This was really necessary on cold nights, because, as I have said, our hair was shorn off close to our
heads. Our day clothes consisted of stuffy uniforms, with
long trousers and single-breasted jackets hooking uncom-
fortably at the throat. They were black in winter, pepper-
and-salt in summer, both with gilt buttons. Beneath
these, winter and summer, we wore ankle- and wrist-length
underclothing, only varying slighty in weight according to
the season. Winter and summer, also, we wore elastic-
sided boots that always seemed to be too tight and were a
tremendous effort for a small boy to pull on, particularly
when they were new. The whole outfit was crowned
with a school cap, a quasi-military affair with the school
cypher, an entwined CDV in gold thread, above the
peak.

The pattern of life was the same for every one of the
boys, from the youngest to the oldest. The older boys had
no more freedom than we had and were under the same
constant supervision. They ate the same food, wore the
same clothes and lived in the same atmosphere of gloom
and darkness.

A series of gravelled playgrounds lay at the back of the
college, one for each division and divided from each other
by iron railings, to which it was unwise to approach too
close, for fear of being suspected of illicit conversation
through the bars. I wonder why we did not die of bore-
dom. No game involving the use of a ball was ever played,
unless you call marbles a ball-game. The only game that
seemed to be played was a rather mild form of prisoner's
base, in which each side in turn had to try to change ends
without being touched by a member of the opposing side;
it was not very exciting, and it was usually too hot in our
uniforms to play it in the summer. The older boys seemed
to content themselves with walking up and down in groups
of three or four; groups of two were not encouraged, as

being too conspiratorial. It is amazing that, after being at the school for ten years, as many of them had, they had retained any individuality at all.

We would go for long walks *en crocodile*, with our division Prefect bringing up the rear. We usually walked west so as to avoid having to trudge through Monte Carlo; this took us along the Lower Corniche Road, along which the newly invented motor-car used to roar at what seemed to us breakneck speed, swaying from side to side, belching out stinking petrol fumes and scaring the lives out of horses, whose riders or drivers would lash at the intrepid motorists with their whips. After pursuing the Corniche Road for some distance, we would leave it and take to the hills, where we were allowed to break forma-tion and find our own way through the olive-groves, pick-ing the sweet locust-beans from the carob-trees.

Occasionally, on special occasions in the summer, we would be taken on pilgrimages to some local shrine, often at some distance away, involving a ride in a charabanc drawn by sturdy mountain ponies. One of these pilgrimages was to the mountain shrine of Notre Dame de Laghet; this was over 1,100 feet above sea-level and meant a whole day's journey, with a church service and luncheon in a restaurant when we got there. Needless to say, this was a great treat. And sometimes we were driven up to La Turbie.

If we went the other way, towards Cap Martin, we walked along the Boulevard des Moulins, from which we could get a fairly close view of the wicked Casino across the gardens. The Casino was to us the emblem and embodiment of all evil. That was the heyday of Monte Carlo, the most fashionable gambling place in the world. Deauville was still a small fishing village. At Nice and Cannes and other seaside resorts they played nothing more exciting than *petite chevaux* and *boule*; but Monte Carlo contained the only legal public roulette rooms in Europe. We pictured to ourselves the wild orgies of worldliness and even paganism that must take place behind those sinister-looking walls, and we had visions of an almost unending procession of suicides, souls hurtling down into the depths of Hell. For we were naturally all intensely religious and believed in the most lurid aspects of Hell as described to us in sermons by our mentors.

When my mother left me at Monaco, I felt that I had indeed been abandoned. My Italian, as I have said, was negligible, so for a few weeks one of the Fathers was given the job of teaching me Italian; but he was due to go to England very shortly, and he spent most of his time practising his English on me. "How," he asked me, "should an Italian address an English nobleman? Should it be 'My Lord' or (phonetically) 'Mee-lord'?" Naturally I had not the vaguest idea, so I took a chance on "My Lord." Most of his questions were connected with the correct way to behave in the presence of nobility and gentry; I do not know whether he ever got to England and met any, but if he did I hope they were suitably impressed.

However, the youthful mind is very retentive, particularly when it is a question of holding one's own with other boys, and I made such good progress that it seemed no time at all before I was taking my place in class with boys of my own age. But it was almost like starting my education all over again. Apart from the drawback of having to do all my lessons in a language which was still strange to me, they were mostly quite different from those to which I had been accustomed.

Latin was an entirely unknown language with its exaggerated Italian pronunciation. Arithmetic seemed somehow to be done backwards. History and geography were the history and geography of the Roman Empire, modern Italy and, of course, the Catholic Church, and seemed to be mainly directed against Protestantism, the Reformation, Henry the Eighth and Good Queen Bess, who was presented as a figure of inhuman cruelty who martyred Catholics wholesale.

Attention had also to be paid to my religious instruction. There were all the prayers to be learnt in Latin, the Mass, the Rosary and Benediction to be explained. And I, who had the usual nebulous ideas about religion of the average English boy, found myself plunged into all the ceremonial and mysticism of the Catholic Church, viewed from the extreme Italian angle, with its tales of all the holy places in Italy, the tombs and relics of the Saints, the Casa Santa, and all the fragments of the True Cross.

Those Italian Jesuits were the gentlest, kindest and most sympathetic body of men that I had so far met in my short life, outside my own family circle. I remember three of them in particular with deep affection: first, my own division Prefect, Father Dominico Giusta, from whom I never had a harsh word that I did not richly deserve. Secondly, Father Alphonso Stradelli, a member of one of the oldest Roman families, who was the Spiritual Father. (The Spiritual Father is the priest to whom any boy in a Jesuit school has access at almost a moment's notice, if he is in any distress, be it religious, moral or mental. In the course of my eight years of Jesuit schooling I never knew one Spiritual Father who was not a help and a comfort to those in trouble.) The third priest, whom I really remember the best, was Father Modesto Cerutti, the chief classical master, and a true friend. He understood my worries and my sorrows and comforted me; and he provided an inexhaustible supply of stamps for my collection. I kept up a correspondence with him for some years after my return to England, but this gradually died for lack of common interest, when he left Monaco and went to Chieri. The last time that I wrote to him was in January 1907.

There was no corporal punishment at the Collegio

della Visitazione. Nevertheless, a boy could be made to feel the error of his ways. Summary justice was administered in the form of a swift cuff on the side of the head. In this the master had an unfair advantage; every time that a boy addressed a fully-ordained priest, he had to kiss his hand; it was the work of a moment for the priest to avoid the salute and to take a swing at the boy's head. However, if one had a guilty conscience, one might be sufficiently wary and quick to anticipate the slap with a well-timed duck; and, rather on the principle of English Law that no man may be put in peril twice for the same offence, if you succeeded in avoiding the sweeping hand you were not attacked again.

This was in the nature of an informal punishment. The official punishments were embarrassing and irksome, though not physically painful. Apart from expulsion, which I suppose existed, although I do not remember a case, the worst punishment that could be inflicted on a boy was to be made to eat his meals kneeling in the middle of the refectory in front of the high table, at which sat all the senior masters. This was not often resorted to; indeed, I do not think I saw it inflicted half a dozen times during the whole time I was at Monaco. Other refectory punishments consisted of not being allowed one's wine ration, or being put on a bread-and-water diet, seated among all one's division mates gorging themselves with good things.

One of the more serious forms of reprisal was to be condemned to silence for a stated period. It might be for only half an hour, or as long as a whole day. To be ordered a day's silence was dreaded almost as much as having to eat one's meals kneeling in the refectory. One could also be confined to one's desk during recreation time, or to a corner of the playground, from which one was not allowed to move.

Only fully ordained priests were allowed to order

punishment. All the Jesuits in Italy were addressed as Father, whether they were ordained or not; for the period of probation is a long one and Jesuits do not usually become priests until they are well over thirty years of age.

My greatest friend at the Monaco school was a boy named Cesare Calciati, who was a nephew of the Spiritual Father. This boy had an amazing gift of being able to mesmerise birds. He would set a box trap in the playground, baited with a small piece of cheese at the end of a string attached to the top end of a twig holding up the box. The unwary bird would peck at the cheese and down would come the box, imprisoning it. Calciati would lift the box just enough to get hold of the bird, which was usually, but not always, a sparrow. Retiring to a corner of the playground, he would spend about ten minutes talking to it and nursing it; then he would turn round and the bird would be sitting on his finger, quite unperturbed, while he stroked it. After a few minutes he would throw the bird up into the air and call out: *"Via!"* and the bird would fly away.

I saw Calciati do this many times; but the priests did not encourage him in this game and eventually forbade him to play it any more, on the grounds that it was cruel to the bird. My own belief is that they thought Calciati possessed some occult power, probably closely connected with the *gettatura*, the dreaded Evil Eye in which nearly all Italians implicitly believe.

Some years later I had definite proof that the Church took such matters seriously. I was in Stazzema with Charles Scott-Moncrieff, the talented translator of Proust into English, and in going round the thirteenth-century church during the siesta period I came across a printed notice in one of the two confessionals, instructing the priests as to which sins were to be referred to higher authority before absolution could be given for them. These consisted of five: murder, blasphemy, abstention from the

Oscar Wilde at the height of his career in 1892.

Constance and Cyril in about 1889, taken by the
Cameron Studio which was founded and run by
Julia Margaret Cameron's son.

Vyvyan in his favourite sailor suit; see page 44.

Vyvyan and Cyril in "Aesthetic Costume"; see pages 43–4

Oscar Wilde in the ruins of the Forum in Rome in April 1900,
probably taken with his own camera.

Constance in Heidelberg in 1896.

Constance's grave in the Staglieno Cemetery in Genoa. The words "Wife of Oscar Wilde" were added in 1963.

Vyvyan in
Heidelberg in
1896.

Cyril in
Heidelberg
in 1896.

Cyril at Radley College in about 1902.

Vyvyan at Lausanne in the winter
of 1904/5.

Vyvyan at the age of 69, the year in which he wrote
Son of Oscar Wilde.

Sacraments for over a year (which implied excommunication), the seduction of minors and, finally, indulging in sorcery of any kind, and particularly the *gettatura*. At about the same time I found, in a secondhand bookshop in Florence, a copy of *Il vero Drago Rosso (The real Red Dragon)*, giving instructions in sorcery and witchcraft, and on the preparation of magic potions, love-philtres and the like. It was a heinous crime in the eyes of the Church to be in possession of a copy of this book, and although I myself had no belief whatever in witchcraft I guarded it from the eyes of my Italian friends, who might easily have been shocked.

My other great friend was a boy named Moreno. He was a Monegasque, i.e. a citizen of Monaco, a status which in those days was (and probably still is) very difficult to acquire; both one's parents had to have been born in the Principality, and one had to have been born there oneself. Moreno's father was a croupier at the Casino, which was almost an hereditary appointment.

Moreno spoke French, Italian and Provencal. The fact that he spoke French first drew us together. We collected stamps, I taught him a little English and he taught me a lot of Provençal, using the works of Frederi Mistral as textbooks, particularly *Mirèio*. We used to talk Provençal together, though this was not much approved of, as not being in the set curriculum.

Twenty-five years later I was in the Casino at Monte Carlo when a little man approached me and asked me if I was Mr. Holland. When I said yes, he introduced himself as Moreno. He was a croupier, and croupiers never forget a face. I took him out to luncheon the next day, and he told me the most fascinating stories about the Casino. According to him, there is one way in which you can be certain of winning, in the long run, at *trente-et-quarante*. An Austrian syndicate had been doing it for years; but it meant someone from the syndicate being in the rooms whenever they were open, and sometimes not putting anything on for days at a time.

Calciati, Moreno and I were all indefatigable philatelists at school, and spent a great deal of our recreation time poring over each other's collections and cadging stamps from masters and other boys. My brother Cyril was also an enthusiastic stamp-collector and we wrote to each other frequently on the subject.

I have before me a letter to my brother in November 1897, which reads:

Darling Cyril,

I have got some used Portuguese stamps that were issued for 18 days and if you send me 1s. 8$^1/_2$d. I will bye you a set of 4 or even better I will send a letter to you for the dealer in these stamps and you could send him a postal order of 1 mark 8$^1/_2$d. I don't know what it would be in pfennigs but any way one and a tanner for the stamps and 2$^1/_2$ for return post. They were issued to commemorate the 7th centenary of St Antony, and are postal stamps and are very rare; one of them is like that which I gave Mother you know. Would you like stamps for Christmas? Johore and the Portuguese stamps 4 of each the Johore ones like the one you have the 1, 2, 3 and 4 cents they would cost me 2/11$^1/_2$ and then I would add some odds and ends. There is no news and I must finish now. Your loving brother Vivian Holland.

We usually signed our names in full when we wrote to each other, though I must say it looks rather odd now.

A great part of my mother's letters also dealt with philatelic matters, and she had to use a great deal of tact in dividing up anything that came her way, as we were like a couple of nestlings fighting for worms. We were always badgering her, as we knew that the Ranee received letters from Sarawak and the Dutch East Indies and the Federated Malay States. And my mother had a cousin married to the British Consul in Yokohama, who could always be relied upon to produce something new.

My pride in my stamp collection was such that I could

not bear the thought that some day in the remote future I would have to die and someone else would get hold of it. I even wondered if I could have it buried in my coffin with me. This was, I think, my only regret at the inevitability of death, because the joys of Paradise were so constantly and vividly put before us at school that many of us, including myself, were looking forward to the time when we would get there. I do not think we ever considered the possibility that we might qualify for the Other Place.

The school assembled late in December and broke up in the following August; there was no break for either Christmas or Easter. These holy days had to be passed at the school because of their religious importance. No work was done for some time before or after these feasts, so one really had holidays at school.

My mother thought it cruel to deprive me of my Easter vacation; but the Jesuits insisted upon all the boys being at the school during Easter Week, with its services, sorrows and rejoicings. So my mother arranged for me to go to Nervi towards the middle of March. I spent three weeks with her there, airing my newly acquired Italian, of which I was inordinately proud. And as soon as I returned to Monaco she had to go to Freiburg, to stay with the Blackers and cope with my brother, whose own school broke up shortly before Easter. In a way this was good for her, as she had one or the other of us with her during the six weeks preceding my father's release, which took place on May 19th, 1897.

My mother naturally felt that this was to be another great crisis in her life. But her family interfered, persuading her to let an interval elapse before she saw my father. She should have returned to England and taken charge of him, instead of leaving him to his own devices. But what her family really wanted was for her to sever connection with him once for all; they succeeded admirably in this, for my father and mother never met again.

The first time I went to the Monaco Palace, before going to school, I just bowed to the Princess, as I was told to do, but on subsequent occasions, when one of the Jesuit Fathers took me, I was ushered into the Presence and was told to go down on both knees and kiss her hand. Having done this, I was sent out into the Palace gardens to play with the children, who were a little older than I. The gardens were extensive and rambling and we used to play hide-and-seek until tea-time.

On my visits to the Palace I did not always see the Princess. She was often away and she had troubles of her own. The Prince was being a little wayward and she was trying, to the best of her ability, to follow in his footsteps. Many years later, when I was driving down to the south of France, I and a friend called at the chateau in which she was then living in retirement. She had long ceased to talk English, and when my friend introduced me to her as *le fils cadet d'Oscar Wilde,* she registered surprise and remarked: *"Tiens! J'avais même oublié qu'Oscar avait eu des enfants!"* When, however, I reminded her of my school-days in Monaco, she was very penitent and we indulged in reminiscences of my father and my mother and the Ranee.

The winter of 1897 passed and so did the spring, and with the coming of summer the great feast-day for all Italian boys approached: June 21st, the feast-day of St. Aloysius of Gonzaga, upon which all young Italians made their first Holy Communion. It was a terribly sad day for me, because one of the conditions of my being allowed to go to this school was that I should not be received into the Catholic Church. And yet there was I, as devout by this time as any boy in the school, seeing my little companions admitted to the Sacraments and being denied them myself. Of course I pleaded, but it was no good. There was no definite evidence, such as all Catholic boys can produce, that I had ever been baptised into any Church, even the

Protestant Church, so I could not go to Communion as I so ardently wished to do. I had to kneel ashamedly in my place in the chapel while all the others went to the altar. It was a bitter experience to see them with their white armbands decorated with gold tassels while I mingled with them as an outcast.

In the following year, 1898, the Bishop of Turin came to the school to give the new boys their First Communion. Again I was told that I could not be one of them, but I was slightly consoled by being appointed to follow the Bishop to the altar carrying the episcopal crozier, while another boy walked by my side carrying the mitre. I remember that there was a bit of a tussle over this, as we both wanted to carry the crozier. This very nearly resulted in neither of us being allowed to carry anything, but I won in the end. I was also presented to the Bishop and knelt before him and kissed his ring; he blessed me and promised me that if I was still at the school in the following year he would give me my First Communion whatever happened.

Shortly before this, on May 19th, my father was released from Reading Gaol. He was accompanied to Dieppe from Newhaven by his friend More Adey where they were met by Robert Ross and Reginald Turner who were already in France.[35] On his arrival he assumed the name Sebastian Melmoth, after the central figure in *Melmoth the Wanderer*, a book written by his great-uncle, Charles Maturin; and under this name he took rooms at the Hôtel Sandwich in Dieppe. At first he appears to have been quite happy there with his friends, many of whom came over from England to see him; but his identity gradually leaked out and visiting English and American people went out of their way to slight him and even to insult him. So after about ten days he moved to the Hôtel de la Plage at Berneval-sur-Mer, a small sea-side resort some five miles east of Dieppe.

His sympathisers had subscribed a sum of money to

help him regain his feet and he lived for some time on this while deciding what his next move was to be. Meanwhile my mother promised to make him an allowance of £3 a week until further notice, and this payment was kept up until her death.[36]

By a strange coincidence, on June 21st, 1897, the very day on which I was longing to make my First Communion, my father gave a children's party at Berneval, which he describes as follows in a letter written to a friend[37] on June 23rd:

My fête was a huge success; 15 *gamins* were entertained on strawberries and cream, apricots, chocolates, cakes and sirop de Grenadine. I had a huge cake with Jubilé de la Reine Victoria in pink sugar just rosetted with green, and a great wreath of red roses round it all. Every child was asked beforehand to choose his present: they all chose instruments of music!!

> 6 accordions
> 5 trompettes
> 4 clairons

They sang the Marseillaise and other songs, and danced a ronde, and also played "God save the Queen": they *said* it was "God save the Queen" and I did not like to differ from them. They also all had flags which I gave them. They were most gay and sweet. I gave the health of "La Reine d'Angleterre," and they cried "Vive la Reine d'Angleterre"!!!! Then I gave "La France—mère de tous les artistes"—and finally I gave "Le Président de la République": I thought I had better do so. They cried out with one accord "Vivent le Président de la République et Monsieur Melmoth"!!! So I found my name coupled with that of the President.

They stayed from 4.30 to 7 oc. and played games: on leaving I gave them each a basket with a Jubilee cake frosted pink and inscribed, and bonbons.

They seem to have made a great demonstration in Berneval-le-Grand, and to have gone to the House of the Mayor and cried "Vive Monsieur Le Maire! Vive la Reine d'Angleterre! Vive Monsieur Melmoth !"—I tremble at my position.

When I had acquired enough Italian to be able to follow the sermons in church, I was greatly puzzled by something called *immodestia,* which appeared to be one of the most heinous sins that a human being could commit—a mortal sin, in fact. It slowly dawned upon me that it had to do with the exposure of the human body, and I became even more perplexed. In my natural innocence it had never occurred to me that to expose one's body to the public view, let alone to one's own view, could possibly be a sin—though it might well be embarrassing. And I found myself suddenly pitchforked into a world in which one's own body was indecent and the bodies of other people were more indecent still. This really gave me my first sense of evil: I can imagine nothing so calculated to make a boy body-conscious and unhealthily inquisitive about its functions.

My spiritual adviser was very grave when I told him that in English schools the boys usually all bathed together naked and that they were sometimes joined in this by the masters. He held up his hands in horror and said: *"Peccato mortale!"* I was in a terrible state to think that I had been committing countless mortal sins over a period of years, but the good priest comforted me by declaring that, as I had not known it was a sin, I had not committed one; but I must be more careful in the future. Having thus had my hopes of salvation almost shattered, I refused during my next holidays to undress in front of my brother or to be present when he was doing so. Quite rightly, Cyril regarded me as an insufferable prig.

The holidays came at last. As nearly all the boys were going back to Italy, and a great many of the Fathers were going to Rome, it was quite easy for me to be dropped at Nervi, which is on the direct line from Monaco to Rome. Next day my mother and I went to Freiburg-im-Breisgau. Cyril was already there, having travelled down from Heidelberg alone, and we made our way, by various means of transport, to the little village of Hoechenschwand, one of the highest points in the Black Forest.

We spent about a month at Hoechenschwand. It was a glorious time of flowers and thunderstorms. The woods and the meadows were a mass of colour and we would bring great armfuls of flowers back to the hotel to decorate our mother's room. And the thunderstorms were magnificent. I have never had the slightest fear of thunderstorms since that summer; to have experienced one of the really heavy storms in the higher parts of the Black Forest gives one a contempt for other thunderstorms for ever. One storm was so heavy that there was no interval at all between the thunderclaps; it was just overhead and the noise was one continuous roar, with the lightning flickering like an early cinema-projector. Everyone in the village crowded into the church, being convinced that the Day of Judgment was at hand. My mother, who always had a headache in a thunderstorm, shut herself in her room, drew the curtains and lay down; but my brother and I stood at our bedroom window and watched the lightning playing round the lightning-conductors on the church spire, along the telegraph wires and on the belvedere from which, on fine evenings, visitors watched the sun setting behind the trees. And it was not bravado, either; we really enjoyed it.

Before we left, Cyril taught me to ride a bicycle. It took me a long time to learn, and then I lost control of my bicycle riding down one of the steep roads out of the village. Down, down I went, until I crashed into a wooden fence at a turn in the road; I shot over the fence and landed in the middle of a field of standing corn, escaping with a few bruises and abrasions. But the bicycle was an almost total loss.

Hoechenschwand is over 3,300 feet above sea-level, and at that altitude it was beginning to grow chilly by the beginning of September, so we returned to Freiburg and spent the remainder of the holidays with the Blackers. It was at Freiburg that I first fell foul of the Law. Proud of my new-found accomplishment of riding a bicycle, I persuaded my mother to hire one for me in the town. I was gaily riding on the pavement in the outskirts of the town when a policeman barred my way and asked for my name and address. Apparently the riding of bicycles on pavements had increased enormously with the advent of the motor car, and the authorities were determined to stamp it out. I was not made to go to court, but I was fined five marks, which was an enormous sum to me in those days, and I had to find it out of my own pocket.

The holidays ended all too soon, and Cyril and I returned to our respective schools. The prospect of ten uninterrupted months at the Collegio della Visitazione was too much for me. Feeling as though I were entering an almost endless tunnel, I wrote a tearful letter to my mother imploring her to take me away. I had a great advantage over the other boys in the school in being able to write English. All letters, both in and out, were read, but as there was no one in the school who could read English my own letters escaped censorship. They could not very well forbid me to write to my mother and my brother. However, my mother wrote me a soothing letter and I soon calmed down and got back into the scholastic groove.

My mother's health was fast failing and she could not stand the hotel life at Nervi any more. She also felt that she ought to make a home for her sons, and that they should not be condemned to spending all their holidays in hotels. So, finding that there was an apartment to let in the Villa Elvira, at Bogliasco, almost next door to the Ranee, she took it for two years. I think she was really happy there for the first time since she left London. Her letters to me at that period are full of her activities; in addition to the Ranee, she seems to have acquired a circle of friends, and she had an Italian servant who adored her and ran the apartment like clockwork.

Cyril went to stay with her during the Christmas holidays, while I had to remain in Monaco to take part in the religious ceremonies. I remember being ashamed of myself for falling fast asleep in the course of the three midnight masses that were said on Christmas Eve. I had to be carried bodily to bed. I was only eleven, and I had been up since seven in the morning, if not earlier; but I felt that if I had had more faith or had been more devout it would not have happened.

To console me for having had no Christmas holiday, my mother visited me for a week in the middle of February 1898. She was, if possible, more sweet to me than ever and kept me close beside her all the time. She even obtained leave for me to sleep away from the school, and I shared a room with her at the Hôtel Bristol. At the end of the week, when one of the priests came to take me back to the school, she cried a little. But neither she nor I knew that we were never to see each other again.

Her health continued to deteriorate. Her domestic troubles had lessened her powers of resistance, and the injuries she had sustained in her fall downstairs in Tite Street were more severe than had at first been realised. Paralysis had developed in her spine and in her right arm. For some months she had been having difficulty in writing and she had taken to using a typewriter for her correspondence. But one day, at the beginning of April, I received a long letter from her in her own handwriting, which must have cost her a prodigious effort. In it she mentioned my father. She wrote: "Try not to feel harshly about your father; remember that he is your father and that he loves you. All his troubles arose from the hatred of a son for his father, and whatever he has done he has suffered bitterly for." This was her last letter to me. She went into a nursing home in Genoa shortly afterwards, for an operation to relieve the pressure on her spine that was causing her ceaseless pain. Both the Ranee and my uncle told me that my mother had no suspicion that she might die, but I can only think, from the contents of her last letter to me, that she knew in her heart that her sorrows would soon be over.

One day Father Stradelli, the Spiritual Father, sent for me to come to his room just as night was falling. As I stood beside his desk he said to me: "My child, do you know that your mother has been very ill?" I did not know it, but some instinct told me the truth and I asked: *"La mia madre è morta?"* Father Stradelli paused for a moment and looked at me; then he replied: *"Sì, fanciullo."*[38] I cried a little, then I asked him about my father, for I wanted to know where he was. He shook his head and said that he did not know. And again I instinctively asked him: "He has been in prison, hasn't he?" Again a pause, then: "Yes, but he is free now." Although I had suspected this for a long time, I had never asked anyone about it, and this was the first time that I was certain. I had a great sense of relief at the words: "He is free now." He had, in fact, been free for nearly a year and was living in Naples.

My grief for my mother was very genuine and deep. I worshipped her, and all the weight of the world seemed to descend upon me with her death. Typically, one of the questions that worried me most was whether my mother, being a Protestant, was eligible for a seat in Heaven; but Father Stradelli quickly reassured me on that point.

The first thing I did was to sit down and write to my brother Cyril. My letter has not been preserved, but I have my brother's letter to me, which crossed mine. It runs:

Darling Vyvyan, Isn't it awful? Poor, poor Mother! It's hard to realise. One's so used to having her. What shall we do in the holidays with no Mother? I went to the theatre last night, it was awful fun. I have bought a revolver. It shoots six times. I paid 12/- for it. I got it about four weeks ago, when mother sent me 10/- for being top of my class. Think of Mother always and remember she sees everything you do. Your loving brother Cyril.

The best tribute to my mother comes from Robert Sherard's *The Life of Oscar Wilde*, in which he says:

Constance Wilde, who had long been ailing, and who never recovered from the horrible shock of the catastrophe which shattered her home, was released from a world so full of cruel surprise to the simple and gentle, by death. She died in Genoa about one year after her husband had left prison. She was a simple, beautiful woman, too gentle and good for the part that life called upon her to play. Her death was to O.W's affectionate heart a sorrow which accentuated his despair. His love for her was pure, deep and reverent.

The day after I heard of my mother's death a charabanc excursion took place for the whole school. I was sent on it because it was thought that it might distract me from my sorrow. I remember feeling curiously light and ethereal; almost disembodied and quite remote from the things of this world. I could not yet realise how great a loss to me my mother's death meant. My brother and I had very little in common, but thenceforward, like the Butcher and the Beaver in *The Hunting of the Snark*, "purely from nervousness, not from goodwill, we walked along shoulder to shoulder."

A fortnight later my uncle Otho came to see me from Genoa, where he had made all the funeral arrangements for my mother. He was kind and sympathetic as always, but was very much wrapped up in his own sorrow for the beloved sister with whom he had grown up. Also, he had a wife and family of his own in Bevaix, to whom he was anxious to return.

Letters, too, came from members of my mother's family, who were thenceforth to have charge of us. I think these relatives were genuinely affected by the tragic circumstances in which my brother and I now found ourselves, but they also felt that we were a bit of a nuisance, and were rather apprehensive of the effect that our paternity might have upon us.

The whole of the school was deeply sympathetic, and

for about a month I was put on what I might describe as light duty, not doing much work and being taken out for walks by any Father who happened to be unoccupied.

Shortly before my mother died, *The Ballad of Reading Gaol* was published.[39] I myself never saw a copy of it until I went to Cambridge in 1905. I do not think that my mother ever saw it at all. The conspiracy of silence about my father was very efficient and I doubt whether anyone would have called her attention to it.

My main preoccupation, now, was to be allowed to continue my religious education. My remaining at Monaco was out of the question; but the Rector of the school wrote to the Rector of Stonyhurst College in Lancashire and received some pamphlets and a prospectus from him, which he gave me to take back to England.

I remained behind when the school broke up, awaiting instructions from home. Eventually I returned to England in charge of a priest whom I did not know, and who read his breviary all through the journey and never spoke to me except in answer to some question of mine.

CHAPTER V

Return from Exile

My destination on my arrival in London was the house of my mother's aunt, Mrs. Napier, who lived in Cottesmore Gardens, Kensington, with her daughter Eliza, whom my brother and I had always known as Lizzie. My Jesuit escort duly delivered me to the door of the house and departed on his way.

These two ladies were thenceforth to stand *in loco parentis* to my brother and myself. We had an official guardian, whose duty it was to administer the small estate left by our mother, which was sufficient to secure our education; but he did not take any other duties he had towards us very seriously. We scarcely ever saw him and he delegated his authority entirely to the Napiers. My brother and I were also Wards in Chancery, but this did not affect us very much. The Judge to whose charge we were officially confided was Mr. Justice Kekewich. I saw him only once, when my brother and I were taken to his chambers in Lincoln's Inn and he delivered to us a short homily on behaviour.

My great-aunt Mary was a very intelligent old lady, who took a deep interest in a vast number of subjects, including politics. She was an ardent Liberal. Born in the reign of William IV, she was not unlike Queen Victoria in appearance. She had seven children, all of whom survived her, and with that she considered she had done her duty by the world in which she lived. Her life ran in a very pleasant groove from which nothing would deflect her; our upbringing was therefore left in the hands of her daughter Lizzie, an angelic woman with the most austere ideas on deportment and a very strong sense of duty.

Both these ladies adored our mother, but the spectre of our father was always hovering in the background, and all our movements were constantly watched as though there was something strange about us—whereas we were just two very normal and rather unhappy little boys. The Napiers were ultra-Scotch and very proud of it, and the fact that my brother and I were ultra-Irish did not help in any way. We were strongly discouraged from referring to our Irish ancestry, as this might conceivably have given a clue to our identity.

I must have been a strange sight to the conventional Napiers when I first appeared from Monaco, with my cropped head and my school uniform. I wonder what my father would have thought if he could have seen me. The contents of my luggage, too, must have been rather baffling; school uniforms, a spare pair of elastic-sided boots, a few Italian schoolbooks, and the oddest assortment of Italian underwear. I had, of course, outgrown any English clothes I had ever possessed.

I was also the proud possessor of a crab, which I regarded as my dearest friend, and which I had transported all the way from Monaco. It had been alive when I had started on my journey, but it was very dead on my arrival.

The process of turning me back into an English boy was embarked upon immediately, and I had to readjust all my ideas and most of my values. As the process involved my being supplied with an entirely new outfit of clothes, I thoroughly enjoyed it at first. Cyril did not arrive until several days later, as he was waiting for someone to be found to bring him from Germany. Eventually he travelled the whole way from Heidelberg to London entirely by himself, which showed initiative in a boy of thirteen. The lateness of his arrival was a blessing so far as I was concerned, since when he arrived he also was found to have outgrown all his clothes. Had he arrived at the same time as I did, his clothes would no doubt have been handed over to me. As it was, we both started afresh.

Of course I asked for my toys, thinking that they would be there to receive me, and it was a grievous disappointment to learn that they had gone for ever. Not only was I disappointed, but I suffered from a deep sense of injustice. They were my own toys and no one had any right to lose them, let alone to dispose of them in any way. To deprive a child of his favourite toys is just as cruel as to break a promise to him. It weakens his faith in human nature. In this case it was naturally no fault of the family that my toys had disappeared, and they must have felt very keenly the fact that they could not explain the circumstances to me.

On the ground floor of the Cottesmore Gardens house was the morning-room, which was also the library, and there I came across a copy of *The Happy Prince*, a book which I had not seen for over three years. I was delighted to see it again and took it out of its shelf. But I had a great shock when I saw that the name Oscar Wilde had been scratched off the cover and that a piece of stamp-paper had been pasted over it on the title-page. Once more I puzzled and wondered what it was all about.

On returning to England my main efforts were directed towards persuading my mother's very Protestant family to allow me to continue my Catholic education. Shortly before my mother died she wrote in a letter to my brother:

Vyvyan is keener than ever about Roman Catholicism; and, as it is the religion of law and discipline and as Vyvyan has very little sense of either, I think it is a very good thing for him.

I have already said that I was not allowed to be received into the Catholic Church while I was at school in Monaco, which was a perpetual source of grief to me. Italian boys make their First Communion at the age of eight or nine, but I could not do so. I was eventually admitted to the

Confessional, as, had I been denied that, I would undoubtedly have become very ill mentally, feeling that all
my sins were crowding in upon me.

So religious was I at this period of my life that I regarded all civilians with pity, wondering how they could
be so blind to their own interests and happiness as not to
become priests. And even secular priests I regarded with
some suspicion. It was a religious order or nothing for me.
I was quite determined to become a Jesuit when I grew
up.

Almost my first act on my arrival in England was to
hand over to my cousin Lizzie the prospectus of Stonyhurst College with which I had been provided at Monaco.
I expected to have a long tussle; but the fact that my
mother had sent me to Monaco and that I was obviously
deeply concerned with the Catholic Church must have
influenced my guardians. I was duly told that at the end
of the holidays I was to go to Stonyhurst.

While my own efforts were being devoted to gaining
entry into a Catholic school, those of my mother's family
were being directed towards obliterating all memory of my
father from the minds of both Cyril and myself; and at the
same time towards destroying all evidence that might conceivably connect us with the family of Wilde.

The first step in that direction was to give us to understand that our father was dead. We were not told this in
so many words, as that would have been a lie and I do not
suppose that anyone in the family ever told a deliberate lie.
But the impression was conveyed and we accepted it as
fact. And it was once more impressed upon us that we
must never mention our father's name to anyone, particularly in connection with ourselves.

The next move was to separate us from each other. It is
much easier to keep a secret by oneself than to share it with
someone else. One become careless and is apt to blurt out
indiscreet remarks.

I rather suspect that, apart from my unhappiness at Neuenheim College, this may have been one of the reasons for my being sent to school in Monaco while Cyril remained in Germany. All decisions affecting our lives at that time were taken by a kind of Family Council, and the fact that I was not allowed to be received into the Catholic Church, although I was sent to a Catholic school, may have been due to a compromise between the Family Council and its Protestant conscience. However, when I was sent to Stonyhurst this compromise could no longer be maintained. And the fact that my brother's religious beliefs now differed from mine provided an excellent excuse for keeping us apart.

From his earliest years Cyril had always wanted to go into the Navy. But the Navy would not have him—another bitter blow to his childish pride. So he was entered for Radley, with a view to his going into the Army, which was not so squeamish.

What remained of the holidays we passed pleasantly with one of my great-aunt's sons, who was a regular soldier and was stationed at Weymouth in Dorset. This cousin made friends with us and allied himself to us on more than one occasion when we were misunderstood by his mother and sister. Never was the saying truer that "the female of the species is more deadly than the male" than in its application to English people at the close of the nineteenth century. The male would have been much more broadminded if he had dared, but Victorian matriarchy was at its height. During the previous few years social restrictions and distinctions had been tightened up, in an attempt to curb the efforts towards emancipation made by the more progressive elements of the nineties, led and encouraged by the Prince of Wales. All social occasions were ruled over by the women with an iron hand. One word from a prominent society hostess, or a breath of scandal, and the unmarried girl (or even the young matron) was hurled into outer darkness and her name struck from all invitation lists. Within limits, men could do what they liked, so long as they were fairly discreet about it; but they too had to tread warily, avoiding the toes of the matriarchs.

At the end of the holidays Cyril and I departed on our separate ways, he to Radley and I to Stonyhurst. From that time onwards I saw very little of him. The family did their work of keeping us apart very efficiently, and used our religions as a pretext. There was no acceptable reason for this, particularly as I spent most of my holidays boarded out with Protestant families. I think my relatives were a little frightened of seeing too much of me; in their eyes a boy educated at a Jesuit school was, to all intents and purposes, a Jesuit himself, and there was no knowing what he might say or do next. And my two years in an Italian school were, from their point of view, bound to have affected me adversely.

One of the reasons given for estranging my brother from me was that we did not get on well together. But we surely did not quarrel more than most brothers; and if our mother had been alive we would always have spent our holidays together. And although my brother and I hardly ever met after we had been sent to our different schools, the family could not prevent us from writing to each other. We corresponded regularly and were always scheming to get together again.

Poor Cyril! He had a much more tragic youth than I had. My own youth was filled with perplexity; his with the weight of knowledge which he was too young to bear. From the moment that he discovered the implication of the placard which he saw in Baker Street, he began to form a resolution which consolidated itself as the years proceeded. He hinted at it to me on several occasions, but it was not until June 1914 when he was twenty-nine, that he wrote to me from India in reply to a letter of mine about the years of our childhood:

When I returned to England in 1898, I naturally realised our position more fully. Gradually, I became obsessed with the idea that I must retrieve what had been lost. By 1900, it had become my settled object in life. I told Ross of this years ago. I told him that by his magnificent labours and self-sacrifice he had almost accomplished my end. But he cannot do all. All these years my great incentive has been to wipe that stain away; to retrieve, if may be, by some action of mine, a name no longer honoured in the land. The more I thought of this, the more convinced I became that, first and foremost, I must be a *man*. There was to be no cry of decadent artist, of effeminate aesthete, of weak-kneed degenerate. That is the first step. For that I have laboured; for that I have toiled. As I roughed it month after month last year in the terrible plateau of Tibet, as I trekked hour after hour, day after day, but lately, over difficult country in dangerous times, when I was weary and ill with dysentery and alone in a strange and barbarous land, it was this Purpose which whispered in my ear: "It is the cause, my soul, it is the cause." Many years ago, I laid to heart the awful truth we hear in *Hamlet*

"Purpose is but the slave to memory
Of violent birth, but poor validity."

This has been my purpose for sixteen years. It is so still. I have often fallen away. I have despaired, I have cursed my fate and mocked at the false gods. It is my purpose still. I am no wild, passionate, irresponsible hero. I live by thought, not by emotion. I ask nothing better than to end in honourable battle for my King and Country.

I have quoted these passages to prove how the iron entered into his soul. And how well he succeeded in avoiding the accusation of effeminacy is shown by his school record.

At Radley, which is a school well known for athletics, he was always the outstanding athlete among boys of his own age. In 1902, his last year at school before going to the Royal Military Academy at Woolwich, he stroked the Radley eight in the Ladies Plate at Henley, at the age of seventeen. Radley won their first heat, against Jesus College who were fourth on the River at Cambridge, but they were beaten in the second round by University

College, who were Head of the River at Oxford and eventually won the Plate. A report of the race said: "It was generally agreed that the young Radley stroke had rowed one of the best races of the day and had shown a judgement far beyond his years." That year, too, he won the mile, the half-mile and the steeplechase in the annual sports and received a silver medal as *victor ludorum*. He was the best swimmer in the school. He was also a prefect and the head of his house.

People who knew my brother at Radley, such as Nicholas Hannen and Louis Wilkinson, assure me that none of the boys in the school had the slightest inkling of his parentage. Indeed, it was this perpetual sailing under false colours that militated against both my brother and myself ever forming any great school friendship. School friendships depend so essentially on their participants having no secrets whatever from each other. To this day, in the *Radley School Register*, which is a list, published periodically, of all the boys who have been educated at Radley, my brother's is the only name against which the words "son of——" are still omitted.[40]

At Woolwich in 1905 he won the mile and the two miles against Sandhurst—one of the few occasions on which Woolwich beat Sandhurst in the sports. Later, he stroked the Artillery four at Henley. And he was an officer cadet at the "Shop," as the Royal Military Academy is known in the British Army.

With all his intelligence, my brother was quite unable to spell. He regarded accuracy in spelling as pedantic and a waste of time. I once remonstrated with him for spelling gnat "knat," to which he replied, "What does it matter? You understood what I meant; and it can still sting!" I have letters written to him by our mother, distressed at the poorness of his spelling at school and giving him long lists of mis-spelled words in his letters. In one she says that his spelling is so bad that it would prevent him from passing any examination. But sometimes it was actually difficult to get his meaning when his mis-spelling encroached upon other words. In one letter to our mother, he wrote *were* for *where*, *newsance* for *nuisance*, *nickers* for *knickers*, *couch* for *cough* and *stoped* for *stopped*.

When my brother went into the Army, I saw even less of him than before; indeed, the last time I saw him was three years before his death, when he was about to go to India with his artillery brigade. He was not popular with his brother officers, who considered him pompous and intolerant. He would not join in the small-talk of the mess, mostly scandal or about sport. And they could not understand anyone who spent his ordinary leave in travelling about Europe, studying architecture and visiting art galleries instead of hunting, shooting, yachting or fishing. He adopted a pose of despising athletics, except as a means to keep fit, and yet with his athletic record there could be no accusation of sour grapes. And he was always getting special leave on "military duties," which sometimes caused him to disappear for weeks at a time. I gathered some idea of the nature of these duties from the fact that he spoke German like a native, was an efficient draughtsman and sometimes grew a beard.

In 1913 my brother got six months' leave, which he spent in a solitary shooting expedition, ending up with an overland journey to Pekin through Tibet. He sent me a postcard from Leh in June, franked with a Queen Victoria one-anna stamp, probably a relic of the Younghusband expedition. And I had a long letter from him in August, written from Payum in Baltistan. This letter is such a mixture of description, philosophy and self-examination, and is so typical of him that I think I am justified in quoting an extract from it. After referring to some short stories of mine that had been published in the *Morning Post*, he describes the first part of his journey, which he has just completed and goes on to say:

Nature only laughs at us when we try to translate her into words. The most that we arrive at is some dull picture of still life. If I sit down with a will and try to give expression to my aesthetic impressions, I am at a loss for words. Words may fix ideas, concepts; they are employed in logic, in science. But they fail to catch life on the wing, they fail to give more than a hint, a suggestion of artistic feeling. Sometimes I catch a phrase which seems to be true to the fact. But after a moment's reflexion, I recollect that it is an old phrase, used many times before, hackneyed, stereotyped.

And yet these phrases are the truest to life. *Au fond*, the generality of mankind is and has long been much the same. The theoretic functions are generic. Aesthetic, as Croce has demonstrated with sad, grieving logic, is at once impression and expression. The salient features of life, of nature, remain the common data of humanity. If we go further and agree with the "Practism" of Bergson, if we follow his train of thought on the subject of Time and Space, we cannot fail to see the futility of describing Nature in its manifold phenomena in a new way. We cannot change the content of Nature, though we may alter the intellectual attitude of man towards the Universe. I consider that Bergson has propounded the truest and most subtle materialism and egoism that the world has yet seen. Not the least interesting deduction to be drawn from his theory of motor-activity is that it affords an explanation of the apparent paradox which has enabled humanity to develop almost entirely without the aid of Philosophy.

It has been said, and truly, that the man of action is the executive officer of the man of thought, as Robespierre was to Rousseau. It has been shown that thought, not crystallised into habit, nor a reflex, precedes action, insofar as thought be regarded as choice or judgement. But such thought has always borne the nature of virtual action and not of pure theoretical speculation. The *Contrat Social*—that oft quoted and seldom read work—was, I conceive, merely an excuse, a *post facto* argument, to support a political attitude towards the political status, an attitude already formed, an attitude which had been brought about, not by speculation, but by life itself.

We often reconstruct our own past in this manner; in fact, whenever we join some phenomena of the present with analogous phenomena of the past, for the purpose of creating a conceptual or general idea—be its immediate object action or speculation—we *ipso facto* reconstruct the past and revise our previous judgements in the light of later acquired knowledge.

Fascinating though such idle musings may be, they are scarcely the subject for a letter. I hope you are flourishing. Your affectionate brother, Cyril.

The first world war had long been foreseen by Cyril. He had a deep knowledge of international politics and I was told by one of his brother officers in India that when the news of the assassination of the Archduke Ferdinand was announced in the mess, Cyril declared, in a challenging voice: "That means that within six weeks there will be war in Europe in which England, France, Germany and Russia will be involved." "Why are you so sure?" asked the Colonel. "Because I have made a special study of European politics." "That's all very fine, but will you bet?" went on the Colonel. "Certainly," replied Cyril. "Five pounds?" suggested the Colonel. "No," my brother retorted. "It's not worth my while. But I'll bet you fifty." The Colonel could not very well back out, and fifty it was—a sum which my brother duly collected.

Towards the end of August 1914 Cyril received the shattering news that his own Field Artillery brigade was to remain behind for the defence of India against possible aggression. At that time no one thought that with modern weapons a war could last more than three or four months, so this looked like no war at all for those left, even temporarily, behind. My brother, pulling every string upon which he could lay his hands, arranged for a transfer from the Field Artillery to a cavalry regiment in India which was going to France to fight. This would have meant the sacrifice of his whole nine years' seniority, as he would have had to take his place as junior subaltern in his new regiment. This in itself shows in what direction his thoughts lay. In the end, plans were changed and all the regular soldiers in India went to France to be replaced by Territorials from England. So my brother arrived in France with the Meerut Division in 1914 and was killed on May 9th, 1915, in what amounted to a duel with a German sniper.

I was in the line myself when I heard of his death, scarcely three miles away from him. I was informed of it in a letter from our family solicitor, whose name he had given to the authorities as his next of kin.

When Cyril went to Radley, I myself went to Hodder Place, the preparatory school attached to Stonyhurst and about a mile distant from it. It was a very exciting adventure. The photographs of the school in the prospectus had shown me Stonyhurst as a vast romantic place compared with the cramped, shut-in premises of the Collegio della Visitazione at Monaco. Indeed, the main entrance to the old Shireburn Hall, from which the school developed, is a singularly beautiful sight, viewed from the end of the straight drive half a mile in length, flanked by the school football fields and two rectangular lakes on which swans lazed beneath the walls of the house.

Hodder was part and parcel of Stonyhurst, since, although it had its own masters and organisation, its curriculum was dictated from Stonyhurst and its examinations conducted from there. On my arrival I was received by the Superior, Father Francis Cassidy, a middle-aged and in every way an admirable priest. He was adored by the small boys, whose ages ranged from seven to about twelve. He had a long experience of them and he understood them perfectly. This was a gift which, with very few exceptions, I found to be possessed by all the Jesuits. They tried to understand the boys and to help them: they had no axes to grind; and they were all our friends, even if at times they were rather severe ones. They would not stand any nonsense, and woe betide the rash individuals who tried to play tricks on them.

At Hodder I had to start my education all over again, but with the important difference that my lessons would in future be done in English. I had, of course, to readjust my Latin pronunciation; yet I knew far more Latin than any of the other boys of my age in the school, since Latin was the most important subject taught at Monaco. My mathematics, too, were much above the average, as I had been attracted to their study as the one subject in which the handicap of language was reduced to a minimum.

To my great joy, one of the first things that Father Cassidy told me was that I was to be received into the Catholic Church. Of course I needed no preliminary instruction, other than learning to say my prayers in English instead of in Latin, and within a week I was a fully-fledged member of the Church to which I had been pleading for election for the past two years. Father Cassidy baptised me *sub conditione*; although I had no doubt been thoroughly baptised into the Christian Community as a baby, there was always the haunting fear that someone might have made a mistake or omitted something and that I might depart this life unbaptised and therefore be inadmissible to Heaven.

I was a little uncomfortable at Hodder at first, just as I had been at Monaco. Boys hate other boys to be different from themselves. I was different in that I had been to foreign schools and could speak French, German and Italian. To the other boys there was something very un-English and rather unsporting about this. They were suspicious and frightened of me, and perhaps a little jealous because I was popular with the masters, who were very interested in all that I had to tell them about the Collegio della Visitazione.

I soon found that I had returned to the realm governed by corporal punishment—mild enough at Hodder, it is true, and consisting mainly of being tapped on the hands or the buttocks without much force behind the stroke; but none the less daunting to one who had suffered the injustices of Neuenheim College.

Another cause for my initial unpopularity at Hodder was that I was now almost twelve, and as most of the other boys of my age in my class had been at Hodder for at least two years and some for longer, I was regarded as something of an interloper. Particularly as, at the end of the first term, I passed top in examinations and was therefore head of the school. I was also a convert and had not yet taken my First Communion, which was unusual for boys of my age. This became a bond between myself and a boy named Antoine Sellier who, although he was a Catholic by birth, had not taken his First Communion either.

The Michaelmas term drew to an end, and I was eagerly looking forward to going south to the England that I knew, when my hopes were dashed to the ground. Room could be found for Cyril somewhere, but I was just a dead weight with which no one wished to be burdened. The solution, however, was quite easy. A number of boys, both from Stonyhurst and from Hodder, lived so far away that it was impossible for them to go home for Christmas, particularly as we were only given a fortnight's holiday. These were herded together and sent in charge of one of the Jesuit Fathers to some salubrious spot in which to relax.

My Christmas holidays were therefore spent at Southport, which is no doubt a delightful place in the summer. There were about a dozen of us altogether. We were in charge of the Sub-Minister of Stonyhurst, Father Sydney Canning, who left us pretty much to our own devices, such as they were. The boys who came from the West Indies, from India and from South Africa were quiet and left us alone, but there were four Spaniards and an Italian, who were natural bullies and combined together to make the lives of the smaller boys unbearable.

There was nothing at all to do except go to the Winter Gardens—a series of leaking glass-topped structures containing waxworks, a few neglected tanks housing weary-looking fish, and a concert-hall in which, at long intervals, a small dejected band would play the popular tunes of the moment. The sea-front was windswept and deserted and even the shops seemed to be only half-open. For all the care and affection we got we might just as well have been in an orphan asylum. The other boys got letters from home.

I got none. And the smaller boys spent most of their time trying to keep out of the way of the bullies.

One of the stultifying things about having no parents is the perpetual consciousness that there is no one to whom you are the most important person in the world. There is no one who, if you died, would shed a single tear or, indeed, give you another thought. I was in fact constantly in my father's thoughts, but, as I was given to understand that he was dead, I could not know about that.

We were given two shillings a week pocket-money, which did not last very long, especially as we were allowed to play *vingt-et-un* in the evenings or on wet days. It hardly seems a suitable game for very young boys when played for money; but there was no question of it not being allowed, as Father Canning sometimes joined in. Chips were ten for a penny, and the maximum bet was ten. No doubling was allowed, but a natural would nevertheless cost us threepence if we had been staking the maximum.

What we did not lose at *vingt-et-un* was usually extorted from us by the Latins, using threats. They had discovered, to their delight, all about the English schoolboys' code of honour, and they worked on it to the utmost. They had not quite grasped its full implications, however, as nothing prevented us from complaining to other boys. Another Hodder boy and I, tired of being robbed, complained to the senior of the holiday-makers, a boy named Davis, from St. Lucia, who was head boy at Stonyhurst. There was a considerable disturbance and the bullying ceased. I am glad to be able to say that most of these bullies were expelled from Stonyhurst at a later date.

The holidays came to an end at last and I returned thankfully to Hodder, there to remain until the summer. There were no Easter holidays at Stonyhurst in those days, though not much work was done in Easter Week, most of which was spent in the church or the school chapel. But the summer term was a very pleasant one. There was no

nonsense about not playing games on Sundays. After
High Mass on Sunday morning the rest of the day would,
weather permitting, be devoted to cricket, somewhat to
the scandalisation of the local Protestant inhabitants.

By the beginning of 1899 I was convinced that my
father was dead, though in fact in February 1899 he made
a special journey to Genoa to visit my mother's grave.[41]
Robert Ross told me in later years that he was continually
wondering where we were and asking after us. We were
completely hidden. No inquiries as to our whereabouts
were ever answered. None of my father's friends knew
where we were.

I have mentioned that in Italian Jesuit schools the
boys make their First Communion on June 21st, which,
besides being Midsummer Day, is also the feast of St.
Aloysius of Gonzaga, who is, as it were, the patron saint
of youth. At Stonyhurst, however, the Feast of Corpus
Christi was reserved for this ceremony. This is a movable
feast, occurring always on the Thursday after Trinity Sunday, and in 1899 it fell on June 1st. This was the great
day for which I had waited for two and a half years. The
First Communicants went into retreat for two or three
days, in order to get into the right frame of mind. The
emotional strain of the moment of receiving Communion
was almost unbearably ecstatic, and the feeling of holiness which it gave one persisted through the day. I felt
safe, sanctified and with one foot firmly on the path that
leads to salvation.

At the end of the summer term at Hodder I returned
to London with three prizes, one for mathematics, one for
classics, and one for being top of the school. I wrote to my
guardian telling him of my success, but he never even
acknowledged the receipt of my letter. My mother's
family were scarcely more enthusiastic. I cannot help
thinking that they were a little annoyed that I should have
been in any way distinguished among my fellows. But I

knew how proud my mother and how pleased my father would have been.

Gradually my mother's old friends began to become aware of our existence. I spent the 1899 Christmas holiday, all too short, at Babbacombe Cliff with Lady Mount Temple, now a very old lady confined to her room. She was very sweet, but tired easily, and I only saw her for a few minutes each day. Then, in the summer of 1900, I had my first real glimpse of home since my mother's death.

My existence had in some way been brought to the notice of one of the sweetest women who ever lived, my aunt Cornelia Cochrane. She was no real blood relation of mine, but was connected with my mother's family by marriage. Her husband was a pillar of the Anglican Church, but she had become a very devout Catholic, and a member of the Third Order of St. Francis. The fact that I also was a young convert to Catholicism must have carried some weight; at any rate, she invited me to spend the summer holidays at her home, Windlesham House, near Bagshot. I arrived there feeling very strange, once more pitchforked into entirely different surroundings, with a summer cold and a large boil on my bottom. The summer cold could not be concealed, but I hid the other infirmity as best I could, until my inability to sit down with any comfort was noticed and its cause analysed.

My aunt Nelia, as I called her, took me into protective custody, as it were, against the hotbed of Anglicanism constituted by the Napier household, and set out to be a real mother to me. She had loved my mother very much and was also a friend of the Ranee of Sarawak. Her husband was a distinguished sailor, Admiral Basil Cochrane, and she herself came from the famous naval family of Osborne.

She drew me out of my shell and made me tell her everything that was in my mind. She comforted me and even went so far as to tell me not to be distressed about the attitude of my mother's family, and that all would come right in the end.

After these delightful holidays I returned to school feeling that life might not be so bad after all. I was growing strong and spent a great deal of time in the gymnasium, as I found that I had a natural aptitude for gymnastics and boxing, the only forms of athletics at which I ever excelled at school.

One day, about a month after my fourteenth birthday, the Rector of Stonyhurst, Father Joseph Browne, sent for me during the morning break and told me that my father was dead.[42] "But," I said, "I thought he died long ago." This rather puzzled Father Browne, who naturally did not know what we had been led to believe, and had undertaken to break the news to me on his own responsibility. He had no doubt seen the obituary notice in *The Times* and had wanted to anticipate anything that I might myself have seen. But he looked at me and said: "No. He died two days ago in Paris. He was received into the Church just before the end. So he is happy now at last."

The surprise, the perplexity, the shock that always come to the young in the presence of the announcement of death were too much for me and I cried. I wanted desperately at that moment to ask the Rector what had happened to my father, but my courage failed me. Father Browne said to me: "He wrote beautiful stories." I said: "Yes, I know." There was not much more to be said on either side and I left the Rector's room to join the other boys in the playground.

Children always like the solemnity of going into mourning, so I immediately procured a black arm-band for myself, as I had done on my mother's death. This naturally led to inquiries from the other boys. I said that my father had just died; to which they replied that I had always told them that my father had died years before. This was awkward, and I had to do some rapid thinking and draw upon my imagination. I told them what I thought was a very good and convincing story, which was that my father had been an explorer who had disappeared when a ship in which he was travelling went down, and that he had eventually been presumed to be dead; but that he had been recently discovered in a South Sea island, suffering from loss of memory as a result of his hardships, had been identified, and had died shortly afterwards. I really think the boys believed my story, and I became something of a hero.

The Christmas holidays came shortly afterwards and I returned to London. I had not been at my aunt's house for more than four minutes when my black arm-band was ripped away, and it was once more impressed upon me that my life was not like that of other boys and I could not go into mourning for my father. I was given to understand that I could never make any sort of a life for myself in England, but must seek my fortune elsewhere. I then managed to pluck up enough courage to put in a tentative inquiry as to what it was all about, but I was told: "We need not go into that now."

I have no doubt that my father's death came as a great relief to my mother's family. While he was alive there was always the danger, from their point of view, that he might succeed in getting into touch with us as we grew older, and so wreck their plans for us. For my own part, I know quite well that if I had received a letter from him I would have answered it, family or no family, and that I would not have mentioned the fact to a soul.

No letters passed between my brother and myself on my father's death. It was as though the revelation of his continued existence was to remain a secret even between ourselves. But again Cyril was not so lucky as I was, for he saw the announcement in the newspapers and heard it discussed by the older boys over the breakfast-table at Radley.

At this time Robert Ross wrote a letter to us, care of the family solicitors. The letter was sent to my brother to answer, and I never saw it myself; indeed I never heard about it until after my brother's death, when Ross showed me Cyril's reply and gave me a copy of it. It must be remembered that my brother was only fifteen and a half at the time, and had over five years of bitterness behind him. His letter ran as follows:

Dear Mr. Ross,

Thank you so much for the kind letter you sent me. It was very kind of you to give the flowers for us. I am glad you say that he loved us. I hope that at his death he was truly penitent; I think he must have been if he joined the Catholic Church and my reverence for the Roman Church is heightened more than ever. It is hard for a young mind like mine to realise why all the sorrow should have come on us, especially so young. And I am here among many happy faces among boys who have never really known an hour of sorrow and I have to keep my sorrow to myself and have no one here to sympathise with me although I am sure my many friends would soon do so if they knew. But when I am solemn and do not join so much in their jokes they stir me up and chide me for my gloominess.

It is of course a long time since I saw father but all I do remember was when we lived happily together in London and how he would come and build brick houses for us in the nursery.

I only hope that it will be a lesson for me and prevent me from falling into the snares and pitfalls of this world. On Saturday I went up to London to see Mrs. Napier and came back on Sunday afternoon.

I first read of his death in a paper at breakfast and luckily one cannot realise so great a loss in cold print or I don't know what I should have done. . . . And yet the ordinary person reads it without emotion and quite dispassionately.

I cannot put my thoughts into words, so I will end.

Yours very affectionately,
Cyril Holland.

During the Christmas holidays of 1900, which I spent with one of my great-aunt Mary's sons, there occurred an unhappy incident which had the effect of altering the whole course of my life. A short distance away lived a cousin of my hosts, a retired General, in the largest house in the district. He lived there with his three daughters and his two grandsons, boys of about my own age, whose father was at the South African War. He was a gentleman of uneven temper, caused by gout. He always sat in an armchair by the fire with one heavily bandaged foot reposing on a stool before him, and he spent a great deal of his time playing chess with one or other of his daughters.

Towards the end of the holidays, on the morning of the day before I was to return to London en route for Stony-hurst, I was asked to go and spend the day with the boys. I duly arrived on my bicycle at about ten in the morning, to be met by one of the daughters who said that she was very sorry, but I could not come in. I asked why and was told that it was something I had said to one of the boys. I then asked if I could see the boys to say good-bye, and, after some hesitation, I was allowed to do this, and so found out what had happened.

The day before I had repeated a silly rhyme which Cyril had heard at school and repeated to me as being very funny. It had a rather obvious double meaning, which I could not see myself, but as it was supposed to be funny I repeated it to the boys. They, in their turn, repeated it to their aunts, who decided that I was no fit companion for their nephews. It was a ridiculously bad piece of psychology as, if they had reflected for a moment, they would have realised that if any of us had suspected that there had been anything wrong about the rhyme we certainly would not have repeated it to our elders.

As I was supposed to be spending the day at the General's house playing with the boys, I found myself in a terrible fix. The jingling rhyme, which was actually be-ing delivered at one of the London music-halls at the time, suddenly became full of hidden meaning at which I could only guess in a vague way. I imagined there must be

something terrible about it, though it was really more vulgar than indecent. But I could not go home without giving some sort of explanation, and I dreaded doing this.
Once more I felt that everyone's hand was against me, and
I began to think that there must be something monstrous
about my family that caused me always to be in disgrace.
And as I drew near the house in which I was staying, my
footsteps dragged until finally I came to a full stop.

There had been a light snowfall in the morning, but
now it had begun to snow in real earnest. So I wheeled my
bicycle past the house and started walking, with no particular idea of what I was going to do. Presently the road
ran through a wood, and I decided that I would get away
from all my troubles and not try to carry on the struggle.
I had read, probably in one of Jack London's books, that
people who lay down in the snow and went to sleep never
woke up again, but died quite painlessly. And with this in
the back of my mind, I left my bicycle against a tree and
wandered into the wood. When I thought I had gone far
enough to be lost, I found a place in a clearing where the
snow had drifted against a low bank and I lay down on it
and closed my eyes and reviewed my life to date. I thought
of the Tite Street days, and of my wanderings. But most
of all I thought of my parents and of the enigma of my
father and pondered over the misery of being an unwanted
orphan. I did not seem to feel the cold and eventually I
fell asleep.

Actually, before I arrived at the General's house and
was refused admittance, they had already telephoned to
my cousin to stop me coming. Unfortunately, as I had already
started, I knew nothing of this, though I think they might
have told me on my arrival and so saved me from considerable mental anguish, but it did not seem to occur to them.
When time passed and I did not return, my hosts began
to be worried, particularly as the snow was now falling
more heavily than ever. And when a couple of hours went

by without my appearing, they thought that something should perhaps be done about it, and search parties set out to find me.

It did not take very long to get on my tracks, as my bicycle leaning against a tree by the roadside led them practically straight to me. I was found and taken home and put into a warm bath. I had gloves on my hands, which did not, therefore, suffer. But my ears, exposed to the air, were slightly frost-bitten and I got a chill in the inner part of my left ear which turned to a mastoid, for which I had an operation on the day of Queen Victoria's death. The operation was a serious one and resulted in my staying away from school for the whole of the year 1901.

This wretched affair did not end there. A full report of my misdemeanour, probably with a transcript of the salacious rhyme and almost certainly with added details and mental eyebrow- and hand-raising together with rhetorical questions such as "What else could you expect?" was duly sent to my cousin Lizzie. I was hardly out of the anaesthetic before I came in for a terrifying lecture into which my father's name entered; the general idea being that unless I was very careful I would come to a bad end. There was also a suggestion that if I had not been ill I would have had a beating, though I do not know who would have been chosen to administer it. Certainly not my cousin Lizzie.

My illness had left me deaf in one ear. This, though it has not been a very great handicap to me, excluded me from entering any of the professions for which a strict medical examination or exceptionally good hearing is required. And it prevented me from satisfying my main ambition at the time, which was to become a civil engineer by way of Cooper's Hill.

I spent most of the year 1901 in a salubrious town in the Midlands, boarded out with a well-meaning gentleman who had been the High Church Anglican incumbent of a

very good living in the West Country, but who had become
a Roman Catholic in middle age. With the loss of his living, my host also lost his only source of income. Being
married, with a wife living, he could not become a Catholic priest. So he compromised by leading an ascetic life and
spending a great part of the day in reading the Catholic
breviary. I imagine that the first part of this programme
was not particularly difficult to adhere to. His wife, poor
woman, worn out by child-bearing and parochial duties,
was well past her prime; she had refused to adopt her husband's new religion and became a dipsomaniac instead;
with whisky at three shillings a bottle it was very difficult
to prevent a determined woman from indulging in her
hobby.

I had a room in the attic. It was rather eerie going up
at night, carrying an unshaded candle, particularly as the
attic was cut off from the top floor of the house by an enclosed staircase with a door at the bottom. But the com-
pensations were tremendous. I had a table and a chair and
a bookshelf, and by the expedient of draping canvas round
these I made myself a kind of den in which I imagined myself to be a hermit, well away from the turmoil of life. And
there I would sit writing my letters to Lizzie Napier and
my brother, and I would also try to compose poetry.

I began to read a great deal. I am afraid that for a time
my favourite authors were Marie Corelli and Ouida,
though in my more serious moments I favoured Henty
and Fitchett. What I liked doing best was to hire a Canadian canoe and paddle some way up the Leam. There I
would get into a backwater and read and imagine myself
in all kinds of heroic rôles. But all this time I never saw a
book by my father. Indeed I doubt very much whether
there were any on sale except in secondhand bookshops.

In the second week of January 1902 I returned to
Stonyhurst. During my year away from school I had grown

much stronger physically, and I began to enter much more into the spirit of school life. And yet I was never completely happy at school. I had too much behind me and too many problems before me. The only experiences that most of my school companions had were confined to their home lives, occasional short visits to relatives and perhaps a yearly visit to the seaside; so the patterns of their lives were always much the same. But I, even more than my brother, had been chased from pillar to post through nearly half of my short life.

Life at Stonyhurst differed in many respects from that at ordinary public schools. As at Monaco, there were no boy prefects with disciplinary or punitive powers. There were monitors who kept younger boys from lolling in chapel and who were supposed to report any grave irregularities to the Jesuit prefects—four in number—in charge of law and order. In those days none of the boys had studies; indeed, there was very little difference in the treatment of any of the boys. This is quite understandable, as it carried out the principles of religious orders in which a priest may be Provincial one day, with complete power over every member of the Order in his particular country, and the next day may be a humble teaching priest owing implicit obedience to the new Provincial, who might, on the previous day, have been at his beck and call.

I have mentioned that I was a little daunted, when I arrived at Stonyhurst, to find that I was back in the area of corporal punishment, which was resorted to with the utmost freedom and was a very great deterrent to the more nervous boys. It consisted of being beaten on the palm of the hand with a "ferula" or, in our schoolboy slang, a "folly." This was a gutta-percha instrument about a foot long, two inches broad and half an inch thick. The usual ration was nine or twelve, though some of the smaller boys received only from one to six. The maximum was eighteen at any one time and any one day; this was known as "twice nine." In order that no personal animus should be allowed to influence the degree of severity with which the ferulas were administered, the originator of the punishment was not allowed to inflict it. You had to go in cold blood to one of the four prefects and say: "I want twelve ferulas for Father So-and-so." That was the correct formula, though the word "want" was singularly inappropriate. The Prefect gave you the number you asked for and entered it in a book. It was an extremely painful business at best, but there was considerable difference in the severity and also the speed with which the different Prefects laid it on. We were allowed to choose our own executioners and we very soon discovered which one was the least heavy-handed and the most expeditious. Actually, he was by no means the most humane. The most dreaded performer was really the most kind-hearted, who used to lay on hard and slowly, in order, we came to the conclusion, to discourage customers from coming to him. I came in for my fair share of follies, but I only once had twice-nine, and that was for something I had not done, but for which the real culprit would not own up; he would really have been much better advised to have done so, as the summary justice meted out to him afterwards by the bigger boys was, I am sure, much more painful than my twice-nine.

They say that somewhere in nature there exists an antidote for all evils, and I certainly discovered a defence against ferulas, about which I told no one but my own particular friend and confidant among the boys. Electric light had not yet been introduced and the whole school was lit by gas; if you struck the palms of your hands smartly with the bristly side of a hair-brush and then held them over an unlit but turned-on gas-jet for about half a minute, this acted as a local anaesthetic and made ferulas almost painless. Even now I shudder to think what my punishment would have been if I had been found out, thus defeating the ends of justice.

For very grave offences, or repeated insubordination, boys might be birched. Indeed, birching was usually concomitant with expulsion. I never suffered it myself, so I cannot speak of it at first hand. But from one of the boys I gathered that it was a tremendous ceremonial, taking place in the presence of the Rector, one's class master and the Prefect of Studies, who was the Father in charge of all our scholastic work. The instrument was a somewhat longer folly than that used on the hands and it was administered on the bare body, the usual number of strokes being twelve. I wonder whether my ferula antidote would have been efficacious in the case of a birching.

Fighting at Stonyhurst was a heinous offence, always punished by follies if detected. And as we were nearly always under the supervision of one or more of the Prefects, detection was almost unavoidable. This put one into a very awkward position because, terrifying though the ferula was, the scorn of one's schoolmates, if one refused a challenge to fight, was even worse. It was like the quandary of the Prussian officer under the old regime who, if challenged to a duel, had to choose between being driven out of his regiment by his brother officers if he refused to fight, and being expelled by the Army Council if he accepted. I had a few fights, but we were always caught and always beaten.

I wish to lay stress on the fact that the descriptions I have given of life at Stonyhurst are as it was fifty years ago. As in many other English public schools, conditions have altered considerably since that time. Tollies are given with far less frequency, the strict supervision has been drastically reduced, and the senior boys have their own studies. When I submitted this chapter to one of the present-day Fathers who was almost a contemporary of mine at school he wrote back:

What you say of Stonyhurst is very true of fifty years ago, as well I know! We took a very long time to shed some of the habits acquired during two centuries of foreign life in France or Belgium.

At the age of fourteen I was stopped from studying Greek and made to substitute extra mathematics, languages and science. I suppose this was done with the connivance of my guardian. If so, it was singularly thoughtless of him. By that time it was almost certain that I would be going to the University, and he must have known that Greek was a compulsory subject in one's preliminary examinations, as I found later, if not to my cost, at any rate to my very great personal inconvenience. I suspect that the fact that my father was such an outstanding Greek scholar may have had something to do with my being made to abandon that language.

One's place in class was decided by examinations at the end of each term called Compositions, the boy with the highest aggregate being placed top. As the marks given for Greek and Latin were higher than those given for modern subjects, I was at a considerable disadvantage in the fight for position, as I missed marks in Greek altogether. Even so I always managed to be somewhere near the top, and in my last year I was second.

Father Reginald Colley, the Prefect of Studies, who was always very kind to me and with whom I was on excellent terms, thought I was too conceited about my Latin prose and was always criticising it. So one day I inserted a passage from a little-read speech of Cicero's into one of my compositions. When I showed it to Father Colley, he said that it was verbose and flowery and stilted. Whereupon I triumphantly pointed to the passage I had cribbed. Without a moment's hesitation, Father Colley looked up at me blandly and said: "Yes, my dear fellow: Cicero can get away with that kind of thing, but you can't."

Our recreational reading matter was very carefully controlled. Every book that one brought to the school was carefully scrutinised and, if passed, was stamped on the fly-leaf with an oval rubber stamp reading: STONYHURST at the top and ALLOWED at the bottom. One of the boys in the school once brought in a copy of Tolstoy's *Resurrection*, which was hardly the sort of book to be encouraged in a Jesuit school. The owner managed to gain access to the "Allowed" stamp and used it on the book. It was a long time before this fraud was discovered, and by then the book had passed through so many hands that the original owner could never be traced, and even we ourselves did not know for certain whose it was. So the whole school was kept in one holiday morning until the culprit owned up. It was a birching, if not an expulsion, matter, and no one quite liked to admit his guilt. So, after about half an hour, it being obvious that no admission was forthcoming, we were allowed to go, and only the poor wretch who was caught red-handed with the book got twice-nine.

I really began to enjoy school life for the first time in 1902. I took up gymnastics and played lawn tennis reasonably well. I never excelled at football or cricket, and seldom played these games after leaving school. But I did fairly well at my work and passed the Oxford and Cambridge Lower Certificate Examination with first class in Latin, French and Mathematics.

In the summer of 1903 I was sixteen and a half and I began to be interested in girls. It was very tentative and fairly innocent, a kiss and a hug and a giggle, usually followed by headlong flight and slight embarrassment the next time we met. But it was all part of one's education and, as I remember it, extremely pleasant. Sometimes one might go a little far, but there was no real harm in it.

After the summer holidays I rushed up to the Carmelite church in Church Street, Kensington, to go to confession, as I felt shy of confiding my peccadillos to the priests at Stonyhurst. I had a vague feeling that I was somehow cheating and not playing the game properly. And I had scruples of conscience too, because I had too logical a mind to be able to say with much conviction that I was determined never to flirt again.

At the end of that scholastic year I had passed the Higher Certificate Examination, had won a five-pound mathematical prize and a *Praemium Primi Ordinis,* a prize awarded to all boys who obtained two-thirds of the possible year's total in all examinations. These *Primi Ordinis* prizes were much coveted. I received one every year I was at school.

When I left Stonyhurst I had no idea that I was not to go back into Rhetoric, which was the equivalent of the Upper Sixth at other English public schools. I was not told until I got back to London. I thought this a little casual on the part of my guardian, but then he was like that. All through our schooldays neither my brother nor myself ever saw a school report, though we must have had about fifteen each. I suppose they were sent to my guardian, who was not interested and forgot about them, or threw them into the waste-paper basket. He died in 1904. I could not mourn him much, as I had only seen him three times during the six years that he had charge of me, and he never wrote to me once.

CHAPTER VI

Adolescence

THE lives of my brother and myself could have been made much happier after our mother's death if we had been allowed to mingle with those friends of our father who had remained loyal to him; this would have enabled us to retain much of the natural self-confidence of youth, which was slowly drained out of us. There were so many people who were willing and even eager to take us to their hearts. They inquired after us and our whereabouts, only to be met with coldness and the statement that we were quite happy where we were and must not be disturbed. The principle was that there should be complete severance of ourselves from anything Wildean. My first cousin, Dorothy Wilde, Willie Wilde's daughter, was born about the time of our return to England.[43] So far from being allowed to meet her, I was not even aware of her existence until she was twenty-two, when she was brought to my house by a mutual friend. My brother never heard of her at all.

If the family could have obliterated all memory of our parentage from our minds, it would have been a great relief to them. Although it was clearly impossible for them to do this, they did their utmost. When one is entered for the Bar, the name of one's father has to be given and appears on the list of those who are being called to the Bar when one has eaten one's dinners and passed one's examinations. In my own case, I found myself on the list as "son of Wills Wild, gentleman."

Robert Ross was always particularly bitter about this attitude of the family's. The day after I met him he wrote to me, on August 7th, 1907:

I regret very much that I was not allowed to see both you and Cyril in the years that have intervened since the tragedy which has darkened your life and about which I know you yourself must feel so bitterly. I believe that I could have made your childhood happier, and it would have made me happier too to know that you realised how fond and devoted I was to you both, because you were the sons of my greatest friend and the most distinguished man of letters in the last years of the last century.

I was, I suppose, as ambitious as most boys, but from a very early period in my life, whenever I dreamed of distinguishing myself, I saw my origin being mocked and the finger of scorn being pointed. And I foresaw the insults. I had my father continually as a spectre behind my shoulder. At the same time there was always a slightly conspiratorial feeling at the back of my mind; a question of what *would* people think if they knew the truth about me? Would they ostracise me? Would they be sympathetic? It was a perpetual secret locked in my mind; one which I felt I could share with no one and which, I thought at the time, I would have to carry to the grave with me.

All papers connected with my father, including most of his letters to my mother, some of them written shortly before her death, were destroyed. Some of the earlier ones, it is true, were said to have found their way to America, and have been published there. I never knew anyone who had seen the originals, and I can only conclude that they are either forgeries, or, if genuine, were stolen from Tite Street during the sale in 1895. These letters to my mother were kept in a locked blue leather case: I often saw my mother poring over them. But even the case disappeared.[44]

After my father's death the memory of him, under the influence of my mother's family, gradually receded further and further into the background. I do not altogether blame the family for their attitude. Even before the catastrophe they had all heartily disliked him, because he represented everything of which they fundamentally disapproved.

Everything in their little world had to conform to an immutable pattern. Poetry was all right, and indeed some poetry was quite fashionable; but not poets. Painters, if they were portrait-painters, were somewhat better, because one had to come into personal contact with them—not, however, painters of classical subjects, who used nude models. And dramatists were little better than actors. Most gentlemen owned property and administered it; but apart from being a landlord the only professions to which a gentleman might belong without losing caste were the Services of the Crown, Politics and the Church; and if you were very liberal-minded, Medicine and the Law.

Even the clothes you wore had to adhere to a rigid standard. In your dress-shirt, for instance, you could only wear one stud, and that might only be plain gold or a single pearl. Two or three studs in the shirt-front indicated a man who was "not quite out of the top drawer," or a foreigner, which amounted to much the same thing. And the wearing of any kind of jewellery other than plain gold or pearls as studs or links branded a man as "a cad, sir!"

My father had, at one time or another, offended against all these canons of good taste, and was therefore a sharp thorn in the side of my mother's family. His eccentricities, the peculiar clothes he wore during his early days in London when he was trying to attract attention to himself, his unorthodox views on art and on so many of the quasi-sacred institutions of the upper and middle classes in England, all combined to make him incomprehensible and therefore an object of loathing and contempt.

It has been said that it is an obstinate and familiar habit of the English to get rid of facts by pretending that they do not exist. Although I cannot claim to be very English, my upbringing from the age of twelve had been thoroughly English and so, by the time I left school in 1904, I had succeeded in putting my father so far out of my mind that I had ceased to have much curiosity about him, except in an objective kind of way. I knew that he had written fairy stories and plays, though I had forgotten what they were. Beyond that, my father's tragedy was still wrapped in mystery and I avoided making inquiries about it, partly out of a sense of delicacy and partly for fear of stirring up some terrible scandal which seemed to have died a natural death. On the other hand, I knew that my enlightenment would be bound to come in the course of time.

During my last year at Monaco and my first years at Hodder and Stonyhurst, I had but one idea for the future, and that was to become a Jesuit. Most of the more devout boys harboured the same ambition, openly or secretly. It was such a calm, dignified, sheltered life, with few temptations and even less chance of succumbing to them; and if one could remain in the Order until the end, it was moreover a certain passport to Paradise. I was, however, never encouraged in this, being told that I had no vocation and that I would probably do better in the outside world. But I think the real reason was my father. Although Catholics are, in general, much more broad-minded than Anglicans, my father's misfortunes were still too recent to be viewed in their right perspective, and the Jesuits were always particularly careful of the parentage of the members of their Order.

Be that as it may, I had to abandon the idea of becoming a monk and to turn my mind in some other direction. At first I wanted to become an engineer, because of my interest in mathematics and mechanics. But in the eyes of my guardian, engineering was only a respectable profession if one went through the semi-military Engineering College at Cooper's Hill. This entailed passing a very severe physical examination, which I had no chance of achieving owing to my deafness in one ear—though this was no bar to my joining the Army in 1914. My next choice was to become a doctor. But this was quickly vetoed, because the family feared that my connection with Sir William Wilde might come to light and all their good work be undone; moreover, the main objective of getting me out of the country could not be guaranteed in this way.

No, it was to be the Far Eastern Consular Service. Of course, following the now well-established principle that I should be kept in the dark concerning anything connected with my own life, I never heard anything about this decision until my return from Stonyhurst in the summer of 1904. The programme was for me to spend six months in Switzerland and six months in Germany, to go to the University to pass my Foreign Office examination—and then good-bye for ever. The family now proceeded to put the first part of this programme into operation, and I was packed off to Lausanne at the age of seventeen.

It may seem odd that people even so vague and unworldly as my guardians should have chosen Switzerland as the country in which my French should be improved, but the reason for this was that I had an aunt living there. My uncle Otho had married his first wife, Nellie, at about the same time that my father had married my mother; the marriage was not a great success and, after divorcing my uncle, my aunt married a Swiss doctor, Henri Grandjean, who practised in Lausanne.

I left Stonyhurst on Thursday, July 28th, 1904, and started for Switzerland on the following Tuesday. Friday was therefore a busy day, as I had to be fitted out for this new phase in my life. My old school trunk and my play-box were discarded and I was given a brand new portmanteau and suitcase with my initials on them. I bought a new bicycle, and I had two new suits, the trousers of one of them being promptly ruined by the Napiers' dog eating a piece out of the seat. Luckily I was not occupying them at the time.

I spent the week-end at Windlesham with the Cochranes, and felt that I had indeed reached manhood at last when the Admiral offered me a cigarette after dinner. And on Tuesday, accompanied by my new luggage, my new bicycle, and an oak treasure chest I had made for myself at school, I set out for Switzerland.

The Grandjeans had already gone to Champéry, a summer resort in the mountains about three and a half hours' diligence-ride from St Maurice, in the Rhône Valley, and there I joined them. I spent a very pleasant summer, mountain-climbing, playing lawn tennis and dancing. Towards the end of September we all returned to Lausanne and I was put to work at Ouchy, at a day school for older boys run by a German professor, Dr. Kümmer.

The discipline at this school was non-existent, as Dr. Kümmer had no authority whatever over the boys. The only punishment he could inflict was to send them home, which suited most of them admirably. The scholars were a motley collection of youths, all studying for different professions, and this made organised teaching very difficult. Boys in the same class, particularly in a cramming establishment, should have a community of interest in their studies; in this way they learn much more, as they can discuss and argue between working hours, and help to solve one another's difficulties.

Among other necessaries with which I had provided myself before leaving England was a blank manuscript book, containing some two hundred pages, in which I intended to keep a diary; and I actually did keep this diary with fair regularity for about seven months. In its way it is an interesting document, as it shows the intensity of passion and emotion with which an adolescent can be stirred by young love. Until quite recently I had not looked at these pages since I wrote them, and I was fascinated by their simplicity and sincerity, punctuated by wild flights of heroics; at the same time they are a queer mixture of arrogance and extreme diffidence.

The object of all this devotion was a young woman whom I met at a dancing class.[45] She was about the same age as myself and attended the École Supérieure de Jeunes Filles in Lausanne. My diary is mostly about her. If there was ever unrequited love, it was there. In the six months that I knew her I never even kissed her; yet her memory is sweet to me now, even after all these years. The greatest tragedy of *jeunes amours* for a young man is that though they appear to be undying and ageless, he knows perfectly well that they can never come to anything because he has his way to make in the world before he can dream of marriage, and at the age of eighteen he never dreams of anything less than marriage.

I must have made myself an abominable nuisance to this poor girl. She, too, had her own tribulations, as she had leanings towards a somewhat older gentleman who did not reciprocate her feelings. My release from her toils came from her own action, when I found that she used to read my letters to her girl friends amid shrieks of merriment. Not that I blame her now, as I kept copies of one or two of those I thought the best, and I can see the cause for amusement; but at the time I compared them favourably with the letters of Abélard and Héloïse.

It is a curious coincidence that, at the time I was weathering this emotional storm and recording my feelings in very immature prose, my father's *De Profundis* was being published in England. I knew nothing of this; the first time I saw a copy of the book was nine months later. And it was within a week of the publication of *De Profundis* that my aunt told me the truth about my father.[46]

Up to the age of eighteen, whenever I tried to broach the subject to my mother's family, or even to my brother, my inquiries were always side-tracked. But one day in Lausanne I put the matter bluntly to my aunt, and she, being a simple woman, not gifted with overmuch tact, gave me an equally blunt answer. The full import of this information did not immediately strike me, and my first feeling was one of great relief. The reticence of my mother's family through the years had led me to conjure up all kinds of pictures of what my father might have done. My imagination showed him to me alternately as an embezzler or a burglar. Sometimes I thought that he might have committed bigamy in marrying my mother, and that Cyril and I were illegitimate; indeed, that was my most frequent fear. And when I say I was relieved, it was because I discovered that we were legitimate after all, and that whatever my father had done had not brought distress to anyone but his own immediate family. My entry in my diary for that day includes the following: "After tea Aunt Nellie came to my room and talked to me about my father. She was surprised to hear that I knew so little about him and she told me the *truth.*" That is my only reference to my father in the whole diary.

I subsequently discovered that my aunt, who was, to say the least of it, broad-minded, regarded all this secrecy about my father as absurd and had told all her friends in Lausanne who I was. She told me herself once that she could not see what all the fuss was about. Indeed, I believe that the news had filtered through even to some of my own friends, for in one of her letters to me, my *inamorata* wrote: "Poor Boy, I don't think that you have had a very happy life."

The end of my sojourn in Switzerland came in an unfortunate way. There was a considerable English colony in Lausanne at that time; there was even an English club, full of retired Service men who found Switzerland cheaper than England. There was a Lausanne football club for which I occasionally played, and there were at least two tea-shops patronised exclusively by English and American residents and visitors. There were also a good many English boys studying French and German at the University, and at the end of term, when a batch of them were due to return to England, farewell parties would take place. I myself was quite unused to alcohol, my consumption rarely going beyond a glass of wine at dinner and perhaps a glass of beer at the Bar Automatique in the Place Saint François. But one day in April, at one of these parties, someone produced whisky. I had never before drunk whisky or spirits of any kind, and this had a delayed-action effect upon me. I was quite coherent so long as I was in a warm room, but when I went out into the cool air to go home at about ten o'clock, I collapsed and had to be assisted by a friend. Not a very creditable performance, I admit, but hardly a mortal sin.

Now, some days before this, I had left my keys at home when I went to the Institut Kümmer in the morning; my aunt found them and immediately pounced upon my treasure chest and my diary; she knew of its existence and often asked to be allowed to see it, a request to which, of course, I could not possibly accede. Unfortunately the diary contained some rather slighting reference to my aunt and her standard of education and intelligence, and she took her revenge by scribbling rude comments, in ink, on nearly every page. She was particularly scathing about my love rhapsodies. It was a disgusting thing to do, and when I discovered it I went into her boudoir in cold and deliberate fury and told her exactly what I thought of her.

I suppose, therefore, that she was still smarting under my scathing remarks and saw in this alcoholic lapse of mine a heaven-sent opportunity of getting even with me. So she wrote a long letter to my cousin Lizzie in England, accusing me of idleness (true), immorality (untrue) and intemperance (only true on this one occasion). I never saw this letter, but it drew forth a most terrible tirade from Lizzie, to whose Victorian mind even mild intemperance was a crime almost akin to murder. I have preserved her letter as an outstanding example of the mentality of the good, upright Victorian woman. It went as follows:

My dear Vyvyan, I wonder if you realise how shocked and how distressed I am at the report of you that I have had from your Aunt Nellie: that you were brought home dead drunk on Saturday night by some men who picked you up in the street.

(There is a great deal of difference between being assisted home by a friend and the foregoing description which was, no doubt, taken verbatim from my aunt's letter.)

To think that I have to hear such a thing of you, Vyvyan, you who have had everything done for you to teach and help you to do right, you who know you have loving relations and friends who care immensely what you do, you to whom we have tried in every way to make up.

Do you realise what a dreadful thing you have done? What a sin against God? Think of your Stonyhurst tradition. Think of the prayers you have said in chapel and yet 6 or 9 months after you leave the good fathers you are picked up drunk in the street.

Vyvyan, my hope for you is that you are plunged in grief and penitence for your sin.

Surely you do not want to sink into the mud. Yet you are playing with sin now. Oh, my dear boy, if ever you made a true confession in your life, go and make one now. And don't slur over anything. There is forgiveness, there is hope for you if you will only look for it, if you will only care. And God knows how anxious we are about you, how glad and thankful we shall be if you turn your back on all this and give up the bad companionship you have evidently fallen into . . .

The letter went on to say that I was obviously not to be trusted alone, that all idea of my going to Germany must be abandoned, that I was to return to London forthwith, and that I would be put somewhere where I would be subjected to strict discipline.

When I returned to England I was naturally in a state of some trepidation, and I did not derive much consolation from the reflection that the family seemed to have a distorted sense of values. Only a few months before, my cousin Lizzie had treated me to a long lecture on blasphemy because she had heard me say "Oh, Lord!" And

my fears were fully justified. Almost on the very thresh-
old I was treated to a further homily on sin, and the cupboard
in which the drink was kept was pointedly locked after
every meal. Lizzie's soldier brother, now a Major, happened to be home from India on leave, and so I told him
exactly what had happened and appealed to him to put in
a good word for me. He shrugged his shoulders and replied: "What can you expect, with the way girls were
brought up twenty-five years ago. It's no use my saying
anything in mitigation. Lizzie either would not understand or she would think I am as bad as you are and only
distress herself further. Your misfortune was to be found
out."

The collapse of this Swiss venture decided my guardians to abandon the German part of the programme for the
time being, and to send me to Cambridge straight away.
I myself wanted to go to Oxford, because my father
had been there, but that was not allowed for that very
reason. But a difficulty which they had not foreseen now
arose; namely, that before starting serious reading at either
University one had to pass one's Preliminary Examination
at Cambridge (or Responsions at Oxford), or be excused
it. And Greek was a compulsory subject. If my Higher
Certificate had included Greek as one of the subjects in
which I had passed, I would have been excused this Preliminary Examination (known as the Little-Go). As it was,
I had to take the whole examination and to learn Greek
into the bargain.

Luckily, the summer term at Cambridge had not yet
begun, and, as I would naturally not be going up until after the Long Vacation, this gave me the whole summer
term in which to prepare for my Little-Go in June. So I
was sent up to Cambridge to prepare for the examination
in charge of Joshua Goodland, with whom I lived in rooms
in Trinity Street. I resented this very much, as I considered I was once more being thrown to the lions.

Goodland was about twelve years older than myself. He was a very sympathetic man, who afterwards became one of my greatest friends, but at the time I resisted all his attempts at friendship. I was not yet a member of the university and knew no one there, whereas he had taken his degree in Law the previous year and knew a great number of people. I felt that I was in the way in his sitting-room and tried to keep out of it as much as possible. I worked hard and neither drank nor smoked. Neither did I talk much. I spent most of my time, when not attending lectures or being coached in Greek and Paley's *Evidences of Christianity*, reading in my bedroom.

One day, when this had been going on for a fortnight, Goodland tackled me on the subject after dinner. And I told him frankly that I knew I was redundant in his scheme of things and I thought it was more tactful to efface myself as much as possible. He then said: "Look here, there must be some mistake somewhere. When I first saw your guardian, he told me that you were a most difficult case, that you were idle, drank to excess and frequented bad company. Yet you work very hard, refuse to drink even a glass of beer, and so far from frequenting bad company, never seem to speak to anyone at all." That was typical of the "family," who delighted in being able to find fault with me and to prove to themselves that I was thoroughly bad.

So keen was I to pass my Little-Go that I overdid it and got a first class in Part I, which included Greek, and a second class in Part II, which was wasted effort, as all I needed was a pass, and I might have spent more time playing lawn tennis, which was my passion at the time.

When the Long Vacation came, the problem of my disposal once more became acute. Goodland was going to Scandinavia with his great friend Peter Wallace, who had been at Trinity Hall with him. He offered to take me with them and my guardian accepted the proposition and obtained the permission of the Chancery Court for me to leave England and go to Norway, Denmark and Sweden.

In point of fact, we altered our minds at the last moment and went to Riga instead, by a Russian freighter through the Kiel Canal. From Riga we went to St Petersburg, Moscow and Nijni-Novgorod and back to St Petersburg, where we took a coasting steamer to Stockholm. We eventually ended up in a little village called Bydalen, about three hundred miles north-west of Stockholm, where we remained for about a month before returning to England. I had to keep very quiet about having been to Russia, as the country was in a very unsettled state after the massacres in front of the Winter Palace in St Petersburg, and the Chancery Court would never have given me permission to go there.

Having been duly entered as an undergraduate at Trinity Hall, I spent the remainder of the Long Vacation at Seaford, with Goodland and another Law coach. And there I had the misfortune to learn to play golf, an affliction from which I have never wholly recovered.

Trinity Hall specialises in Law and has provided the Bar with many of its greatest lawyers. So I was made to read Law, thus once more completely altering my life. Not only had I to start an entirely new train of thought in studying Law, but I also took up rowing. Trinity Hall was a famous rowing college, and the sport was almost compulsory if you were there as an undergraduate. It almost amounted to treason to prefer another form of athletics, and although we had cricket and football blues in the college, they were looked upon with disfavour and even grave suspicion.

The Trinity Hall first boat went to the Head of the River in my first year and kept its position during all the time that I was at Cambridge, and I do not think it had been lower than fourth for nearly forty years. In my last year we had five blues in the boat.

When I say that my life was once more entirely altered,

I am not complaining. I do not envy the man whose education has, from his pre-preparatory school until he reaches his desk in the City, progressed along one narrow groove. He starts learning Latin at the age of seven and Greek a little later, and after twelve years he is still studying Latin and Greek and trying to take his degree at the university. It is the same with his games. He plays cricket and football or rows at his schools, and does the same things when he reaches the university. His great shock comes when he goes down.

My life at Cambridge was uneventful. I tried to be as much like other undergraduates as possible, wearing the same sort of clothes, using the same slang and getting into the same scrapes. I made a number of new friends and became a member of the Pitt Club, the only purely social club at Cambridge worth belonging to; and, like many another undergraduate, before and since my day, I took too great an advantage of my new-found freedom.

We all had a most exaggerated idea of our own importance. We interpreted the word "university" as being the centre of the universe, round which everything else revolved. The prominence given in the press to events like the Oxford and Cambridge Boat Race fostered this illusion; during my first year the President of the C.U.B.C. was even the subject of a cartoon in *Vanity Fair*, an honour reserved for the most prominent men in Great Britain. We sincerely thought that for all practical purposes a man's life was over when he went down and started on a weary round of grinding work to keep body and soul together. And we thought that at the age of forty a man might just as well be dead.

I remember someone in London saying that the Boston Waltz was going out of fashion and was being superseded by some other dance step. Without hesitation I adopted a very superior air and said: "Oh, no! You are quite wrong there. At Cambridge the Boston is still all the rage!" It was, I suppose, part of the general intolerance of youth and a sign of healthy enthusiasm. Sometimes we wondered how on earth people amused themselves in the outside world while we, the real lords of creation, were up at our universities during term time.

It was soon after I went up that I first saw a copy of *The Ballad of Reading Gaol*, on the book-shelf of one of my new-found friends. Until then I had not even known of its existence. It may seem odd that my aunt Nellie had not mentioned it to me in Switzerland, but very likely she had not heard of it either. I asked if I could borrow it and took it away to read.

My literary education at this period was in a peculiar state. No one had ever made any attempt to guide my choice of reading, and my knowledge of poetry was confined to such works as *The Lays of Ancient Rome, The Hunting of the Snark* and *The Bab Ballads*, with a small smattering of Swinburne and Barham. On the other hand, I had a fair knowledge of Verlaine, Baudelaire and Mallarmé. So *The Ballad of Reading Gaol* had a curious effect upon me.

My first feeling was that it reminded me of *The Dream of Eugene Aram*. I also thought it was too harrowing. Then I went back to the beginning and read it through again. Slowly the beauty and force of the poem came home to me and I felt a great urge to read more of my father's writings. Until then the only other book of his that I remembered having seen was *The Happy Prince*, in Cottesmore Gardens, with the name Oscar Wilde obliterated.

I returned the poem to its owner and went to the library of the Union Society, to see what I could find. But though there were several entries in the catalogue under Wilde, the books were all missing from the shelves, with the exception of a very battered copy of *Intentions*.

Intentions fascinated me with its beautifully constructed phrases and its melodious cadences. Particularly did I like

The Decay of Lying, which I read over and over again. There were my brother's name and my own set out for all to see, and I began to feel nervous lest someone should catch me reading the book and connect me with it in some way.

Books by Oscar Wilde were very difficult to get at that time. The first collected edition had not yet appeared and no authorised edition of any of his works had been published for years. Even the copies sometimes to be found in secondhand bookshops were usually badly printed and were often inaccurate piracies. I wrote to my brother and told him of my discoveries, and he replied by sending me a copy of *De Profundis.* I read it on my nineteenth birthday.

De Profundis, as first issued in 1905, consisted of extracts from a long letter written in Reading Gaol by my father to Alfred Douglas, showing him how he had contributed to the catastrophe. The whole letter has since been published, but for reasons inherent in the letter itself it could not be published in Douglas's lifetime. The 1905 *De Profundis* consisted of the more lyrical passages in the letter, and when I first read it, it struck me as being a little artificial. I thought that beneath the beauty of the language I could detect a certain striving after effect, as though it were written for its literary style rather than as the sincere reflections of a sorely stricken man. Two years later, when I met Robert Ross and he showed me the whole letter, I began to appreciate it at its true value and to understand what an amazing piece of work it is. I think it was a mistake to publish the shortened version in 1905, instead of waiting until the years had mellowed the story.

About this time my fellow-undergraduates began to show a certain curiosity about me. Who was my father? What had he done while he was alive? Why did I go to school in Monaco? Parrying these questions was hard

work, especially as I was caught unawares by the first
question and replied, without thinking: "He was an
author." "What books?" "Oh, just books." "But what
books?" "None you've ever heard of." And I reverted to
the explorer story and said that he wrote rather dry eth-
nological and anthropological books which were not very
good anyhow.

The family never visualised the complications of the
deception they had compelled me to practise, and they
would have no doubt been appalled by the tissue of lies
that I had to weave in support of this deception. I suppose
all the dons were aware of my identity; the Master of my
college must certainly have known. But although so
many people seemed to be in the secret, I was not supposed to know that they knew, which put me into a cruelly
awkward position.

I remained up at Cambridge for a great part of my first
Long Vacation, pursuing the study of the Law, which I
was growing increasingly to dislike, and towards the latter
part I went to Babbacombe to stay with Lady Mount
Temple's adopted daughter, Juliet, who had inherited the
Cliff. And there, for the first time in my life, I met women
and girls of my own age on an equal footing. I do not
count my life in Lausanne, where one's feminine companionship was confined to dancing classes twice a week,
occasional tea-parties and private dances. Nor do I count
the rather stilted and formal meetings in May Week
with the girls of my undergraduate friends' families, with
whom there was always a certain shyness and awkward-
ness. It was a new experience to be able to go and call
whenever I wanted, to play golf with them, and go on
motor tours over the moors, in an early motor car with
a body like an open governess cart, which one entered by
a small door at the back. Of course I fell in love with
most of the girls, but I was becoming more immune with
each attack. I was growing up rapidly and was an entirely

different person from the callow youth of eighteen months before at Lausanne.

In the Michaelmas Term, 1906, Ronald Firbank arrived as an undergraduate at Trinity Hall. No college at the university, with the possible exception of Pembroke, could have been less suited to his character and temperament. He was quite unfitted for playing any games, and I do not think he ever did much work. I never knew what he read, but he must have read something or he would not have been allowed to stay up.* His arrival created a great sensation, as it was rumoured that not only was he an author, but that he had actually had a book published! So any of us who had literary ambitions called on him at a very early date. And he and I soon became friends. He gave me a copy of the published book, containing two stories, "Odette d'Antrevennes" and "A Study in Temperament." It had been published in 1905 by Elkin Mathews in light blue paper covers, with its price announced on the front cover as "One Florin Net." Like my father as an undergraduate, Ronald had not yet simplified his name, and his full name appears across the top of the cover: Arthur Annesley Ronald Firbank. The first of these stories was re-published in 1916. Certain adolescent faults were eliminated in the new edition, the title of the book was shortened to *Odette* and the name of the author to Ronald Firbank. Even the price of the book was shortened to one shilling.

At the time of Firbank's arrival I was editor of the college magazine, the *Crescent*, named after the ermine crescent appearing in the centre of the college arms. The magazine appeared at the end of every term and was not a very learned publication, being devoted largely to record-

* I have already written my reminiscences of Ronald Firbank at Cambridge in *Ronald Firbank: A memoir* by Ifan Kyrle Fletcher. With personal Reminiscences by Lord Berners, V. B. Holland, Augustus John, R.A., and Osbert Sitwell. Duckworth, 1930.

ing the athletic prowess of the members of the college. Ronald sent me in a contribution. Unfortunately, his style was hardly one to appeal to the hearty, rowing, drinking, swearing undergraduates of the period, and when he submitted a fantasy in true Firbank vein for publication in the magazine, I had, in self-defence, to refuse it. I wish I had at least kept the manuscript, as I do not think it was ever published.

By the end of the summer term of 1907, after two years at Cambridge, I felt that if I was to go into the Far Eastern Consular Service, as my family wished me to do, I was really wasting my time in studying for a Law degree. I was in danger of forgetting all the subjects in which I would have to pass my Foreign Office examination.

Besides, the study of Law, and particularly of jurisprudence, required a major effort on my part. I found it difficult to retain what I learnt, as I invariably put it out of my mind as soon as I put down my books. Criminal Law, the Law of Torts, and the Law of Evidence were, it is true, fascinating subjects, but they were of comparatively minor importance in the eyes of the teachers and examiners beside the Institutes of Justinian and Gaius, Constitutional Law and the Laws of Real Property and Procedure, and all the rigmarole of Pleadings and the Courts, which I could only manage to learn parrot-fashion.

I have a logical mind, and it seemed to me that with a properly drawn-up code of law nine-tenths of the business of the Civil Courts could be avoided. In other professions men at the top might occasionally make mistakes. A doctor might make a wrong diagnosis, a surgeon's knife might slip, or a parson might go over to Rome, yet by and large they were all pretty good at their jobs. But in every case before the Civil Courts, one side or the other had to lose, which meant that half the Counsel employed had to be wrong, however eminent they were; and in important cases which went to the Court of Appeal and to the House of

Lords a large proportion of the Judges had to be wrong too.

So after another May Week I said good-bye to Trinity Hall and my friends there. It seems strange to me now that all the time I was at Stonyhurst and Cambridge my most intimate friends, such as Joshua Goodland, Gerald Seligman and Ronald Firbank, were quite unaware of my identity. But before I went down I told one or two of them. When I told my great friend Joshua Goodland, he said: "I always thought there was something mysterious about you. And now I know why. But what does it really matter? Your father was a great writer." And that cheered me as nothing else could have done.

During that summer I began to realise that everyone seemed to know who I was. And yet when I told the family this they refused to believe it and said that the only person who could possibly know was Juliet Mount Temple, who would never have breathed a word about it to anyone. Juliet was a garrulous woman, not overburdened with tact, and it was quite beyond her nature not to talk in the circumstances. Yet the family still kept up a conspiracy of silence among themselves, furious, I suppose, at seeing all they had striven for come to nothing.

After the summer holiday I returned to London and found two rooms in Emperor's Gate, Kensington, on the top floor of a dim Victorian house. The rooms had probably been servants' bedrooms in an era when the well-being and comfort of her employees was something into which the average mistress of a household would not have dreamed of inquiring. And it was there that I awaited my twenty-first birthday.

CHAPTER VII

Happy Years Ahead

In spite of the rather dingy surroundings in which I found myself in Emperor's Gate, I was very happy there. For the first time for years I felt myself completely free from the trammels of tutelage, with no one to watch my comings and goings.

It was now arranged that I should go to Scoones', the most important cramming establishment for all Foreign Office examinations. It was situated in Garrick Street, almost next to the Garrick Club, and more than half the Foreign Office candidates passed through it at one time or another. Its teachers had an uncanny instinct for knowing what was in the examiners' minds, and for making their pupils read the right books and learn the obscure philological facts upon which they were subsequently questioned.

I went to Scoones' towards the middle of July, and immediately felt very much a fish out of water; nearly all the other pupils had spent the previous two years abroad, mostly at French and German universities, whereas I soon found that I had forgotten most of my German during those two years, and that my French, though very fluent, was mainly of a conversational kind and of little use for composition. And, to make matters worse, a new subject was thrust upon me—Political Economy.

If Law had appeared to me illogical, Political Economy was simply meaningless. Whereas in Law half the experts were always wrong, in Political Economy no one ever seemed to be right. The authorities all had different theories and contradicted one another and I was quite bemused by it all. My only comfort was that if I failed to pass my examination, I would not be banished to the Far East; but I was keenly conscious of the waste of time, and I was already turning over alternative occupations in my mind.

When I had been at Scoones' for a few days, I struck up a friendship with Sir Coleridge Kennard, who was about to enter the Diplomatic Service. A week later he told me that he knew about me and that his mother, Mrs. Helen Carew, who lived in Hans Place, was anxious to meet me; she had been a friend of my father, for whose memory she retained a deep affection. So that evening, after our studies, I went back to Hans Place with Kennard and stayed to dinner. Mrs. Carew spoke to me about my father, saying what a wonderful man she thought him. I was very much moved by this as, apart from Goodland's remark when I told him who I was, this was the first time since I had left England twelve years before that I had ever heard him spoken of with respect. To hear him talked of as an artist and a distinguished man of letters rather embarrassed me, as it did also to be regarded as an object of envy instead of one of pity.

Mrs. Carew showed me the copies of my father's books which he had inscribed to her, and in them I saw his handwriting for (so far as I could remember) the first time. I must, in fact, have seen it often enough, but I had forgotten what it was like.

Towards the end of the evening Mrs. Carew broached the subject of Robert Ross. Would I object to meeting him, as he wanted to meet me and also, if possible, my brother? And when she discovered that I had no idea of whom she was talking, she could scarcely believe me and gave me a brief resume of what he had done for my father during the past six years. I explained to her all the circumstances of my upbringing. I think she had expected that my mind would have been poisoned against friends of my father's, and was relieved to find that I was most anxious to meet any of them that I could.

It was to Mrs. Carew that Robert Ross had dedicated the shortened version of *De Profundis* that he published in 1905, and it was she who had provided £2,000 with which to purchase the site in Père Lachaise cemetery to which my father's remains were subsequently transferred, and to pay for the monument by Epstein which now surmounts it.

The following week I dined with Mrs. Carew again and there I met Robert Ross, Max Beerbohm and Reginald Turner, all of whom had been Oscar Wilde's intimate friends. It was a highly emotional meeting, and from the moment that I met Robert Ross, I knew that I had found a true friend of my own, one who would be loyal and true and never betray me. And the impression I had at that moment remained with me until Robbie's untimely death almost exactly eleven years later.

Robert Ross's appearance was very different from what I had anticipated. I had pictured him in my mind as a tall, melancholy, clean-shaven man, with a shock of greying hair and a flowing tie; something like W. B. Yeats, in fact. He turned out to be small and neat, with a tidy moustache. The worries of his life had deprived him of a great deal of his hair, but he had a roguish, almost boyish look that attracted me at once. He had an infectious laugh which came very easily.

I suppose that when I first went to Scoones' I had reached my lowest ebb. After a reasonably successful school career, I had idled at Lausanne and done little at Cambridge, except to pass a few Bar examinations, and I was confronted with a very stiff competitive examination, which I knew to be beyond me in the short time at my disposal before the examination took place. I would need at least six months in Germany and three in France, apart from Political Economy and other subjects to be studied; and my examination was to take place in June the following year, less than nine months ahead. And I was living in two dark rooms at the top of a Kensington house, into which my meals were reluctantly brought on a tray, while I worked away at my Political Economy. Then suddenly, with the entry into my life of Mrs. Carew, I found myself, within the space of a few days, no longer the friendless, haunted creature I had been for years, but in the midst of well-wishers in the literary and artistic world of London.

Robert Ross began to take me round to see my father's old friends and I started to learn something about Oscar Wilde and his charm. The first visit was to Miss Adela Schuster, to whom my father refers in his letters as "the lady of Wimbledon." It was she who had provided him with £1,000 to enable him to conduct his defence at the Old Bailey, and she also helped him again on his release. It was the revival of a childhood's memory, because as soon as I saw the lawn sloping away from the house towards an artificial pond at the bottom of the garden, I remembered how Cyril and I had rolled down the lawn as children and I had ended up in the pond and had to be fished out and dried.

Miss Schuster showed me the "Poems in Prose" which my father had told her and which she had written down from memory, and she conveyed to me some of her own enthusiasm about his plays. She was an old lady by this time, and I visited her frequently at her beautiful Wimbledon home. My father always regretted very much that he had not dedicated one of his works to Miss Schuster, so when the first Collected Edition was published in 1908 Robert Ross made up the deficiency by dedicating *The Duchess of Padua* to her.

Another lady with whom I became great friends was Mrs. Ada Leverson, whom my father called "The Gilded Sphinx of Golden Memory." She and her husband had sheltered my father between his two trials and she had been one of his greatest friends. She was a fascinating person, still very beautiful with the aureole of gold-tinted hair from which derived the name my father had given her. She spoke in a low, rather deep voice, pausing in a disconcerting manner at the end of each sentence to gauge the effect that her words were having on you. People like Miss Schuster and Mrs. Leverson gave me a fresh outlook on life and on human nature. They broadened my views, broke down my prejudices and inhibitions and gradually drew me out of the shell into which I had tried to retire.

When I first met Robert Ross he naturally wanted to know my brother too, so I arranged a meeting and we three lunched together at the Reform Club, of which Ross was a member. I warned Ross that he might not find my brother as tractable as myself, and he promised to keep the conversation on safe lines. I confess that I was a little afraid that Ross might say something that would draw an antagonistic reply from Cyril, but during the whole luncheon no mention was made of Oscar Wilde; the conversation was mainly about literature and art, concerning which we all held different views. Cyril and Robert Ross subsequently became firm friends, and when Cyril went to India they carried on a lengthy correspondence. I never saw Ross's letters, but those from Cyril which Ross showed me were, I suspect, addressed more to posterity than to Ross himself.

Three months after I had met Robert Ross, I came of age. No suggestion came from any of my mother's family about any form of celebration. I suppose they thought that nothing in any way connected with my birth was a matter for rejoicing. But Robbie Ross remedied the deficiency and gave me a magnificent dinner-party at 15 Vicarage Gardens in Kensington, where he shared a charming Victorian house with More Adey. We sat down twelve at table, the guests being Sir William Richmond, R.A., Charles Shannon, Charles Ricketts, Henry James,

Reginald Turner, William Rothenstein, Sir Coleridge
Kennard, Ronald Firbank, More Adey and my brother
Cyril. Alas, I have lost the menu of that occasion, though
I had one signed by everyone present. There were
speeches, no doubt, and afterwards Kennard, my brother
and I returned to Kennard's home in Hans Place, where
we discussed philosophy, life and literature far into the
night.

Another month passed, and then one day Joshua
Goodland came to see me and told me that he and Peter
Wallace, with whom I had travelled to Russia and Sweden,
were going to Canada on a shooting expedition in the
north of Quebec, and I asked whether I could come too.
As they were off in about a week, this did not give me
much time for preparation. But the world was free then.
No passports were required for the American continent;
there were no currency restrictions and passages were easy
to obtain. But there was the family to be dealt with, and
that did not promise to be very easy, although on coming
of age I had come into a small patrimony from my mother,
so I was, temporarily at any rate, my own master.

As I expected, when I broke the news of my impending
trip to my ex-guardian and the family, they were very put
out and used every argument to dissuade me from taking
such an irrevocable step. My brother Cyril was the only
one who took my side; that was after I had explained to
him that my two years spent in the study of Law had unfitted me for the examination which I faced, and that
furthermore I did not want to be parted from my new-
found friends and banished from England to the Far East,
there to live the life of a petty Foreign Office official
until either the climate or acute despondency put a mer-
ciful end to my life.

The same arguments failed to carry any weight with the
family, who resorted to vague statements and the old
assertion that they knew best, that everything they had

done for me through the years had been for my own good, and that I was now in danger of undoing it all. My own attitude was that too many people knew my identity for it to be concealed any longer, and that this ostrich-like attitude was a source of embarrassment to me.

Anyway, I surmounted all the difficulties and said farewell to Scoones' and to the prospect of exile to the Far East. And on November 22nd, 1907, I sailed from Liverpool on the R.M.S. *Victorian,* of the Allan Line, bound for Halifax, Nova Scotia.

This American trip lasted altogether five months, during which I spent a great deal of money I could ill afford. Goodland and Wallace were growing restless and decided to move on to Japan. But I began to take stock and I had a feeling of *lusisti satis* and decided to return to England alone. So I left them at Monterey and took the train from San Francisco to New York. I began to have a guilty feeling of "Life is real, life is earnest" and that I must buckle on my armour.

On the train I had a cold and pains in my chest. I was convinced that I was going to die and wrote a lot of letters to various people to be posted after my death. On reaching Chicago and finding I had three hours to wait, I looked up a doctor, who said I had slight bronchitis and was not to worry, so I passed the rest of the journey in comparative peace of mind.

I was now getting near the end of my funds, and when I had booked a second-class passage to England on an American Line boat for £15, I had to watch every cent. So, on this my only visit to New York, I spent the time walking about the streets, admiring the sky-scrapers and going to museums and art galleries during the three days I had to wait before my boat sailed. I daresay that I saw more of the surface of New York in those three days than most visitors see in a month.

The voyage on the ship was uneventful. I played

bridge most of the time at ten cents a hundred and made about twenty dollars, which enabled me to remunerate the stewards adequately; when I arrived in London I had about thirty-three shillings left, which was cutting it a little fine in a journey all the way from San Francisco.

The day after my return I went to see Robert Ross, who received me with affection, but with some disapproval of my gallivanting and wasting my time in America. His greeting was typical of his whimsical sense of humour: "Ah! I see the prodigal has returned. I hear you have been killing the fatted calf at both ends!"

I decided that, whatever else I did, I would continue reading for the Bar. I had paid my fees, eaten most of my dinners and passed some of my examinations, and it seemed a pity to waste all that effort. So I found myself a small unfurnished flat in Kensington Palace Mansions, at £75 a year inclusive of service, and settled down to work. It was then late April 1908.

I saw a great deal of Robert Ross and of Mrs. Carew during these months, and I met most of the literary and artistic figures of the time. Among those with whom I formed friendships were Henry James, Thomas Hardy, Sir William Richmond, H. G. Wells and Arnold Bennett. I found myself at last in the literary milieu to which I had always wanted to belong. Particularly did I make friends with H. G. Wells, whom I saw constantly throughout the rest of his life.

I became very friendly with Max Beerbohm later and used to sit in his room and talk to him while he drew his caricatures. He once told me that he was the world's example of the triumph of mind over matter. He had been born, he said, with a small head and large hands and feet but, by dint of making countless drawings of himself and by continual concentration, he had achieved his ambition, which was to have a large head and very small hands and feet.

Max Beerbohm's half-brother, Herbert Beerbohm Tree, also became a friend of mine. When I met him in 1908 he remembered that, at the age of seven, I had sat on his knee at the Haymarket Theatre and had repeated the remark I had heard about *A Woman of No Importance*. He was undoubtedly the most outstanding actor-manager of his generation, not even excepting Henry Irving; but he affected an almost impenetrable vagueness as a defence against importunates and bores, who always pursued him relentlessly, and he carried this vagueness into all the phases of his life.

Tree told me that my father was an "infernal nuisance" during the rehearsals of *A Woman of No Importance* in 1893, and kept interrupting with objections and suggestions until, a week before the play was produced, Tree gave orders that he was not to be admitted to the theatre during rehearsals, on any pretext whatever. Two days later my father was walking up the Haymarket when he ran into Tree just outside the Haymarket Theatre. It was one of those warm days in April that give promise of an early summer and Tree, clad in a frock-coat beflowered with a carnation, was carrying his top-hat, brim upwards, in his hand. It was a new hat that morning and had a bright red lining. My father eyed it with delight and observed: "My dear Herbert, what a charming lining you have in your hat!" Tree replied: "My dear Oscar, do you really like it?" "Yes," said my father, "I think it is perfection." "Then," continued Tree, plunging his hand into his hat, ripping out the lining and handing it to him, "it is yours!" And he disappeared into his theatre, thus avoiding any possible discussion about the production of the play.

There was one person whom I was never asked to meet, and that was Lord Alfred Douglas. The nearest I ever came to it was one evening at the theatre with Mrs. Carew. Someone in the row behind us attracted her attention in an interval and held a conversation with her. And after the play was over she said to me: "I did not introduce you, because I thought it was better not to do so. That was Bosie Douglas."

In about 1929 I received a letter from an American author who was contemplating writing a book about Frank Harris; he wanted my own opinion about Harris's *Life and Confessions of Oscar Wilde.* I replied that I knew nothing whatever about the matter, but that I had heard Robert Ross say that, although it was a thoroughly bad book, written with the sole object of glorifying Harris himself, it did, on the whole, contain some elements of truth. I think Robert Ross meant that Harris had put Alfred Douglas into his proper perspective. Unfortunately I now no longer possess a copy of my letter. Six months later I received an infuriated letter from Alfred Douglas. As this and one other letter on the same subject constituted the only correspondence I ever had with Douglas, I think it may be of interest to give them here.* The first and only time that I met Alfred Douglas after 1895 was shortly before the last war, at the coming-out ball of his great-niece, Lady Jane Douglas. We chatted on general subjects for about five minutes and then parted. I never saw him again.

Years ago I became friendly with the late Lord Queensberry, who wrote about his uncle Alfred Douglas in *Oscar Wilde and the Black Douglas,* which he dedicated to me in order, as he told me, to make "full cycle." So much for Alfred Douglas.

Coleridge Kennard took his examination for the Diplomatic Service in the summer of 1908, and when it was over we went to Venice together for a short holiday. I had been working very hard and needed a holiday. We had a wonderful time on the Lido for a fortnight, afterwards staying at the Grand Hotel in Venice and lazing through

* See Appendix D, p. 265.

the days in gondolas or roaming about the outer islands in a motor boat.

In Venice, Coleridge Kennard suggested that I should call myself Vyvyan Wilde as an experiment. I accordingly did so, but found it to be an embarrassment, as I was constantly being sought out by reporters from Italian newspapers, who wanted me to give them interviews. So I soon abandoned the experiment.

After about a month of this, we returned to London, via Paris, where Mrs. Carew came out to meet us. She showed me round Paris and took me to the Hôtel d'Alsace, where my father died, and to Bagneux cemetery, where he was buried. Contrary to what has frequently been said by people wishing to suggest that my father died in misery and want, the Hôtel d'Alsace was not a mean and squalid place. It was, and still is, a small but very pleasant and comfortable hotel with a courtyard in the centre. In the middle of this courtyard grows a fig-tree, which was over-looked by my father's two bright, sunlit rooms. I had only been in Paris once before and that for one night only, during the nightmare flight of my brother and myself into Switzerland some thirteen years earlier.

On my return to England my brother told me of a persistent rumour in the family that I had been sent down from Cambridge by the authorities, more or less under a cloud. So, to put an end to that story, I wrote to my tutor at Trinity Hall, G. B. Shirres, and asked if I could come up for another year, explaining my predicament. He readily agreed, so I let my flat in London and went back to Cambridge, in *statu pupillari*, at the beginning of the Michaelmas Term 1908.

After my year of completely untrammelled freedom, it was strange to be back under the comparatively strict col-lege discipline. I found a few old friends still up, notably Ronald Firbank, who was in the same rooms and behaving in exactly the same way as he had done two years before.

I do not think he had started to do any work yet. I got to know Rupert Brooke and A. C. Landsberg, and we used to hold poetry recitals in Firbank's rooms. Unfortunately, I no longer had rooms in college, but was in lodgings looking out over Midsummer Common.

I went to London for the day from time to time, and I attended the dinner given to Robert Ross on December 1st, 1908, on the publication of my father's complete works, a labour of love which had occupied most of his time for the previous two years. From the date of my father's death, Robert Ross laboured to rehabilitate the literary reputation of his friend. His first act was to get himself appointed my father's literary executor. That in itself, in view of the fact that he was not a relative and that the estate was bankrupt, was a real feat. He fought like a wildcat against the opposition he encountered everywhere, extracting royalties from reluctant producers of the plays in Germany.

There were more than a hundred and sixty guests at this dinner, with Sir Martin Conway, the famous explorer and author, in the chair. Among those present were the Duchess of Sutherland, Lord Howard de Walden, Lord Grimthorpe, Mr. and Mrs. Edmund Gosse, H. G. Wells, Gertrude Kingston, William Archer, Oscar Browning, Herbert Trench, Somerset Maugham, George Alexander, Mrs. Belloc Lowndes, Mr. and Mrs. Laurence Binyon and many other people well known in literature, science and the arts. I myself sat next to Somerset Maugham. My brother Cyril was also there, seated between William Rothenstein and E. V. Lucas.

During that last year at Cambridge I had reached the stage at which most young men arrive sooner or later, when the most important thing in life, and almost the most important art, is the art of conversation. We used to amuse ourselves by holding Socratic arguments about the topics of the day in the world at large, as well as in

Cambridge, flattering ourselves that our thoughts were profound, our wit divine and our satire devastating.

One day in May I heard from Robert Ross that he was coming up to Cambridge for the night on some business connected with the Fitzwilliam Museum, and that he hoped I would dine with him and bring along any friends who I thought would enjoy it. Ronald Firbank and I had other ideas and we gave him a dinner instead.

It was arranged that I should supply the food, from the college kitchens, and that Ronald would try to get the wine from his father, who had a considerable cellar. The wine in question was Moët et Chandon 1884, which was really far too old to drink in 1909, unless it had been kept with extraordinary care. However, at that time we knew very little about wine and were rather proud of its age. I still have the menu of that dinner, signed by those present. The guests were Robert Ross, Rupert Brooke, Mario Colonna, Ernst Goldschmidt, A. C. Landsberg, F. G. W. Parish and one other man whose name is undecipherable.

Ronald Firbank and I came down together in June 1909. During the whole of his time at Cambridge, Ronald not only never passed an examination, but never even sat for one.

After I left Cambridge, Robert Ross took me to Paris to be present at the removal of my father's earthly remains from Bagneux cemetery to Père Lachaise.[47] The proceedings were fraught with petty restrictions and regulations, with countless papers to be signed and countersigned and innumerable revenue stamps to be paid for and affixed. One of the regulations, doubtless invented as a perquisite for someone, was that the shell used for the removal had to be made in the workshops on the Bagneux cemetery premises. This annoyed Robert Ross, who had already ordered a sumptuous coffin, which could not be used. The Bagneux coffin was of plain oak, with a silver plate on the lid on which was engraved OSCARD WILDE 1854–1900.

This was the last straw and I thought that Ross was going to explode. However, the undertaker produced a chisel and hacked out the intrusive D, making a bad mess of it but correcting the error.

When the ceremony was over and the vault closed, the undertaker approached Robert Ross and, in an ingratiating manner, suggested that, pending the erection of the Epstein monument, he might put on *"une petite inscription."* Robbie recoiled from him and, raising his hands in horrified protest, cried in his rather drawling Canadian French: *"Oh, ma foi, non! Assez d'inscriptions!"*

CHAPTER VIII

And Now

MY father was only forty-six when he died, an age at which most authors and artists enter upon the period of their greatest achievements. But apart from the letter to Lord Alfred Douglas known as *De Profundis*, and *The Ballad of Reading Gaol*, he wrote nothing after 1895. The spark of genius in him was extinguished by prison life, and it could never be rekindled. He constantly spoke of work which he had in mind, but when it came to actual writing he began to be assailed by doubts and problems; doubts as to how any work of his would be received, and problems as to whether it was humanly possible for him to reconstruct his literary life.

More books have been written, in more languages, about Oscar Wilde than about any literary figure who has lived during the past hundred years. But as people recede further and further into the past, they are apt to assume the aspect of effigies from which all humanity has departed; and when other people write about them they hack them about to make them fit into a pattern of their own making until no flesh and blood remains. This is especially true of Oscar Wilde. Most of the people who have written about him have treated him like a beetle under a microscope, to be examined and dissected and analysed as a psychological problem—not as a human being at all. If they have mentioned any human qualities it has always been in parentheses, as it were, and almost on a note of surprise and deprecation. And yet the most outstanding aspect of my father's character was his great humanity, his love of life and of his fellow-men and his sympathy with suffering. He was the kindest and gentlest of men, and he hated to see anyone suffer. None of his biographers, not even Frank Harris, has suggested that he ever did a mean or an unkind act. Many stories are told of how he helped people in distress, even when he was himself in want.

Once in Reading Gaol he discovered that three small children were in the same place for the heinous crime of poaching rabbits; a fine which neither they nor their parents were able to pay had been inflicted upon them and they were sent to prison in default. This may seem incredible to us now, but not much more than a hundred years earlier they would probably have been publicly hanged. My father was deeply distressed that children who might be the same age as his own could be so barbarously treated by a self-righteous community, and he managed to get a note through to one of the warders with whom he was on good terms, asking what he could do to help and offering to pay the fine. "Please do this for me," the note went on to say; "I must get them out. Think what a thing it would be for me to be able to help three little children. If I can do this by paying the fine, tell the children that they are to be released tomorrow by a friend, and ask them to be happy and not to tell anyone." And the children were freed.

My father has been reproached for disliking all forms of violent collective sport, such as hunting, cricket and football. Yet as his letters to Ward and Harding show, he spent most of his Oxford vacations shooting, fishing and playing lawn tennis. He was an exceptionally strong swimmer and has been described to me as ploughing through the waves in a rough sea at Worthing like a shark, in a way that struck awe into the onlookers.

Oddly enough, too, he was at one time a keen golfer. His biographers have tried to make out that he only pretended to play golf so as to be able to explain his absences from home, and that he would not have known a driver from a putter. But the first golf-clubs I ever saw and handled belonged to my father; they used to stand in a corner of the hall in the Tite Street house; in later years Robert Ross assured me that my father was an enthusiastic, if somewhat inefficient, golfer—characteristics which I seem to have inherited from him.

The phases through which my father's literary reputation passed during the first twenty years of this century have an odd counterpart in the way in which he was built up in my own mind through those same years.

My feelings towards my father's memory have always of necessity been mixed ones. I think of my mother with deep affection and regret. I also have affectionate feelings towards my mother's family, who, however misguidedly, tried to construct a new life for my brother and myself on a foundation of sand. But I am also proud of my father and of his place in English literature, though, as I suppose the sons of all famous men must feel, it is embarrassing to bask in so much reflected glory.

I remember him as a smiling giant, always exquisitely dressed, who crawled about the nursery floor with us and lived in an aura of cigarette-smoke and eau-de-cologne. During his last years we were constantly in his thoughts; he was always asking Robert Ross to try and find out something about us, how we were and how we were getting on at school. And Ross told me that he wept bitter tears when he pondered on how he had failed us and himself and his ancestors. Towards the end he realised that he would probably never see us again and he tried to get messages through to us. He even approached our guardian through More Adey, to ask to be allowed to write letters to us, to be delivered when we came of age, but my guardian's reply was that if any such letters were sent they would immediately be destroyed. All that my father had to remind him of us were the two photographs taken at Heidelberg in 1897, and one or two letters which we had written to him from our preparatory schools before 1895.

When I was parted from my father for ever I passed through the stages of fear, perplexity and frustration. Fear and frustration are more destructive to peace of mind than almost any other mental processes; and as I connected these with my father I gradually began to think of him with dislike, when I thought of him at all. And this feeling, fostered by the attitude of my mother's family, increased as I approached adolescence.

My fear was for what I might one day discover. My frustration came from having it constantly dinned into me that I was different from other boys; that I was a pariah who could not take his place within the framework of the world, except, perhaps, in some remote corner of it.

Fear and frustration are two obsessions of which it is terribly hard to rid oneself. And if I have learnt nothing else in the course of my life, I have learnt that it is impossible to hide one's head and to be happy at the same time, that it is better to sail under one's true colours and to face all corners bravely and resolutely. And I think that this is what our family should have made us do, even though it meant that our entire education must take place away from England; it was not as though we were English anyway.

As one result of the secrecy with which I was surrounded in my childhood, I have suffered all my life from embarrassing shyness. Because of my anomalous and often awkward position it is difficult for me to make friends. Difficult more for the prospective friends than for myself. I always have to be explained—almost apologised for. Men, particularly men of the Anglo-Saxon races, are innately conventional. Women usually take a wider view; consequently I have always felt more at ease with women than with men. As much as women are capable of being understood, I understand them; and I know that they understand me.

I was just nineteen when I began to read my father's works, in 1905. Until a few months earlier he had been nothing to me but a name shrouded in mystery. It was really as well for me that I had been enlightened about my father's life by my aunt in Switzerland, as at Cambridge his name was frequently mentioned. Many references to him were, to say the least of it, unflattering, but already the rising generation was beginning to appreciate the beauty of his language, and his works formed one of the main subjects for discussion in literary undergraduate circles.

After reading the copy of *Intentions* which I found in the Cambridge Union library, I succeeded in getting hold of a secondhand copy of *The Picture of Dorian Gray*. At the time I was passing through a stage of being intensely interested in the supernatural and was avidly reading the books of Algernon Blackwood and Arthur Machen; I had even acquired an early sixteenth-century copy of a work on magic by Albertus Magnus which I endeavoured to puzzle out. So naturally *Dorian Gray* had a great fascination for me, and it was then that I first began to feel proud of being the son of a man who could write such a book. And there, for the time being, my knowledge of my father's writings ceased, as it was impossible to find copies of any of his other books. No reference book of the period even gave a list of his works. And it was not until two years later that Mrs. Carew lent me her own precious copies, each containing inscriptions to her from my father.

Until I was thirty-five, the only biography of my father that I had read was one by Sherard, and I had only skimmed through that. I took the view that my father had plunged my mother into the depths of misery and had caused her premature death. In this attitude I was, of course, encouraged by my mother's family, upon whom the responsibility for my subsequent upbringing devolved. Time, however, which numbs pain and dulls resentment, has caused me to take a more tolerant view, and has convinced me that my father was more the victim of circumstances than of his own frailty. It is no part of my task to discuss the events that led up to my father's débâcle; but had he not had the misfortune to know Lionel Johnson, who introduced him to Alfred Douglas, and if Alfred Douglas's father had not hated his son and used Oscar Wilde as a cat's-paw, a very different story might have been told, and the world might have been richer by many more plays like *The Importance of Being Earnest*.

For many years I had a recurrent dream that I met my father again, rather quietly in a sombrely-lit room, and that he spoke gently to me and asked me to forgive him for the unhappiness he had brought upon his family.

I do not try to defend my father's behaviour; but I do think that the penalties inflicted upon him were unnecessarily severe. And by that I do not only mean the prison sentence; I mean the virtual suppression of all his works and the ostracism and insults which he had to endure during the few remaining years of his life. The worst aspects of Victorian hypocrisy have now disappeared, and today my father would not have been hounded to his death as he was fifty years ago. The self-righteousness of that age was really camouflage to disguise its own hypocrisy, and the people who were loudest in their condemnation of my father were often those whose own lives could least bear investigation. Nothing makes the transgressor so indignant as the transgressions, of a different kind, of his fellow-men; except, perhaps, transgressions of the same kind.

On the other hand, many deeply religious people are naturally cruel and consider that their religious beliefs and practices absolve them from the necessity of possessing any other virtues, particularly charity. When my father was lying battered and broken in his prison cell, a petition was prepared for the reduction of his sentence, but most people were afraid to sign it. Among those who refused was William Holman Hunt, one of the founders of the Pre-Raphaelites, who spent most of his life painting religious pictures, notably "The Light of the World." Holman Hunt's letter of refusal is so typical of the general attitude at the time that I give it in full.

Draycott Lodge,
Fulham,
Novr. 18th, 1895.

My dear Sir,
　　I have not failed to give myself the fullest opportunity of discovering any solid argument in the case which you from feelings of friendly humanity are pressing, to obtain the shortening of the sentence on Oscar Wilde; but I must repeat my opinion that the law treated him with exceeding leniency and state that further consideration of the facts convinces me that in justice to criminals belonging to other classes of society I should have to join in the cry for doing away with all personal responsibility for wickedness, if I took any part in appealing for his liberation before the completion of his term of imprisonment, and while such a course might seem benevolent to malefactors, it would scarcely be so to the self-restrained and orderly members of society. I am sorry that in being obliged to refuse signing the petition I am opposing a desire of yours which is evidently prompted by the kindest instincts.

I am, yours very sincerely,
W. Holman Hunt.

This letter was addressed to More Adey, who was a friend of both my parents. It is only fair to suppose that when Holman Hunt wrote this letter, he had forgotten the quotation which inspired his picture "The Light of the World":

I expect to pass through this world but once. Any good, therefore, that I can do, or any kindness that I can show to any fellow creature let me do it now. Let me not defer or neglect it, for I shall not pass this way again.

I am constantly surprised by the letters I receive from all over the world, from people in all walks of life, expressing their admiration for my father's writings and for his philosophy; I have even received a letter in Japanese which I sent to the School of Oriental Studies to be translated. Indeed, after the publication of the complete *De Profundis* in 1949,[48] I received so many letters that I found it quite impossible to answer them all, much as I would like to have done so.

Oscar Wilde was undoubtedly one of the outstanding figures of his time; he dominated the literary and dramatic world of the early nineties, but he did it in such a way as to make for himself many jealous enemies. His plays, light and airy as they may appear on the surface, are full of deep wisdom. There can be no better proof of this than the fact that when translated into other languages they lose practically nothing. I myself have seen *The Importance of Being Earnest* played in half a dozen different languages, and my wife once saw *Lady Windermere's Fan* acted in South Africa by an all-coloured cast. Oscar Wilde's works are translated into every civilised language in the world. In nearly every European country, including those behind the Iron Curtain, they are standard school and university textbooks for the study of the English language. And in England itself there is hardly a dramatic society or academy that has not performed my father's plays at one time or another.

In these pages I have tried to show what it is like to be the son of Oscar Wilde. On the whole my life has been one of concealment and repression. My descendants will not suffer as I have done, as they become more and more remote from the actual tragedy. As ancestry recedes into the past it becomes more and more impersonal; more than one great English family views with equanimity the fact that an ancestor many generations back was executed at Newgate or at Tyburn for sexual aberrations.

It was a cruel irony that Oscar Wilde should have been singled out by fate to suffer for all the countless artists who, both before and since his day, have shared his weakness.

Last year Sir Travers Humphreys, the eminent High Court Judge, in an article on the Wilde trials in which he himself had taken an active part in 1895, wrote as follows: "Reflecting upon the events of nearly sixty years ago, one fact is plain beyond argument. The prosecution of Oscar Wilde should never have been brought."

Now that Oscar Wilde has regained the position in literature which he lost in 1895, I hope that his spirit is at rest; for he might well say of himself, as the Young King says in *A House of Pomegranates:* "On the loom of Sorrow, and by the white hands of Pain, has this my robe been woven."

APPENDICES

Thirty-three Letters from Oscar Wilde to Reginald Richard ("Kitten") Harding and William Welsford ("Bouncer") Ward 1876–1878

REGINALD HARDING went up to Oxford at the same time as Oscar Wilde.

William Ward occupied rooms on the same staircase as Oscar Wilde at Magdalen. He was a year senior to him, having gone up as a Demy in 1873; when Ward went down, Oscar Wilde took over his rooms, which are now known as the Oscar Wilde Rooms.

The originals of the Harding letters are in the possession of Mr. H. Montgomery Hyde, M.P. The letters to W. W. Ward are in the library of Magdalen College, Oxford, to which they were presented by his daughter, Miss Cecil Ward.[49]

1

TO REGINALD HARDING: 28 JUNE 1876

Magdalen College, Oxford.
Wednesday.

My dear Kitten,

Many thanks for your delightful letters; they were quite a pleasant relaxation to us to get your letters every morning at breakfast. (This is sarcasm.) I think you an awful wretch really for never writing to us, living all alone in this desolate college. However, we have been very pleasant notwithstanding, and have survived the loss of Provincial gossip.

Bouncer's people stayed up till Monday as I suppose you know from a stupid telegram Bouncer would send you.

We were very pleasant and went to Radley and a lot of places together.

I like Mrs. Bouncer immensely and the eldest Miss B. is very charming indeed. We brought them to All Souls and Worcester and a lot of Colleges.

I am more charmed than ever with Worcester Chapel. As a piece of simple decoration and beautiful art it is perfect—and the windows very artistic.

Monday we rode to Abingdon and dined there and Tuesday we had tea at Radley and lawn tennis. Tonight we dined at the Mitre. We have been very jolly together indeed and Bouncer, you will be glad to hear, *most kind!*

Tomorrow I go down to Lincolnshire to stay with my uncle.* I suppose you are too much occupied with croquet and loafing and playing the organ to write to me. In case you have time, however, I will be at The Vicarage, West Ashby, Horncastle, Lincolnshire.

I will have to come up next week for viva voce—about Tuesday or Wednesday and all for nothing probably as I think I have missed my First† and will have to look cheerful under the doubtful honours of a Second.

I will be in Nottingham with the Miles' for a week and then home till September—after the partridge comes the Pope, whom I hope to see about the 1st of October.

Please remember me to Mrs. Harding and your sister.

Yours ever OSCAR O'F. W. WILDE

I hope Puss‡ is reading hard for a First. Give him my love.

---

* The Rev. John Maxwell Wilde, Sir William Wilde's elder brother, Vicar of West Ashby.

† O. W. took a First Class in Moderations in the Trinity Term 1876.

‡ "Puss" was James J. Harding, Reginald Harding's elder brother.

2

TO WILLIAM WARD: JUNE 1876

The Vicarage, West Ashby.
Sunday.

My dear Bouncer,

I am in terrible dread of reading a pathetic account in Reynolds' Police News of "the death by starvation of a *young man* on Lundy Island." The idea of *you* forgetting your food—I hope you got it safe—I sent it off by 12 o'clock on Thursday.

I arrived here in an awful storm—it came down as if the angels thought the earth was on fire and were pumping fire engines on us.

Luckily I met some people who live here in the Manor House in the train so it was not so tedious after all—but two miles in a dogcart and a restive horse in pouring rain did not improve my temper.

I have been kissed and petted and made to examine schools in Geography! and played Lawn Tennis and *talked* and *sang*, and made myself the "bellus homo" of a Tea party. My uncle is milder than ever—says "Dear me now, wouldn't you have found the penny post more convenient than a telegram?" about six times a day. I have found out he had to pay half-a-crown for my enquiry—the whole transaction costing 5/6—while as he. . .

[*The remainder of this letter is missing.*]

3

TO REGINALD HARDING: EARLY JULY 1876

Magdalen College, Oxford.
Wednesday.

My dear Kitten,

I am very sorry to hear that you did not meet the poor Bouncer Boy; see what comes of having rowdy friends fond of practical jokes. I had an awful pencil scrawl from him yesterday, written sitting on the rocks at Lundy. I hope nothing will happen to him.

I had a very pleasant time in Lincolnshire—but the weather was so hot we did nothing but play Lawn Tennis —as probably Bouncer will tell you when you see him next (I wrote a full account to him). I examined schools in Geography and History, *sang* glees, ate strawberries and argued fiercely with my poor uncle, who revenged himself on Sunday by preaching on Rome in the morning, and on humility in the evening. Both very "nasty ones" for me.

I ran up to Town yesterday from Lincoln and brought Frank Miles* a great basket of roses from the Rectory—I found him sketching the most lovely and dangerous woman in London—Lady Desart. She is very fascinating indeed.

I came down on Monday night to read for viva voce— but yesterday morning at 10 o'clock was woke up by the Clerk of the Schools, and found I was in already. I was rather afraid of being put on in Catullus, but got a delightful exam. from a delightful man—not on the books at all but on Aeschylus versus Shakespeare, modern poetry or Drama and every conceivable subject. I was up for about an hour and was quite sorry when it was over.

---

*George Francis Miles. An artist of some repute in his time.

In Divinity I was ploughed of course.

I am going down to Bingham with Frank Miles and
R. Gower* on Saturday for a week. They have the most
beautiful modern church in England, and the finest lilies.
—I shall write and tell you about it.

Being utterly penniless I can't go up to Town till
Friday. It is very slow here—now that Bouncer is gone.
But tonight the Mods. List comes up so I will have some
excitement being congratulated—really I don't care a bit
(no one ever does now) and quite expect a Second after
my Logic—though *of course much the cleverest man in*. (Such
cheek!)

You will probably see the list on Thursday or Friday;
if I get a Second mind you write and condole with me
awfully, and if I get a First say it was only what you expected.

See the results of having nothing to do—10 pages of a
letter!

Yours ever OSCAR F. O'F. WILLS WILDE

My address will be The Rectory, Bingham, Notts. after
Saturday. I hope you will write a line and tell me all extra
news about Bouncer.

4

TO WILLIAM WARD: 10 JULY 1876

4, Albert Street, S.W.

My Dear Boy,

I know you will be glad to hear I have got my First all
right. I came up from Lincolnshire to town on Monday
and went down that night to Magdalen to read my Catullus
but while lying in bed on Tuesday morning with Swinburne
(a copy of) was woke up by the Clerk of the Schools to
know why I did not come up—I thought I was not in

* Lord Ronald Sutherland Gower.

till Thursday—about one o'clock. I *nipped up* and was ploughed immediately in Divinity and then got a delightful viva voce first in the Odyssey—where we discussed Epic poetry in general, *dogs*, and women. Then in Aeschylus where we talked of Shakespeare, Walt Whitman and the Poetics. He had a long discussion about my Essay on Poetry in the Aristotle paper and altogether was delightful—of course I knew I had got a First—so swaggered horribly.

The next day the B.C's and myself were dining with Nicols in Christ Church and the list came out at 7, as we were walking up the High. I said I would not go up to the Schools—as I knew I had a First etc.—and made them all very ill—absolutely. I did not know what I had got till the next morning at 12 o'clock, breakfasting at the Mitre I read it in the Times. Altogether I swaggered horribly—but am really pleased with myself. My poor mother is in great delight and I was overwhelmed with Telegrams on Thursday from everyone I know. My Father would have been so pleased about it—I think God has dealt very hardly with us. It has robbed me of any real pleasure in my First—and I have not sufficient faith in Providence to believe it is all for the best—I know it is not. I feel an awful dread of going home to our Old House—with everything filled with memories. I go down today for a week at Bingham with the Miles'. I have been staying here with Julia Tindal who is in great form. Yesterday I heard the Cardinal at the Pro Cathedral preach a charity sermon. He is more fascinating than ever. I met MacColl and Williamson there who greeted me with much *empressement*. I feel an impostor, and traitor to myself on these occasions and must do something decided.

Afterwards I went to the Zoo with Julia and the two Peytons—Tom is nearly all right. Young Stewy dined with us on Saturday. He said he was afraid he must have jarred you by his indecencies and was going to reform.

Altogether I found out we were right in thinking that set a little jarred about our carelessness about them. Next Term I shall look them up.

I hope you will see the Kitten. I got a very nice letter from him about Mods. Miss Puss* has fallen in my estimation if she is fetched with Swan—who to men is irritable, but to women intolerable I think. Write soon to Bingham Rectory, Nottinghamshire.

Evers Yours, OSCAR O'F. W. WILDE

5

TO WILLIAM WARD: 17 JULY 1876

(Paper stamped Bingham Rectory, Notts.)

Bingham.
Monday.

Dear Boy,

I have never heard from you except your scrawl written from the rocks on your arrival.

However I hope to find some letters at home waiting for me.

I have had a delightful week here. The garden and house are very beautiful. I never saw such lilies—white and red and golden. Nearly all the family are good artists. Mrs. Miles is really wonderful. I suppose you remember my showing you her drawings in Ruskin's School at Oxford when we went there to your sisters.

Mr. Miles père† is a very advanced Anglican and a great friend of Newman, Pusey, Manning, Gladstone and all the English Theologians.

He is very clever and interesting: I have learned a lot from him.

---

*"Miss Puss" was Miss Amy Harding, Reginald Harding's sister.

†Canon Miles, Rector of Bingham, the father of the artist Frank Miles, who was a great friend of Oscar Wilde at Oxford and afterwards shared a house with him at Keats House, No. 3, Tite Street, Chelsea.

If you want an interesting book get *Pomponio Leto*—an account of the last Vatican Council—a really wonderfully dramatic book. How strange that on the day of the Pope publicly declaring that his Infallability and that of the Church were identical a fearful storm broke over Rome *and two thunderbolts fell from heaven*. It reads like the talkative ox of Livy *(bos locutus est)* and the rain of blood, that were always happening.

I don't know what to think myself—I wish you would come to Rome with me and test the whole matter—I am afraid to go alone.

I never knew how near the English Church was to joining with Rome.

Before the Promulgation of the Immaculate Conception Pusey and Liddon and others were working hard for an Eirenicon and union with Rome—but now they look to the Greek Church—but I think it is a mere dream—and very strange that they should be so anxious to believe the Blessed Virgin conceived in sin.

As regards worldly matter, we have had some very pleasant garden parties and any amount of Lawn Tennis—the neighbourhood also boasts of a giant in the shape of the Honble. Lascelles who is sixteen years old and 6 ft. 8 in. height! He is reading with a Mr. Seymour near here, a clergyman—(father of young Seymour of Balliol)—to go up for *Magdalen*—what an excitement he will cause but he is not going up for two years so we wont see him there.

I suppose you will see the Kitten after you leave Lundy. Send me your address like a good boy, mine will be 1, Merrion Square North, Dublin, till I go down to Galway which I hope to do soon.

Ever yours OSCAR F. O'F. WILLS WILDE

6

TO REGINALD HARDING: JULY 1876

Bingham Rectory, Notts.

My dear Boy,

Thousand thanks for your letter. Half the pleasure of getting a First is to receive such delightful congratulations—*I am* really a little pleased at getting it though I swaggered horribly and pretended that I did not care a bit. In fact I would not go up to the Schools on Wednesday evening—said it was a bore—and actually did not know certainly till Thursday at 12 o'clock when I read it in the Times. The really pleasant part is that my mother is so pleased. I got a heap of telegrams on Thursday from Ireland with congratulations.

I went up to Town on Friday and stayed with Julia Tindal—we had a very pleasant time together.

Sunday we went to the Zoo with Algy and Tom Peyton. Tom is all right now—he had got paralysis of his face.

I came down here Monday and had no idea it was so lovely. A wonderful garden with such white lilies and rose walks; only that there are no serpents or apples it would be quite Paradise. The Church is very fine indeed. Frank and his mother, a very good artist, have painted wonderful windows, and frescoed angels on the walls and one of his sisters has carved the screen and altar. It is simply beautiful and everything done by themselves.

These horrid red marks are strawberries—which I am eating in basketfuls, during intervals of Lawn Tennis, at which I am awfully good.

There are four daughters—all very pretty indeed, one of them who is writing at the other side of the table quite lovely. My heart is torn asunder with admiration for them all—and my health going so I return to Ireland next week.

We are having a large garden party here to-day and tomorrow one at the Duke of Rutland's who is quite close.

I make myself as charming as ever and am much admired. Have had some good arguments with Dean Miles who was a great friend of Newman, Pusey and Manning at Oxford and a very advanced Anglican.

Write me a line soon like a good boy.

Ever yours OSCAR F. O'F. WILLS WILDE

I heard the Cardinal preach a charity sermon at the Pro Cathedral Kensington. MacColl was there.

7

TO REGINALD HARDING

1 Merrion Square North.
July 20th '76.

Dear Kitten,

Thousand thanks for the Testimonial—I have of course laid it up in the Family Archives—when found in two or three hundred years by some of the family devoted to Natural History and the habits of the Feline Race it will cause much discussion. In case I become bankrupt I suppose the autographs will fetch something, especially those of the "child Amy" and "Fräulein"?

I want Bouncer's address—will you send it like a good boy as soon as you can remember it?

I found a heap of congratulatory letters from all sorts of people, telegrams from Hammond and the Boy, which Mamma had of course opened and was very much troubled to know why a telegram should begin "Indeed Oscar" and whether S. Aloysius was one of the Examiners.

Don't forget Bouncer's address.

[*The signature has been cut away.*]

8

TO WILLIAM WARD: LATE JULY 1876

1 Merrion Square North, Dublin.

My Dear Boy,

I sent you two charming letters, one from Julia Tindal's lodgings in London, and one from Bingham.

Did you get them? Or are they now used by the litterati of Lundy Island as models of polite letter writing? I hope they are not used to give *laxas tunicas* to "Scombri" —*as our friend Juvenal has it* (see what comes of Mods.).

I came back here yesterday from Bingham. I had a delightful time there—the whole family is charming. Mr. Miles knew your Father when he was rector of S. Raphael's in Bristol and talked much of his great liberality and devotion to the Church. He was much interested to hear about you.

I got a delightful lot of letters congratulating me—the pleasantest part of Mods.—from Mark and Jack Borrow and a lot of fellows I hardly thought would take the trouble. Terribly absurd Telegrams from Hammond and the Boy sent here and of course opened by Mamma, who was greatly troubled as to what S. Aloysius had to do with me, and why when only twenty words go for a shilling a telegram should begin *"Indeed Oscar"*.

I go down to Mayo probably next week and then to Galway to have some fishing. Illaunroe, Leenane, Co. Galway is our address but I am very uncertain about when I shall be there so I hope you will write here and tell me all about the King's Close Cats.

I suppose they told you about the Testimonial sent to me from the whole set including the Child Amy.

I am going to edit an unfinished work of my Father's, the Life of Gabriel Beranger, Artist, for next Christmas, so

between this and Newman will have no time for any reading for scholarship.

About Newman I think that his higher emotions re-
volted against Rome but that he was swept on by Logic
to accept it as the only rational form of Christianity. His
life is a terrible Tragedy. I fear he is a very unhappy man.
I bought a lot of his books before leaving Oxford.

Luckily the life of Beranger is 3/4 finished; so I will not
have much trouble—still it is a great responsibility: I will
not be idle about it.

I hope your mother and sisters are well.

Ever yours OSCAR F. O'F. WILLS WILDE

9

TO WILLIAM WARD: 25 JULY 1876

1 Merrion Square N., Dublin.

My Dear Boy,

I confess not to be a worshipper at the Temple of
Reason—I think man's reason the most misleading and
thwarting guide that the sun looks upon, except perhaps
the reason of woman. Faith is, I think, a bright lantern
for the feet—though of course an exotic plant in man's
mind, and requiring continual cultivation. My mother
would probably agree with you. Except for the *people,* for
whom she thinks dogma necessary, she rejects all forms of
superstition and dogma, particularly any notion of priest
and sacrament standing between her and God—she has a
very strong faith in that aspect of God *we* call the Holy
Ghost—the divine intelligence of which we on earth par-
take. Here she is very strong though of course at times
troubled by the discord and jarring of the world—when
she takes a dip into pessimism.

Her last Pessimist, Schopenhauer, says the whole
human race ought on a given day, after a strong remon-

strance *firmly but respectfully* urged on God, to walk into the sea and leave the world tenantless—but of course some skulking wretches would hide and be left behind to people the world again, I am afraid.

I wonder you don't see the beauty and necessity for the *Incarnation* of God into man to help us to grasp at the skirts of the Infinite. The atonement is I admit hard to grasp—But I think since Christ the dead world has woke up from sleep. Since him we have lived—I think the greatest proof of the Incarnation aspect of Christianity is its whole career of noble men and thoughts and not the mere narration of unauthenticated History.

I think *you* are bound to account (psychologically most especially) for S. Bernard and S. Augustine and S. Philip Neri—and even in our day for Liddon and Newman—as being good philosophers and good Christians. That reminds me of Mallock's *New Republic* in Belgravia—it is decidedly clever—Jowitt especially. If you have the Key to all the actors please send it to me.

I send you this letter and a Book together—I wonder which you will open first.

It is *Aurora Leigh*—which I think you said you had not read.

It is one of those books that, written straight from the heart—and from such a large heart too—never weary one: because they are sincere. We tire of art but not of nature after all our aesthetic training. I look upon it as much the greatest work in our literature.

I rank it with *Hamlet* and *In Memoriam*: so much do I love it, that I hated the idea of sending it to you without marking a few passages, I felt you would well appreciate—And I found myself marking the whole book. I am really very sorry—it is like being given a bouquet of plucked flowers instead of being allowed to look for them oneself.

But I could not resist the Temptation as it *did* instead of writing to you about each passage.

The only fault is that she overstrains her metaphors till they snap—and although one does not like polished emotion, still she is inartistically rugged at times—as she says herself she shows the mallet hand in carving cherry stones.

I hope you will have time to read it—for I don't believe your dismal forebodings about Greats.

I wrote to Kitten for your address and his letter and yours arrived simultaneously. His thoughts and ink rarely last beyond a sheet.

I ride sometimes after six—but don't do much but bathe—and although always feeling slightly immortal when in the sea, feel sometimes slightly heretical when good Roman Catholic boys enter the water with little amulets and crosses round their necks and arms that the good S. Christopher may hold them up.

I am now off to bed after reading a chapter of S. Thomas à Kempis. I think half-an-hour's warping of the inner man daily is greatly conducive to holiness.

Pray remember me to your Mother and Sister.

Evers Yours, OSCAR F. O'F. WILLS WILDE

10

TO REGINALD HARDING: AUGUST 1876

1 Merrion Square N.
Sunday.

My Dear Kitten,

I suppose you are reading much too hard ever to write any letter now. It seems a long time since I heard from you—and as for Bouncer I have not heard anything about him for a fortnight.

In his last letters he complained terribly that his mother and sisters would not let him read—I hope your people are better—and encourage your industry in every way.

I have been waiting for my brother who is on circuit,

and for Frank Miles who could not get away from home till we go down to Galway together.—We expect them both tomorrow. I am rather tired of sea bathing and lawn tennis and shall be glad to be down for the 12th—after this rain too there will be a lot of fish up.

I am just going out to bring an *exquisitely pretty girl* to afternoon service in the Cathedral. She is just seventeen with the *most perfectly beautiful face I ever saw and not a six-pence of money. I* will show you her photograph when I see you next.

Strutt and his wife, or rather Mrs. Strutt and Mrs. Strutt's husband, are in Town. I am going to call and see them on my way.

I hope you will write all about yourself and your belongings soon.

Ever yours OSCAR F. O'F. WILLS WILDE

11

TO WILLIAM WARD: 5 AUGUST 1876

1 Merrion Square N.
Sunday.

My Dear Bouncer,

I feel quite sure you never could have got a book and letter I sent you about ten days ago. You couldn't have been such a complete Scythian as not to write how charmed you were with my delightful letter and Book if you had got them—I sent them to Cliff Court. If you did not get the Book will you ask your Post Office about it as I should be very sorry you did not get it—it was Mrs. Browning's "Aurora Leigh".

I have got three poems (and perhaps four!) coming out on the 1st of September in various Magazines—and am awfully pleased about it—I will send you one of them which I would like you to read. I call it no name but put in as motto that great chaunt αἴλινον αἴλινον εἰπέ, τὸ δ' εὖ νικάτω*.

I am with that dear Mahaffy every day. He has a charming house by the sea here—on a place called the Hill of Howth, (one of the crescent horns that shuts in the Bay of Dublin)—the only place near Town with fields of yellow gorse, and stretches of wild myrtle, red heather and ferns. By dallying in the enchanted isle of Bingham Rectory, and eating the Lotus flowers of Love and the *moly*† of oblivion I arrived just too late to go on a charming party to the North of Ireland—Mahaffy, Seyrs of Queen's, Appleton the Editor of the Academy and my brother. They had a very Royal Time of it—but Circe and Calypso delayed me till it was too late to join them.

Mahaffy's book of Travels in Greece will soon be out—I have been correcting his Proofs and like it immensely.

I hope nothing is wrong with your people or yourself that you don't write.

Ever yours OSCAR F. O'F WILLS WILDE

P.S. I hope you did not write to Illaunroe?—they only get letters *once a week there.*

12

TO REGINALD HARDING: AUGUST 1876

Moytura House.
Wednesday.

Dear Kitten,

Have you fallen into a well, or been mislaid anywhere that you never write to me? or has one of your nine lives gone?

---

* Aeschylus. Agamemnon 159. "Sing a strain of woe, but let the good prevail."

†Moly. A herb said to have been given by Hermes to Odysseus as a charm against the sorceries of Circe.

Frank Miles and I came down here last week, and have had a very royal time of it sailing.— We are at the top of Lough Corrib which if you refer to your geography you will find to be a lake 30 miles along, 10 broad and situated in the most romantic scenery in Ireland. Frank has done some wonderful sunsets since he came down; he has given me some more of his drawings. Has your sister got the one he calls "My little Lady"—a little girl's face with a lot of falling hair? If she has not got it I would like to send it to her in return for her autograph on the celebrated memorial.

Frank has never fired off a gun in his life (and says he doesn't want to) but as our proper sporting season here does not begin till September I have not taught him any-thing—but on Friday we go into Connemara to a charming little fishing lodge we have in the mountains where I hope to make him land a salmon and kill a brace of grouse. I expect to have very good sport indeed this season. Write to me there if your claws have not been clipped. Illaunroe Lodge, Leenane, Co. Galway.

Best love to Puss, I hope he is reading hard.

Evers yours, OSCAR F. O'F. WILLS WILDE

13

TO WILLIAM WARD: 28 AUGUST 1876

Illaunroe Lodge, Connemara.

My dear Bouncer,

So very glad to hear from you at last: I was afraid that you were still seedy.

I need not say how disappointed I was that you could not come and see this part of the world: I have two fellows staying with me, Dick Trench, and Jack Barrow, who took a lodge near here for July and came to stay with me about three weeks ago: they are both capital fellows, indeed Dick

Trench is I think my oldest friend, but I don't do any reading someway and pass my evenings in Pool, Écarté and Potheen Punch—I wish you had come, one requiring sympathy to read.

I am however in the midst of two articles, one on Greece, the other on Art which keep me thinking, if not writing. But of Greats work, I have done nothing—after all there are more profitable studies, I suppose, than the Greats Course: still I would like a good Class awfully and want you to lend me your notes on Philosophy: I know your style, and really it would be a *very great advantage* for me to have them—Ethics, Politics (Republic) and general Philosophy. Can you do this for me? If you could send them to me in Dublin? or at least to Oxford next Term? and *also give me advice*—a thing I can't stand from my elders because it's like preaching, but I think I would like some from you "who have passed through the fire."

The weather is fair but not good for fishing, I have only got one salmon but our 'bag' yesterday of "12 white trout and 20 brown" was not bad. I have also had capital hare shooting, but mountain climbing is not my forte.

I heard, by the same post which brought your letter, from Miss Fletcher—who is still in the Tyrol: she sends her best wishes to you of course—and writes as cleverly as she talks: I am much attracted by her in every way.

Please give my very best wishes to your sister on her approaching marriage—I remember Mr. St. John's *window* very well, and will hope to have the pleasure of knowing him some day. He must be a very cultured artist: will the wedding be soon? *What* form you *will* be in!

Ever yours, OSCAR WILDE

I am going to Longford on Friday to shoot.
Write me at Clonfin House, Granard, Co. Longford.

14

Illaunroe Lodge, Connemara.

Dear Bouncer,

I am very glad you like "Aurora Leigh"—I think it simply "intense" in every way. I am deep in a Review of Symonds' last Book whenever I can get time and the weather is too bright for fishing. Mahaffy has promised to look it over before publication. Up to this however I am glad to say that I have too much *occupied with rod and gun for the handling of the quill* (neat and Pope-like?).

I have only got one salmon as yet but have had heaps of sea trout which give great play. I have not had a blank day yet. Grouse are few but I have got a lot of hares so have had a capital time of it. I hope next year that you and the Kitten will come and stay a (lunar) month with me. I am sure you would like this wild mountainous country, close to the Atlantic and teeming with sport of all kinds. It is in every way magnificent and makes me years younger than actual History records.

I hope you are reading hard; if you don't get your First the Examiners ought to be sent down.

Write like a good boy to Moytura House, Cong. County Mayo, as I will be leaving here this week.

With kind regards to your mother and sisters,

Ever yours, OSCAR F. O'F. WILLS WILDE

P.S. I have Frank Miles with me. He is delighted with all.

15

TO WILLIAM WARD: SEPTEMBER 1876

1 Merrion Square.
Wednesday.

My Dear Bouncer,

Note paper became such a scarcity in the West and I had to put off answering your letter till I came home.

I had a delightful time, and capital sport, especially the last week, which I spent shooting, and got fair bags.

I am afraid I shall not cross to England via Bristol, as I hear the boats are rather of the "Ancient Mariner" type! but I may be down in Bristol with Frank Miles as I want to see S. Raphael's and the pictures at Clevedon.

I would like very much to renew my friendship with your mother and sisters so shall write to you if I see any hope of going down.

I have given up my pilgrimage to Rome for the present: Ronald Gower and Frank Miles were coming: (we would have been a great Trinity) but at the last hour Ronald couldn't get time, so I am staying in Dublin till the 20th. when I go down to Longford, and hope to have good sport.

I have heard from many people of your Father's liberality and noble spirit, so I know you will take interest in the Report I send you of my Father's Hospital—which he built when he was only 29 and not a rich man—it is a great memorial of his name, and a movement is being set on foot to enlarge it and make it still greater.

I have got some charming letters lately from a great friend of my mother, Aubrey de Vere—a cultured poet (though sexless) and a convert to catholicity.

I must show you them; he is greatly interested in me and is going to get one of my poems into the 'Month'. I have two this month out: one in the Dublin Univ. Maga-

zine one in the Irish Monthly. Both are brief and Tenny-
sonian.

I hope you are doing good work but I suppose at home
you are hardly allowed "to contemplate the abstract"
(whatever that means) undisturbed.

I am bothered with business and many things and find
the world an "ἀναρχία" at present and a Tarpeian Rock
for honest men.

I hope you will write when you have time.

Ever yours OSCAR F. O'F. WILLS WILDE

I like signing my name as if it was to some document of
great importance—as "send two bags of gold by bearer"
or "Let the Duke be slain tomorrow and the Duchess
await me at the Hostelry".

I send you one of Aubrey De Vere's letters. I know you
will be amused at them.

Return it when you have committed it to Memory.

16

TO REGINALD HARDING: 17 DECEMBER 1876

85 Jermyn Street, London, S.W.
Sunday.

My dear Kitten,

I have not had a line from you since you rushed away
from Oxford leaving me on a bed of *broken neck-ness*; I suppose your Christmas anthem keeps you too much employed to write to anyone.

I have been having a delightful time here; any amount
of theatres and dining out. On Thursday I brought young
May down to Windsor and we had a delightful day with
Ronald Gower who has got a new house there (one of the
most beautiful houses I ever saw). He brought us to St.
George's Chapel for afternoon service and I did not like
the singing so well as our own.

We had just time after it was over to catch the 6.30 train and go to the Albert Hall to hear the Creation.

Foli sang magnificently and the song about the "sinewy tiger and horrid lion" was very fine, but Lemmens Sherrington was rather horrid and affected.

I have taken a great fancy to May, he is quite charming in every way and a beautiful artist.

He dined with me last night and we went to see Henry Irving in Macbeth—I enjoyed it of course immensely.

I have heard nothing from Bouncer, except a very incoherent telegram the day he got his degree. He promised to write however from "The Palace."

I suppose you know I have got his rooms. I am awfully pleased about it.

I am off to Ireland tonight, and intend "nipping down" to the Oratory for the 3.30 service. Dunskie* went off yesterday, we were at the Court Theatre on Friday together.— He tells me *Lang is* going to become a Catholic. I must know him next term. You are not to tell anyone.

Love to Puss,

Ever yours, OSCAR F. O'F. W. WILDE

Remember Xmas is near, and that there is an old custom of giving presents. I gave you a lovely Arundel lately.

17

TO WILLIAM WARD: JANUARY 1877

1 Merrion Square N.
Saturday.

My Dear Bouncer,

I was very glad indeed to hear from you and to find, what I expected all along, that your philosophy in Greats

---

* Sir David Hunter Blair, Bart., later Abbot of Dunfermline.

was so good! It is a great thing to do well in the subjects worth doing well in.*

Except the Mark I think few people would set laborious industry on any footing with brilliant and original thought: It really was a great pity you did not make up your books, I suppose one ought to be a Gibeonite, a "wood-hewer and water-drawer of Literature" in order to make one's First safe.

I hope greatly you will stay and read for a Fellowship, not merely on selfish grounds of having you at any rate within reach if not at Oxford, but because I feel certain you would get one within a year: at least if *you* don't I don't know who will.

You would see Italy with greater pleasure after having gained what I certainly consider a great honour. After a year you might find yourself disinclined to read up your philosophy again, too tired to return on the road you have already travelled:

The extreme beauty of Italy may ruin you, as I think it has done me, for hard work again: but I think that *now,* with your knowledge fresh, and your brain keen, you could work well and successfully.

However, you are much stronger than I am, and Italy may not unnerve you after all: and I don't think as a rule that people ever mind much what advice friends *of the same age* give them. After all, for effect and persuasion there is nothing like wrinkles and either grey hair or baldness.

I was very sorry you did not come up to Town after Term. I had a delightful week and saw everything from Nelly Bromley and the Brompton Priest-Shop, down to Henry Irving and Gibson's *Tinted Hebe:* a lovely statue by the by, quite Greek, and the effect of the colouring is most life-like and beautiful. I had a charming day at Windsor

---

* This refers to the notes on Philosophy for which O.W. asked in letter 13.

with Ronald Gower—I brought Arthur May with me and have not enjoyed myself so much for years.

We went to St. George's Chapel for evening service after lunch, and just got up in time to hear the Creation at the Albert Hall.

I saw a great deal of Arthur May; he is quite charming in every way and we have rushed into friendship.

Dublin is very gay but I have got tired of evening parties and go in for dining out now which is much more satisfactory especially as the Dublin people all think I am a Fellow of Magdalen, and so listen to all I say with great attention.

I got a long letter from the Kitten asking me to go over for this Fancy Ball, but I have already refused the Miles' who want me to go to Bingham the same week. The fact is I have a lot of things to do in Dublin and cannot manage to leave home so early in the vac.

I am so glad your people liked the ring, and if the Greek lines you quoted to me would fit it would be charming: Perhaps however our initials inside and φιλίας μνημοσύνον outside would be all that would fit conveniently.*

I find I have written about 12 pages! poor Boy! but as I have not heard from you for a long time I had a lot to write about.

It certainly would be a very charming surprise to find you back in Oxford; I need not tell you I shall miss you greatly if you go to Italy. In any case I hope you will come up and see us next Term and we will promise not to call you the Old Crust.

Please give my best wishes for the New Year to your Mother and Sisters.

Yours affectionately, OSCAR WILDE

P.S. How can *you*, an aesthetic youth, dress yourself as a China man and so exhibit yourself to some girl you are

* This ring is now at Magdalen College, Oxford.

fond of? You ought to go as Pico della Mirandola with a Plato under your arm. Don't you think that "Puss in Boots" would be a good dress for Kings Close?

18

TO REGINALD HARDING: MARCH 1877

Magdalen College, Oxford.

My dear Kitten,

I start for Rome on Sunday; Mahaffy comes as far as Genoa with me: and I hope to see the golden dome of St. Peter's and the Eternal City by Tuesday night.

This is an era in my life, a crisis—I wish I could look into the seeds of Time and see what is coming.

I shall not forget you in Rome—and will burn a candle for you at the Shrine of Our Lady.

Write to me like a good boy, "Hotel d'Angleterre", Rome.

Yours ever OSCAR

19

TO WILLIAM WARD: KENT TERM 1877

[*A long letter of four double sheets, the first of which is missing.*]

... Webbe and Jack Barrow, and is blossoming out into the Fast man: however his career has been cut short by the Dean refusing to let him take his degree through his late hours in lodgings! *Wee! Wee* is Mark's expression in consequence.

The Freshmen *in it* are Gore, a great pal of Tom Peyton's lot. Grey a nice Eton boy—and we have all suddenly woke to the idea that Wharton is charming. I like him very much indeed and ran him in for the Apollo lately—I also ran in Gerhardt with whom I have had several rows through *his drunken-noisy-Jewish ways*—and two freshmen Vintor and Chance both of them very casual fellows indeed. I have got rather keen on Masonry lately and believe in it awfully—in fact would be awfully sorry to have to give it up in case I secede from the Protestant Heresy: I now breakfast with Father Parkinson, go to St. Aloysius, talk sentimental religion to Dunlop and altogether am caught in the fowler's snare, in the wiles of the Scarlet Woman—I may go over in the vac. I have dreams of a visit to Newman, of the holy sacrament in a new Church, and of a quiet and peace afterwards in my soul. I need not say, though, that I shift with every breath of thought and am weaker and more self-deceiving than ever.

If I *could hope* that the church would wake in me some earnestness and purity I would go over *as a luxury*, if for no better reasons. But I can hardly hope it would—and to go over to Rome would be to sacrifice and give up my two great Gods "Money and Ambition".

Still I get so wretched and low and troubled that in some desperate mood I will seek the shelter of a Church which simply enthrals me by its fascination.

I hope that now in the sacred city you are wakened up from the Egyptian darkness that has blinded you. *Do* be touched by *it, feel* the awful fascination of the Church, its extreme beauty and sentiment, and let every part of your nature have play and room.

We have had our Sports and are now in the midst of Torpids and tomorrow the Pigeons are shot: to escape I go up to town to see the Old Masters *with the Kitten!*—who is very anxious to come. Dear little Puss is up, and looks wretched, but as pleasant and bright as ever. He is rather keen on going to Rome for Easter with me, but I don't know if I can afford it, as I have been elected for the St. Stephens and have to pay £42 0. 0: I did not want to be elected for a year or so but David Plunket ran me in in three weeks some way rather to my annoyance.

I would give worlds to be in Rome with you and Dunskie. I know I would enjoy it awfully but I don't know if I can manage it. You would be a safeguard against Dunskie's attacks.

I am in for "the Ireland"* on Monday—God! how I have wasted my life up here! I look back on weeks and months of extravagance, trivial talk, utter vacancy of employment *with feelings so bitter that I have lost faith in myself*— I am too ridiculously easily led astray—so I have idled and won't get it and will be wretched in consequence: I feel that if I had read I would have done well up here but I have not.

I enjoy your rooms awfully—the inner room is filled with china, pictures, a portfolio and a piano—and a grey carpet with stained floor. The whole get up is much admired and a little made fun of on Sunday evenings. They are more delightful than I ever expected—the sunshine, the cawing rooks and waving tree branches and the breeze at the window are too charming.

I do nothing but write sonnets and scribble poetry— some of which I send you—though to send anything of mine to Rome is an awful impertinence—but you always took an interest in my attempts to ride Pegasus.

My greatest chum except of course the Kitten is Gussy who is charming though not educated well: however he is 'psychological' and we have long chats and walks. The rest of Tom's set are capital good fellows but awful children. They talk nonsense and smut. I am quite as fond of the dear Kitten as ever but he has not enough power of character to be more than a pleasant affectionate boy. He never exerts my intellect or brain *in any way*—between his mind and mine there is no *intellectual friction to rouse me up*

* Dean Ireland's Scholarship of £50 a year. Subject: Classical learning and taste.

to talk or think, as I used when with you—especially on those dear rides through the greenwood: I ride a good deal now and the last day rode an awful brute which by a skilful back jump threw me on my head on Shotover. I escaped however unhurt and got home all safe.

The Dean comes sometimes and we talk Theology—but I usually ride by myself—and have got such new trousers —quite the dog! I have written a very foolish letter; it reads very rambling and absurd—but it is so delightful writing to you that I just put down whatever comes into my head.

Your letters are charming and the one from Sicily came with a scent of olive-gardens, blue skies and orange trees, that was like reading Theocritus in this grey climate.

Goodbye,

Ever dear boy,

Your affectionate friend OSCAR WILDE

I have a vacant page.

I won't write to you Theology—but I only say that for *you* to feel the fascination of Rome would to me be the greatest of pleasures: I think it would *settle* me.

And really to go to Rome with the bugbear of Formal logic on one's mind is quite as bad as to have the "Protestant jumps".

But I know you are keenly alive to beauty, and do try and see in the Church not man's hand only but also a little of God's.

20

TO WILLIAM WARD: LENT TERM 1877

My Dear Bouncer,

I sent you a long letter to the Poste Restante about a fortnight ago which I hope you got: I have been in for "the Ireland" and of course lost it: on six weeks reading I could not expect to get a prize for which men work two and three years. What stumped me was Philology on which they gave us a long paper: otherwise I did rather well: it is horrid receiving the awkward commiserations of most of the College. I shall not be sorry when Term ends: though I have only a year for Greats work: still I intend to reform and read hard if possible.

I am sorry to say that I will not see the Holy City this Easter at any rate: I have been elected for the St. Stephens Club and £42 is a lot to pay down on the nail—so I will go up to Town for a week and then to Bingham and then home. I am going first to see Newman at Birmingham, to burn my fingers a little more: do you remember young Wise of this place? he is awfully caught with the wiles of the Scarlet Woman and wrote to Newman about several things: and received the most charming letters back and invitations to come and see him: I am awfully keen for an interview not of course to argue, but merely to be in the presence of that divine man.

I will send you a long account of it: but perhaps my courage will fail, as I could hardly resist Newman I am afraid.

Oxford is much as usual and dining in Hall more horrid than ever: now of course Jupp and I are not on speaking terms, but when we were I gave him a great jar: the Caliban came into Hall beaming and sniggering and said "I'm very glad they've given the £15 Exhibition to *Jones*" (put in all the beastly pronunciation for yourself) so I maliciously said "What! the old Jugger got an exhibition! very hot indeed." He was *too sick* and said "not likely, I mean Wansborough Jones" to which I replied "I never knew there was such a fellow up here." Which confined Jupp to his gummy* bed for a day and prevented him dining in hall for two days.

* Archaic word for "sordid". O.E.D.

Some rather good demies have come up this Term, Fletcher an Eton fellow, and Armitage, who has the most Greek face I ever saw, and Broadbent: I have been doing my duty like a brick and keeping up the reputation of these rooms by breakfasts, lunches etc: however I find it is rather a bore and that one gains nothing from the conversation of any one. The Saturday before "the Ireland" I brought up the dear Kitten to Town and saw the old Masters, which brought out his little Popish tendencies very much.

Had afternoon tea with Frank Miles to meet Ronald Gower and his sister the Duchess of Westminster, who is the most fascinating, Circe-like, brilliant woman I have ever met in England: something too charming. Did I tell you that in consequence of Mark's late hours the Dean refused to let him take his degree? however he hopes to take it the boat race day.

Collins, Cooper and old Stewy are giving three dinners on three successive nights in town, for the Sports Race &c., and we are all going to them:

Our Varsity Sports have just been on and were much as usual with the exception of Bullock-Webster's running which is the most beautiful thing I ever saw. Usually running men are so ungraceful and stiff-legged and pigeon-breasted but he is lithe and exquisitely graceful and strides about *nine feet*—he is like a beautiful horse trotting, as regards his action:

I never saw anything like it: he and Stevenson ran a three mile race, he keeping behind Stevenson about a yard the whole time till the last quarter when he rushed in before him amid awful cheers and shouting: you will see in Naples two bronze statues of two Greek boys running quite like Webster:

We have had the Jugger down till we are very tired of him: he is coming up for all the summer term to coach (!) and give concerts.

I hope soon to get a long letter from you with all your Roman experiences in it.

Ever affectionately OSCAR WILDE

21

TO REGINALD HARDING: 2 APRIL 1877

Corfu.

Postcard.

I never went to Rome at all! What a changeable fellow you must think me but Mahaffy my old tutor carried me off to Greece with him to see Mykenae and Athens—I am awfully ashamed of myself but I could not help it and will take Rome on my way back. We went to Genoa, then to Ravenna and left Brindisi last night—catching sight of Greece at 5.30 this morning. We go tomorrow to Zante and land near Olympia and then ride through Arcadia to Mykenae—Write to Athens Poste Restante.

Love to Puss, OSCAR WILDE

22

TO REGINALD HARDING: MAY 1877

1 Merrion Square N.
Tuesday.

My dear Boy,

Thanks for your letter: I had made out the facts by a careful study of the statutes going up to Town, but it was comforting all the same to have it confirmed by such an authority as the School's Clerk.

I had a delightful time in town with Frank Miles and a lot of friends and came home on Friday: my Mother was of course awfully astonished to hear my news and very much disgusted with the wretched stupidity of our College Dons, while Mahaffy is *raging!* I never saw him so indignantly angry—he looks on it almost as an insult to himself.*

The weather is charming, Florrie† more lovely than ever, and I am going to give two lectures on Greece to the Alexandra College Girls here, so I am rapidly forgetting the Boeotian ἀναισθησία of Allen and the wretched time-serving of that old woman in petticoats, the Dean.

As I expected all my friends here refuse to believe my story and my brother who is down at Moytura at present writes me a letter marked *"Private"* to ask "what it *really* is all about and *why* I have been rusticated" treating my explanations as mere child's play.

I hope you will write and tell me all about the College, who is desecrating my rooms and what is the latest scandal.

When Dunskie comes tell him to write to me and remember me to Dick and Gussy and little Dunlop and everyone you like or I like.

Ever yours OSCAR

I am going down I hope for my May fishing soon but I am overwhelmed with business of all kinds.
Get *Aurora Leigh* by Mrs. Browning and read it carefully.

---

* O.W. went to Greece with Mahaffy in April 1877 and was a month late for his term when he returned. For this he was fined £45 and rusticated. The £45 was, however, returned to him when he took his first in Greats.
† Miss Florence Balcombe.

TO WILLIAM WARD: 19 JULY 1877

1 Merrion Square N.

Dear Old Boy,

I hear you are back: did you get my telegram at the Lord Warden? Do write and tell me about the Turks. I like their attitude towards life very much though it seems strange that the descendants of the wild Arabs should be the Sybarites of our day.

I sent you two Mags. to Frenchay*—one with a memoir of Keats, the other religious.

Do you remember your delightful visit to Keats's grave, and Dunskie's disgust. Poor Dunskie: I know he looks on me as a Renegade; still I have suffered very much for my Roman fever in mind and *pocket* and happiness.

I am going down to Connemara for a month or more next week to try and read. I have not opened a book yet I have been so bothered with business and other matters. I shall be quite alone—will you come? I will give you fishing and scenery—and bring your books—*and some Note books for me.*

I am in despair about 'Greats'.

It is roughing it you know but you will have

(1) bed
(2) table and chair
(3) knife and fork
(4) fishing
(5) scenery—sunsets—bathing—heather mountains—lakes.
(6) whisky and salmon to get. Write and say when you can come,

---

* A suburb of Bristol in which William Ward lived.

and also send me please *Immediately* the name and address of Miss Fletcher whom I rode with at Rome, and of her stepfather. I have never sent her some articles of [Walter] Pater's I promised her.

I want you to read my article on the Grosvenor Gallery in the Dublin University Magazine of July—my first art-essay.

I have had such delightful letters from many of the painters—and from Pater *such sympathetic praise*. I must send you his letters: or rather do so but return it in *registered letter* by next Post: don't forget.

Ever Yours OSCAR

After all I can't trust my letter from Pater to the mercies of the Postman but I send you a copy—

Dear Mr. Wilde,

Accept my best thanks for the Magazine and your letter. Your excellent article on the Grosvenor Gallery I read with very great pleasure: it makes me much wish to make your acquaintance, and I hope you will give me an early call on your return to Oxford.

I should much like to talk over some of the points with you, though on the whole I think your criticisms very just, and they are certainly very pleasantly expressed.

The article shows that you possess some beautiful, and, for your age, quite exceptionally cultivated tastes: and a considerable knowledge too of many beautiful things.

I hope you will write a great deal in time to come.

Very truly, Yours Walter Pater

You won't think me snobbish for sending you this? after all it *is* something to be honestly proud of.

O.F.W.

TO REGINALD HARDING: JULY 1877

1 Merrion Square N.

My dear Kitten,

Many thanks for your delightful letter—I am glad you are in the midst of beautiful scenery and *Aurora Leigh*.

I am very much down in spirits and depressed—a cousin of ours to whom we were all very much attached has just died—quite suddenly from some chill caught riding. I dined with him on Saturday and he was dead on Wednesday. My brother and I were always supposed to be his heirs but his will was an unpleasant surprise, like most wills.

He leaves my Father's Hospital about £8,000, my brother £2,000, and me £100 on condition of my being a Protestant!

He was, poor fellow, bigotedly intolerant of the Catholics and seeing me "on the brink" struck me out of his will. It is a terrible disappointment to me; you see I suffer a great deal from my Romish leanings, in pocket and mind.

My father had given him a share in my Fishing Lodge in Connemara, which of course ought to have reverted to me on his death; well, even this I lose "if I become a Roman Catholic for five years"—which is very infamous.

Fancy a man going before "God and the Eternal Silences" with his wretched Protestant prejudices and bigotry clinging still to him.

However, I won't bore you with myself any more—the world seems too much out of joint for me to set it right.

I send you a little notice of Keats' grave I have just written which may interest you. I visited it with Bouncer and Dunskie.

If you would care to see my views on the Grosvenor Gallery send for the enclosed—and write soon to me.

Ever yours, OSCAR WILDE

I heard from little Bouncer from Constantinople lately —
he said he was coming home—
Love to Puss.

25

TO REGINALD HARDING: AUGUST 1877

Illaunroe Lodge, Lough Fee.

My dear Kitten,

So glad to hear from you again.— I have been here fishing for the last three weeks; Jack Barrow and Dick Trench
are staying with me, so I find myself far from lonely—
which is unfortunate as far as reading goes.

The fishing has not been so good as usual—I only got
one salmon, about $7^1/_2$ lbs—the sea-trout however are very
plentiful; we get a steady average of over four a day and
lots of brown trout, so it is not difficult to amuse oneself
and as no fish are going in any of the neighbouring lakes
I am fairly pleased. I have become an awful misanthrope
however—you won't know me next term.

I had two jolly letters yesterday—one from Bouncer
who is quill-driving or going to! the other from Dunskie who
is a Captain now, he says. Did I tell you of my wonderful
letter from Pater of Brasenose about my "Grosvenor Gallery", which I am glad by the by you like. Pater gives me
great praise, so I am vainer than usual.

One week more of this delightful, heathery, mountainous, lake-filled region! Teeming with hares and trout!
Then to Longford for the partridge, then Home.

Love to Puss,

Yours OSCAR

Write to me at the Square.

26

TO REGINALD HARDING: 1877

Magdalen College, Oxford.
Tuesday.

My dear Kitten,

Many thanks for your kind note. I have a childish longing for some flowers—I don't care what—only *not* wallflowers. If you have any spare moments and can get me a few you will be doing as benevolent an action as giving groundsel to a starving canary would be!

I am very wretched and ill and as soon as possible I am to be sent away somewhere out of Oxford—so my Greats work has collapsed finally for ever.

Only that Tuckwell and William are awfully kind to me I should jump into the muddy Cherwell—.

Ever yours OSCAR

Would you steal a branch of that lovely red blossoming tree outside the new buildings for me? I am sick at heart for want of some freshness and beauty in life.—

27

TO WILLIAM WARD: AUTUMN 1877

Magdalen College, Oxford.
Monday.

My Dear Bouncer,

I hope you will come up soon: I am reading hard for a Fourth in Greats. (How are the mighty fallen!!)

I never remembered your kindness in lending me £5 in Rome till I met Grizell the other day. (Idea Association)

I hope you don't think me very careless. Please cash enclosed cheque—if your bankers think the name of Wilde still valid for £5.

How much do I owe you for the Greek rugs? I hope you will bring them with you.

Yours ever OSCAR WILDE

Dunskie talks of coming up on Saturday.

28

TO REGINALD HARDING: 1877

Magdalen College, Oxford.

Dear Kitten,

If there is anything that could console me for being ill it is your charming basket of flowers and delightful letter.

The roses have quite given me a sense of the swift beauty and light of the Spring—they are most exquisite.

And I heard your light quick step down the passage this morning and am awfully obliged for your theft of the pink and white blossoms.—

I can bury my face in them and dream how nice it would be to be out again.

You are the nicest of kittens.

Ever yours OSCAR

29

TO REGINALD HARDING: 1877

Magdalen College, Oxford.

Dear Boy,

You are in Chapel I suppose with a divine calm in your soul.—

The Doomed One is wretched at failure—and no tea.

Ever OSCAR

30

TO WILLIAM WARD: WINTER 1877—78

1 Merrion Square, Dublin.

My Dear Willie,

I am very sorry I cannot come down for your Ball, but I only go back to Oxford tomorrow, and much as I would like it I would not like to ask for leave—and indeed it would not be fair to Milner: it is a great disappointment to me but I don't think I would be acting wisely in going away from Oxford after I got leave to come up and read.

I hope that I will be able to come and see you in the Summer, after I get my 4th.

I find really that I can't read—I have too much to think about. Pray express to your mother how sorry I am to miss your kind invitation.

And believe very truly yours OSCAR

31

TO REGINALD HARDING: 1878

St. Stephen's Club, Westminster.

Dear Reggie,

I was only in Cambridge for the night with Oscar Browning (I wish he was *not* called Oscar) and left the next morning for the Hicks-Beach's in Hampshire, to kill time and pheasants and the ennui of not having set the world on fire as yet.

I will come some day and stay with you—though your letters are rather what boys call "philippic".—

I am going tonight with *Ruskin* to see Irving and Shylock—and afterwards to the *Millais* Ball—How odd it is.—

Dear Reg. ever your OSCAR

Remember me to Tom Peyton.

32

TO WILLIAM WARD: JUNE   1878

St. Stephen's Club, Westminster.
Thursday.

Dear Boy,

Why don't you write to me? I don't know what has become of you.

As for me I am ruined—the Law Suit is going against me and I am afraid I will have to pay costs—which means leaving Oxford and doing some horrid work to earn bread. The world is too much for me.

However, I have seen Greece and had some golden days of youth. I go back to Oxford immediately for viva voce and then think of rowing up the river to town with Frank Miles—will you come?

Yours, OSCAR

33

TO WILLIAM WARD: JULY   1878

Magdalen College, Oxford.

My Dear Old Boy,

You are the best of fellows to telegraph your con‐gratulations—there were none I valued more—it is too de‐lightful altogether this display of Fireworks at the end of my career. I cannot understand my First except for the essays which I was fairly good in. I got a very compli‐mentary viva voce.

The Dons are "astonied" beyond words—the Bad Boy doing so well in the end! They made me stay up for the Gaudy and said nice things about me. I am on the best terms with everyone including *Allen*!* who I think is remorseful of his treatment to me.

Then I rowed to Pangbourne with Frank Miles in a birch bark canoe! and shot rapids and did wonders everywhere—it was delightful.

I cannot, I am afraid, yacht with you. I am so troubled about my Law Suit—which I have won but find my own costs heavy—though I was allowed them. I have to be in Ireland.

Dear old boy I wish I could see you again.

Ever yours, OSCAR

*The Rev. W. D. Allen, M.A., Junior Bursar of Magdalen.

Oscar Wilde: An Oxford Reminiscence

BY W. W. WARD

ONE of my greatest friends at Oxford—certainly the most intimate during my last year—was Oscar Wilde. I should like those who come after me to know something of the charm of his companionship and conversation, to see him for a moment as he was in those far-off College days, a laughing but always an interesting personality.

How brilliant and radiant he could be! How playful and charming! How his moods varied and how he revelled in inconsistency! The whim of the moment he openly acknowledged as his dictator. One can see now, reading his character by the light of his later life, the beginnings of those tendencies which grew to his destruction. There was the love of pose, the desire for self-realisation, the egotism, but they seemed foibles rather than faults, and his frank regret or laugh at his own expense robbed them of blame and took away offence. I daresay we were a little dazzled by his directness and surprised by the unexpected angle from which he looked at things. There was something foreign to us, and inconsequential, in his modes of thought, just as there was a suspicion of a brogue in his pronunciation, and an unfamiliar turn in his phrasing. His qualities were not ordinary and we, his intimate friends, did not judge him by the ordinary standards. Of course there were many who disliked him, those whom he naturally offended by his unconventionality and whom he did not attempt to conciliate. But, speaking generally, I would say that during my last year at Magdalen he had gained a much larger amount of popularity than might have been expected. This, I think, may be accounted for partly by the fact that at that little College more importance was attached to social ability than to individual or athletic superiority. And certainly Oscar Wilde was socially distinguished. It was impossible to overlook him in any company of College men. He might be disliked by some as a poseur and as being conceited and affected, but he was a brilliant talker and said clever things and could, if he tried, make himself a pleasant companion to the ordinary undergraduate, and he had a reputation of being something out of the common. So, speaking of my own time, I would say that the College was proud of him and that though some disliked him he had a considerable circle outside his intimate friends with whom he was on very friendly terms. It may have been different afterwards. I believe that he became more exaggerated in his behaviour, his older friends went down, and his popularity declined, but I should say that in 1876 he had a few really intimate friends and a large number of friendships, in and out of College.

I have been reading lately a bundle of old letters written to me by him, during his undergraduate days at Oxford, and they show him as he lives in my memory, radiant and humorous, affectionate and natural. Much has been reported of him in the later years of his brilliant decadence, but I think that the following extracts from letters, written straight from the heart and fresh with the dew of youth, present him in an aspect which only few knew, and fewer still remember. They may, I think, at any rate, serve to exhibit something of the charm of his conversation and companionship, something of the gleam of his opalescent mind.

They show, too, that his final decision to find refuge in the Roman Church was not the sudden clutch of the drowning man at the plank in the shipwreck, but a return to a first love, a love rejected, it is true, or at least rejected in the tragic progress of his self-realisation, yet one that had haunted him from early days with a persistent spell.

One dim morning I remember well in my rooms at Magdalen when he and I and Hunter-Blair, a new and eager convert to Roman Catholicism, a man of singular enthuasism and vivacity, had talked through the short summer night till there was the sound of waking birds in the trees that fringe the Cherwell, and Oscar had hung, poised in a paradox, between doubt and dogma—I remember that Hunter-Blair suddenly hit him on the head and exclaimed: "You will be damned, you will be damned, for you see the light and will not follow it!" "And I?" I asked. "You will be saved by your invincible ignorance," was the reply.

[*Here follow numerous extracts from the letters published in full in Appendix A.*]

I dined with him sometimes at Romano's or at his mother's house, when he told me of his doings, how he had introduced Ruskin to Mrs. Langtry and so on. He came to stay with me at Frenchay and at Coombe, the last time was for a lecture which he gave at the Victoria Rooms, shortly before his American tour. And I remember looking in at his rooms off the Strand one morning on my way to Lincoln's Inn, when I found him still in bed and his sitting-room in great disorder. He explained that he had given a supper party the night before, at which Sarah Bernhardt had been present and that she had tried to see how high she could jump and write her name with a charcoal on the wall. From the scrawl on the side of the room and not much below the ceiling it seemed that she had attained considerable success in the attempt.

His was, to use the current phrase, the artistic temperament *in excelsis et profundis*. Money he wanted, no man more, for lack of it was an impediment, but to get it only after long and forced labour and at the price of lost liberty, this he thought was a sacrifice of ends to means. What is the use of the open door to the bird so long caged that its power of flight is gone? The drudgery of business, according to his view, made men not themselves, wearers of masks of which their faces by natural mimicry took the dull shape and lifeless likeness. Life itself was in his hands to be a work of art, he and the free and happy artist to give it shape and colour according to his idea and technique.

Later I saw him only fitfully for a few years, when I happened to be in London, and then, as our ways were more and more parted, all intimacy died out, and at length we never met and never corresponded. The last time I saw him was by accident, at the first night of a play written by Miss Fletcher, the lady referred to in his letters whose acquaintance we had made in Rome and whose gifts of intellect, and whose romantic engagement to Lord Wentworth—an engagement broken off by her—had attracted us both. But he—*Quantum mutatus ab illo!* The shadow of approaching disaster had already fallen upon him, to me at least he had lost all his old gaiety of nature and frankness of heart, his appearance seemed altered by something more than mere lapse of time. I am glad that but for that passing glimpse my recollections of him are confined to the bright and happy period of his early youth.

It is perhaps an idle thing to speculate upon the tragedy of his life. The law of *corruptio optimi* obtains, and he himself has told the story, in his own inimitable way, in *De Profundis*. I know that some say they detect in it the false ring of self-pity, the Neronian cry of *Qualis artifex pereo!* I hear no such note. Deliberately he had cultivated, as it seems to me, moods and feelings and appetites and states of thought so warring and so contradictory that at length the mould of sanity and self-control broke. He had made his mind a stage on which incongruous scenes continually shifted, across which strange characters, each the protagonist of the moment, passed and repassed in a carnival of mad confusion, while he himself sat, as he fondly thought, a passive spectator in the stalls and watched the play proceed—with appropriate emotions. He had turned his mind into a laboratory in which he might test his own experiences and he fell a victim to his own experiments. For the search on these lines, the γνῶθι σεαντόν—individualism—self realisation as he called it, was his Philosopher's Stone, or rather the Helen for whom he lost all. He disdained the role of a "creature moving about in worlds unrealised." Here was this wonderful and beautiful world on the one side and he—Oscar Wilde—on the other, and his vocation was to realise himself in it so far as in him lay, during the short span of human life. That was his creed from his youth up. Browning's *Dead Grammarian* view of life was the antipodes of his horizon. To him the "Now" was supreme, imperative, justified of all her children. The Heavens might fall, as they did for him, but the crash would find him unshaken in this belief. The two years in Reading Gaol did not destroy the major premise of his life—rather they confirmed it and gave it added scope. Boldly and consistently he maintained his thesis that self-realisation is the one pearl of great price, the beginning and the end of life worth living. His mistake had been, so he reasoned, that he sought it solely in pleasure.

Through the prison bars this new light broke. The long watches on the plank in the cell did their work, their gracious work. Wisdom through suffering, the heart bleeding through the black hours with pain and remorse, this is the stern mercy which the great poet tells us is forced on men against their will by throned and awful powers.

And so with a certain reverence he lifts to his lips the cup of bitterness; slowly he drains it to the dregs; drop by drop he rolls the wine of humiliation over his tongue to taste to the full its exquisite flavour; he becomes an epicure of suffering, an *arbiter miserarum*. He treads the thorns of his *Via Dolorosa* more vibrant with discriminative sensibility, more critically recordant than ever he walked down the Primrose Path to the sound of flutes. He passes through the prison gate as through a *janua vitae novae*, the same man bent on the same quest of self-realisation, but with wonder, as the discoverer of a new world and—what to him is still more important—of a new Self, voyaging on strange seas and under changed skies. *Insuetum miratur limen Olympi.* How long did this attitude of mind last? Ah! That is the hard question to ask and to answer. For the moment I am sure he was sincere, but I do not know and cannot tell and hardly dare to inquire.

In the spring of 1877 I was in Rome; Hunter-Blair was also there, and Oscar Wilde came out in the Easter Vacation and joined us. We used to go about a great deal together, riding on the Campagna with Miss Fletcher, who wrote under the name of George Fleming, making expeditions together and generally dining at some Italian Restaurant with Grissell and Ogilvie Fairlie—who were, like Hunter-Blair, Chamberlains to the Pope. Oscar Wilde all but embraced Catholicism. He was granted a private audience by Pius IX, wrote him, I think, a sonnet, which was graciously accepted; was welcomed in cultivated and interesting Roman society.

One day Hunter-Blair received as a present from a nameless donor an unmounted diamond, a very beautiful stone. He found it on his dressing-table; the gift was altogether mysterious, and we supposed that it had been sent to Hunter-Blair by some admirer, as he was a very attractive person and in every way one of Fortune's Favourites. Eventually he gave the stone to Ogilvie Fairlie, on condition that as soon as Oscar was converted it should be presented as a votive offering to the famous Madonna of the Church of St. Agostino. Years passed, and there seemed little chance that the condition would ever be fulfilled, and

indeed the stone was set and worn by the lady whom Fair
lie had married. But the great downfall came; the term of
imprisonment ended; soon ended, too, the short life of the
exile, and all the world read in the newspaper that Oscar
Wilde had died a Roman Catholic, having received on his
deathbed the full consolations of the Church. The diamond is now in the safe keeping of the monks of S.
Agostino, and is surely not the least precious of the votive
offerings that adorn that *Mater Amabilis* of Sansovino.

When I go to Rome, I visit that shrine. The last time
I was there, I saw stretched on the ground before the
beautiful and gracious face that looks down so pitifully, a
rough and rugged *contadino*, sobbing and praying in some
agony of soul. He, too, seemed like one who might be saying:

> Orribil furon li peccati miei,
> Ma la bontà infinita ha sì gran braccia
> Che prende ciò, che si rivolge a lei.
>   Dante, *Purgatorio*, III, 121–3.

Unpublished Poems in Prose [50]
Told by Oscar Wilde

THE POET

THE poet lived in the country amongst the meadows and the woods; but every morning he went into the great city which lay many miles away over the hills in the blue mist. And every evening he returned. And in the dusky twilight the children and the people would gather round him while he told them of all the wonderful things that he had seen that day in the woods, and by the river, and on the hill-tops.

He would tell them of how the little brown fauns peeped out at him from among the green leaves in the woodland.

He would tell them of the green-haired nereids who had risen out of the glassy lake, singing to him on their harps.

He would tell them also about the great centaur who met him on the hill-top, and had galloped off laughing in a cloud of dust

These, and many more wonderful things, did the poet tell the children and the people as they clustered round him every evening whilst the shadows grew thick and the grey twilight fell.

He told them marvellous tales of the wondrous things which his mind had created, for he was filled with beautiful fancies.

But one day the poet, returning from the great city through the wood, really did see the little brown fauns peering at him through the green leaves. And when he came to the lake the green-haired nereids did indeed rise from the glassy water and sang to him on their harps. And when he reached the hill-top a great centaur went galloping off in a cloud of dust and laughed.

On that evening when the people and the children gathered round him in the dim twilight to hear of all the wonderful things he had seen that day, the poet said to them: "I have nothing to tell you, for today, I have seen nothing"; for on that day, for the first time in his life, he had seen reality, and to a poet, fancy is reality, and reality is nothing.

THE ACTRESS

There was once a great actress. A woman who had achieved such triumphs that the whole world of art worshipped at her feet.

The incense of their worship had for many years filled her life and dimmed her eye for other things, so that she wished for nothing else.

The day came, however, when she met a man whom she loved with all her soul. Then all her art, and all her triumphs, and the clouds of incense were as nothing to her —love was her whole life. But even though this was so, the man she loved grew jealous—jealous of the public that the woman no longer cared for.

He asked her to give up her career and to leave the stage for ever. She did so easily, for she said: "Love is better than art, better than fame, better than life itself." And so she left the stage and all its triumphs gladly, and gave up her whole life to the man whom she loved.

Time rushed by, and the man's love grew steadily less and less, and the woman who had given up everything for it knew it, and the knowledge of it fell on her like a chill mist at evening, and wrapped her from head to foot in a grey shroud of despair. But she was a brave woman, and strong, and she looked the horror full in the face without flinching. She knew that she had reached the crisis of her life, the crisis on the issue of which her whole fate hung.

She saw the situation with a cruel, sharp clearness,

which cut into her heart. She had sacrificed her career to her love. And now that love was failing her. If she could not find means of reviving that light which was now fading away it would soon burn out altogether, she would be desolate in the midst of the ruins of her spoilt life.

And now, the woman who had been a great actress, realised that her art, instead of being a help and an inspiration to her in this darkest strait of her life, proved, on the contrary, a drawback and a hindrance. She missed the stage-manager's directions, and the author's ideas and words. Hitherto she had never done aught without them, every thought, every intonation, and well-nigh every gesture had been indicated to her, for such is the actor's art. And now when called upon to think and originate and act for herself she felt helpless and without resource, like a child might who was suddenly confronted with a great problem. But with every day that passed, the necessity for action, prompt and strong, imposed itself on her more and more. One day, whilst she was pacing to and fro with the feeling of wild despair which was within her increasing with every minute that passed, a man came to see her. He had been the manager of the theatre where she had acted in former days. He came to ask her to act a part at short notice in a new play. She refused. What had she to do with the stage, and with that false art which turned those who practised it into puppets, helpless puppets moved by strings which were in the hands of the stage-manager and the author?

Today she was face to face with a tragedy of real life, beside which all the mock sufferings on the stage were but as so much tinsel and cardboard. But the manager persisted, it meant money to him, and so he buzzed round her with the perseverance of a fly in autumn, who will not be beaten off.

Would she not at least read the play? To be rid of him she read it, and she found that the tragedy of the play was the tragedy of her life. The situation was the same, and a solution of the problem was given.

Fate had come to the actress's help in a stage-play. She would act it so as to master entirely every detail of the situation. And so she studied the part, and soon played it to a large audience. She acted with a fervour of genius which she had never surpassed during the whole of her career, and the applause that thundered from all sides was the irresistible homage paid by the hearts and souls of men to all-conquering genius.

When it was all over she returned home weary and half stupefied, with the cries and shouts of the multitude still ringing in her ears. She had given them her best, had poured the power and wonder of her soul at their feet. All that was left to her now was a sense of powerlessness and weakness. She arrived at her house weary and flower-laden. Suddenly she noticed the two places that were prepared at the supper table, and then remembered that tonight was to decide her fate. She had forgotten it till then. At that moment the man she had loved came in, and he said, "Am I in time?"

She looked at the clock and said, "You are in time; but you are just too late."

SIMON OF CYRENE

The old man sat with bowed head and patient back, while the futile recriminations of his angry wife beat about his ears.

Like an endless cascade splashed the full reiteration of her reproaches: "Senseless grey-beard, why did ye lose your time loitering on the way? Your father, and his father, and his father before him, all were keepers of the temple gate; and, had you been prompt when ye were sent for, ye would doubtless have been made keeper likewise. But now a readier man hath been chosen.

"Oh! most foolish old man who did prefer to loiter on the way, so that, forsooth, you might carry the cross for some young carpenter, a seditious criminal."

" 'Tis true," said the old man, "I met the young man who was to be crucified, and the centurion bade me carry his cross. And after that I had carried it to the top of the hill, I still lingered, because of the words which he spake, for he was sorely grieved, but with a grief which was not for himself, but for others, and the wonder of his words held me there, so that I forgot all things."

"Yes, in verity, you forgot all things, and the little sense you ever had, and so came too late to be made keeper of the temple gate! Are you not ashamed, to think that your father, and his father, and his father before him were all keepers of the gate of the Lord's house, and that their names are written thereon in letters of gold, which will be read by all men in times to come for ever and for aye? But thou, vain old dotard, alone of all thy kin, will never be heard of again, for who in all the world, when thou art dead, will ever hear the name of Simon of Cyrene?"

JEZEBEL

The Queen stood on her marble terrace gazing on the fair lands which lay far and wide around her palace. Her blood-red hair hung in thick braids on each side of her white face. She was wrapped from head to foot in a robe of woven gold, and long strands of emeralds coiled about her, flashing and glinting in the twilight like green snakes at play. Her long pale hands were circled with gems, and she looked like some marvellous idol in her gorgeous and deadly beauty.

She sighed a deep and heavy sigh, and Ahab the king said to her:

"Wherefore sighest thou, O Queen of Beauty? Is there aught in heaven or on earth which, lacking, thy heart cloth desire? Hast thou not all that gold can buy and that men can make with the labour of their hands? But if there be aught else that thy soul desireth, am I not here to give it to thee? For am I not thy slave, even though I be King of Syria?"

And the queen answered, and with slow and languid accents did she speak, as one who is wearied with a great weariness and stricken unto death with the satiety of fulfilled desires:

" 'Tis true, O King! that I have all that the earth can give, gems and gold and garments of Tyrian purple and woven silver, and marble palaces filled with slaves and dancing girls; all these are mine. Also have I rose gardens, and palm trees, and orange groves, where the scent lies heavy at noon.

"And the camels with their swinging tread ceaselessly cross the great desert, heavy laden with perfumes and treasures for my delight. And every man is my slave, for I am almighty in my beauty. Even thou, O King! doest bow before me unto the dust, and thou art Ahab, King of Syria.

"But at my palace gate there is a vineyard; the grass is green and the doves fly there, and it belongs to another; therefore do I sigh."

And Ahab said:

"Sigh not, O Jezebel! for most surely shalt thou have the vineyard where the grass is green and the doves do fly. It is the field of Naboth, my standard-bearer, and the friend of my bosom, for he hath twice saved my life in battle."

Then he sent for Naboth the Syrian.

Now Naboth was a youth of twenty years, and good to look upon as he stood before the King in all his strength and stature.

And the King said:

"The Queen cloth desire thy vineyard; I will therefore

cover it with gold pieces and with precious gems, which thou shalt take in the place of the land, or whatsoever else thou shalt appoint either in honours or in treasure that shalt thou have; for the Queen cloth desire thy vineyard."

But Naboth said:

"Nay, King, my vineyard was the vineyard of my fathers, their heritage to me, all that I have; and I may not part with it; nay, not for all the treasure upon the earth."

Then Jezebel, the Queen, spake, and her voice was low and soft, like unto the summer breeze at evening:

"Do not trouble him; the vineyard is his and should not be taken from him. Suffer him to go in peace."

And Ahab went forth and likewise Naboth.

But later in the day did Jezebel call for Naboth, and he stood before her. Then she said unto him:

"Come hither and seat thyself beside me on this throne of ivory and gold."

But Naboth said:

"Nay, Queen, that may I not do, for the throne of ivory and gold is the throne of Ahab, the King of Syria, and on it may no man sit beside thee, save only the King."

But the queen answered:

"I am Jezebel, the Queen, and I command thee to be seated."

And he sat beside her on the throne of ivory and gold. Then the Queen said to Naboth:

"Here is a drinking-cup carven from a single amethyst. Drink from it!"

But Naboth said:

"Nay, for it is the drinking-cup of Ahab, King of Syria, and from it should no man drink save the King alone."

But the queen answered:

"I am Jezebel, the Queen, and I command you to drink from it."

And he drank from the drinking-cup that was carven from a single amethyst. Then the Queen said to Naboth:

"I am very fair. There is none so fair on all the earth. Kiss me!"

But Naboth said:

"Thou art the wife of Ahab, the King of Syria; no man may kiss thee save only the King."

And the queen said:

"I am Jezebel, the Queen, and thou shalt kiss me."

And she twined her ivory arms around his neck, so that he could not go. And then she cried in a loud voice, saying:

"Ahab! Ahab!"

And the King did hear her, and coming, did see her lips on the lips of Naboth, and her ivory arms twined round his neck. And, mad with blind rage, he ran his spear through the body of Naboth the Syrian, who died and fell in his blood on the marble floor. And when the King saw the friend of his bosom lying in his blood, killed by his hand, his wrath left him and his heart was filled with remorse and his soul with anguish. And he cried out:

"Oh Naboth! my standard-bearer and friend of my bosom, who twice didst save my life in battle, have I with these hands indeed killed thee, and is the blood upon them indeed thy young heart's blood? Would that it were mine own, and that I were lying in my own blood where thou art now!"

And his grief ate into his very soul and his lamentations filled the air. But Jezebel, the Queen, smiled a strange, sweet smile and said, with her voice which was like the sighing of the summer breeze at evening, so low and soft was it:

"Nay, King, thy lamentations are foolish and thy tears are vain; rather shouldst thou laugh, for now the vineyard where the grass is green and where the doves fly is mine own.

Letters from Lord Alfred Douglas
referred to on page 193

Dear Mr. Holland,

I have been sent from America a copy of extracts from a letter written by you to a Mr. Gertz, who is bringing out a book about Frank Harris. You are quoted as saying (1) that Harris's book *The Life and Confessions of Oscar Wilde* contains the truth about my association with your father. May I point out that, firstly, you are in no position to judge on that point? You were a small child when the affair took place and you can have no personal knowledge of the matter; and, secondly, Harris himself has admitted that his story about me is untrue in almost every particular. It is true that he now tries to repudiate his withdrawal, but the fact remains that he admitted his lies (or errors, if you prefer so to call them) and that this admission was made chiefly on the strength of evidence as to money I gave your father on various occasions. This evidence is still available and can be produced at any moment.

You are also quoted as saying that Harris cannot come to England "for political reasons." But perhaps you do not even know that what prevents Harris from coming to England is nothing to do with politics. He is "wanted by the Police." There is at least one warrant for his arrest which would be put into force the moment he landed in England.

I pass over what you say about Ross, because although it is not true I can appreciate your feelings of loyalty towards him. There is no reason, on the other hand, why you should show loyalty to a blackguard like Harris, who robbed your father of his play *Mr. and Mrs. Daventry* and who was to a great extent the cause of his death, which was hastened, if not actually caused, by his rage and indignation against Harris. The full story of this episode has been written by Mr. Bell, who was Harris's private secretary at the time, and it is to be published shortly.

I feel very sorry that you should persist in carrying on a feud against me. I was your father's greatest friend and I was also a great friend of your mother's. I knew you as a child. The legend you have imbibed about me in relation to your father is almost entirely false. It is true that I attacked him in my book *Oscar Wilde and*

Myself, but I did it under frightful provocation, and I have now re-pudiated the book.

Could you not manage to get out of your mind the ill-feeling which you appear to cherish? I have only good feelings towards you.

Yours sincerely, ALFRED DOUGLAS

Luckily for me, I had kept a carbon copy of my letter to the American author. I promptly sent this carbon copy to Alfred Douglas, telling him, at the same time, that, so far as I was concerned, I had heard so many contradictory stories about my father and had read so many statements and retractions and repudiations, that I was seriously beginning to doubt whether any such person as Oscar Wilde ever existed! I added that I did not think that any meeting between him and me could serve any useful purpose since we seemed to be in such diametrically opposed camps, so far as Robert Ross was concerned. To this letter, Alfred Douglas replied as follows:

Dear Mr. Holland,

Thanks for your letter, which satisfactorily explains everything, as far as you are concerned. Gertz, however, by quoting fragments of your letter and dove-tailing them between comments of his own has succeeded in conveying the impression I complained of in my first letter to you; namely, that you are supporting Harris against me. Gertz, is as you say, an infernal nuisance. He pestered me with questions which ultimately I felt bound to answer in self-defence, because he gave me to understand that, if I did not answer, he would print Harris's lying version of the "Preface" affair uncontradicted. I might just as well not have answered him, for he has completely misrepresented everything, and his pro-Harris bias is obvious. However, this, of course, does not concern you in any way. The only thing I wish you would do *is* to write and tell him that you must not be quoted as appearing to uphold Harris against me. Your threat to injunct him in this country will not deter him from printing your letter in America, I fear.

There is only one thing in your letter to me to which I feel I must demur. You say "your own declarations upon several occasions have made it impossible for any friend of Ross's to be a friend of yours." But many of Ross's former friends are now friends of mine. For instance, Reggie Turner, who wrote me a touching letter about my autobiography, and Roy Kennard, who has been friendly with me since I saw him again in 1925. I could mention at least three other names. Several other friends of Ross's have changed their views since reading my book, although unacquainted with me. Your own case is different, I allow, though I cannot admit that I have ever done anything which ought properly to prevent your being friendly with me.

                              Yours sincerely, ALFRED DOUGLAS

I wrote to America as suggested, but I received no reply to my letter. In due course the proposed book on Harris appeared. It is such an amazing piece of effrontery that it might well have been written by Harris himself.

Stages of Public Opinion on Oscar Wilde's Works

IN this centenary year of Oscar Wilde's birth it seems appropriate to pass in rapid review the progressive stages by which public opinion has altered with regard to his works and his place in literature.

After the 1895 trials the press was unanimous in its condemnation of all Wilde's work, whether dramatic, poetic or critical.

The *Echo*, one of the leading London evening papers of the period, came out with the following on the afternoon of the verdict in the Queensberry libel action:

> And so a most miserable case is ended. Lord Queensberry is triumphant, and Mr. Oscar Wilde is "damned and done for." The best thing for everybody now is to forget all about Oscar Wilde, his perpetual posings, his aesthetical teachings and his theatrical productions. Let him go into silence, and be heard no more.

On the Monday following his conviction, the *Daily Telegraph* came out with a leading article, in the course of which it said:

> The man has now suffered the penalties of his career, and may well be allowed to pass from that platform of publicity which he loved into that limbo of disrepute and oblivion which is his due. The grave of contemptuous oblivion may rest on his foolish ostentation, his empty paradoxes, his incurable vanity.

At Portora Royal School, Wilde's name was removed from the "Honours Board."

In about 1933 the Headmaster of Portora Royal School, the Rev. E. G. Seale, restored the name of Oscar Wilde to the "Honours Board." And in September 1953 the Rev. D.

L. Graham, who was then Headmaster, wrote to me: "A portrait of Oscar Wilde now hangs in the school and we have from time to time produced his plays over the last thirty years."

In 1895 Oscar Wilde's books were withdrawn from circulation, his plays were withdrawn from the stage and thereafter the press was completely silent about him until the appearance of *The Ballad of Reading Gaol* in 1898.

As though this were not enough, publishers of obscene and salacious books, of the kind that are hawked around the Boulevards in Paris, began attributing their authorship to Oscar Wilde. This was particularly galling to my father's friends, because it was well known that he never used an obscene or even a vulgar word in anything he wrote or said.

To add to his humiliation, my father was made bankrupt shortly after he had begun to serve his sentence, and immediately shady publishers in England, France and America began re-printing his books and selling them openly, with a blatant disregard for the laws of copyright. There was nothing to prevent them from doing so. My father's literary estate was vested in the Official Receiver in Bankruptcy, who took the attitude that the works were of no value and that if people were foolish enough to waste time and money in printing them, they were at liberty to do so.

The Ballad of Reading Gaol itself was received with great caution by the Press, but favourable reviews appeared in both the *Daily Telegraph* and the *Echo,* both of which had heaped violent abuse on his work three years before. *The Times* ignored the poem completely.

On December 1st, 1900, the day after my father's death, *The Times* contained a long obituary notice of him, in the course of which his plays were praised in the words: "They were packed with witty sayings and the author's cleverness gave him at once a position in the dramatic world." But it goes on to say: "The revelations of the trial in 1895 naturally made them impossible for some years." Yet *The Importance of Being Earnest* was already being played in the English provinces.

In 1901, shortly after my father's death, Robert Ross applied to the Court of Bankruptcy to be appointed his literary executor. An official of the Court smiled tolerantly at him and assured him that "Wilde's works will never command any interest whatever." However, the application was granted, for what it was worth, and then began Ross's long struggle against literary pirates and the Official Receiver. Of this struggle Robbie said, in the course of the speech he made at the dinner given in his honour in 1908: "The laws of bankruptcy I confess never to have mastered. So far as I can make out the copyrights of an author in bankruptcy belong to everyone except his creditors, his family or his literary executor, for forty years or the temper of the Official Receiver, whichever lasts longer."

So well did Robert Ross's efforts succeed that by the middle of 1906 he had paid off the bankruptcy and had even satisfied in full all my father's French creditors, according to his last wishes.

By December 1901 *The Importance of Being Earnest*, which had been bought from the Official Receiver by George Alexander together with *Lady Windermere's Fan*, was revived at the Coronet Theatre, going to the St James's Theatre in 1902. This play has been revived about a dozen times in London since then.

In 1905 Robert Ross published part of the letter written by my father to Alfred Douglas, under the title of *De Profundis*. This was translated into all the principal languages in the world, and started a Wilde revival; and in 1908 his complete works were published by Methuen & Co. in a limited edition of one thousand copies which was over-subscribed before publication.

February 1st, 1910, was the twentieth anniversary of George Alexander's management of the St James's Theatre. A special performance of *The Importance of Being Earnest* was given on that occasion, and George Alexander gave each member of the audience a specially bound copy of the printed play.

In 1911, when the new Chelsea Town Hall was built, it was decided to decorate the Council Chamber with four mural paintings representing people famous in history, science, literature and art who lived in Chelsea. A competition was held among Chelsea artists for these murals, and the competitors were told whom they were to include. In the picture representing literature they were told to include Swift, Smollet, Carlyle, Leigh Hunt, St Evremonde, Oscar Wilde, George Eliot and Charles Kingsley. The picture chosen was one by George Woolway. There was some protest in the Chelsea Borough Council about the inclusion of Oscar Wilde, but it was brushed aside.

Between the two wars Oscar Wilde's plays and books were filmed and re-filmed and there were frequent stage revivals of all his plays, which became part of the stock-in-trade of Repertory and Amateur Theatrical Companies all over the world. At the beginning of the last war *The Importance of Being Earnest* started on a run which lasted for nine months, one of the longest revivals in the history of the English stage.

On April 11th, 1946, a special command performance of *The Importance of Being Earnest* in aid of King George's Pension Fund for Actors and Actresses took place at the Haymarket Theatre and was attended by King George VI, Queen Elizabeth and the two Royal Princesses.

On the occasion of the fiftieth anniversary of Oscar Wilde's death, in November 1950, *The Times Literary Supplement* devoted its first three pages to him and his works, summing up his place in English Literature.

In this year 1954, the centenary of Oscar Wilde's birth is being commemorated in a number of different ways in many different countries. The London County Council is putting a plaque on the house in Tite Street in which he lived. And, finally, a special display of manuscripts and books connected with Oscar Wilde was held this summer in the library of Trinity College, Dublin.[51]

Addenda and Corrigenda

[1] Pleasingly romantic idea though it may be that we were descended from a Dutch soldier of fortune who came to Ireland in the seventeenth century, there is sadly no evidence for it at all. The origins of the Wilde family name are to be found in an article on Sir William published in the *Dublin University Magazine* 85 (1875): 570–89, which, since it was published in his lifetime, may be assumed to be correct. Also Brian de Breffny writes on "The Paternal Ancestry of Oscar Wilde" in *The Irish Ancestor* 5 (1973): 96–9.

[2] Since the first publication of this book in 1954, several dozen biographies about Wilde have appeared. Most have trodden carefully around Sherard's inaccuracies and many have made extensive use of Wilde's *Letters* which were first published in 1962. A brief annotated bibliography follows these notes.

[3] Sir William in fact founded St Mark's Hospital in 1844 which was amalgamated with the National Eye and Ear Hospital in 1890 to become the Royal Victoria.

[4] Sir William can only be credited with the first of these works (1852); *Ancient Races* was a lecture delivered in 1874. Apart from this, outside the medical field he published *The Closing Years of Dean Swift's Life* (1849); *The Beauties of the Boyne and the Blackwater* (1849); *Lough Corrib* (1867); and his magnum opus, *A Descriptive Catalogue of the Antiquities in the Museum of the Royal Irish Academy* 3 vols (1857–62).

[5] Jane was born on 27 December 1821; see Richard Ellmann, *Oscar Wilde* (1987), p. 6.

[6] Wills was not given to Oscar at his christening; he adopted it later from his father.

[7] There is no evidence at all that this operation took place. It would undoubtedly have been referred to in the *Dublin University Magazine* article (see n. 1, above) if it had occurred. Enquiries at the Swedish Royal Archives, where details of such an operation would have been recorded, were without result.

[8] Willie, Oscar's elder brother, did not share the name Wills; he was christened William Charles Kingsbury.

[9] Vyvyan was christened Vyvyan Oscar Beresford; for his subsequent changes of name, see p. 76.

[10] Isola's full name was Isola Emily Francesca. She was born 2 April 1857 and died on 23 February 1867. An envelope decorated by Oscar and containing a lock of her hair was found among his possessions after his death in Paris in 1900.

[11] A more thoroughly researched and accurate biography was written in 1994 by Joy Melville.

[12] *For* Enniskill *read* Enniskillen.

[13] The drawing no longer exists. Wilde's rooms were converted into meeting rooms in the 1950s and the window was smashed during the course of some college festivity.

[14] Constance met Oscar for the first time in 1881. See *Letters of Oscar Wilde*, ed. Rupert Hart-Davis (1962), p. 152 n. 3.

[15] Charles Hemphill was a Liberal MP.

[16] My father's personal views on Frank Harris reflect the views of many who met him and they must stand as a personal appraisal. However, to dismiss Harris's *Life and Confessions of Oscar Wilde* (1916) as he does, is unfair. Like most of what Harris wrote, it pulled no punches and its totally frank treatment of Wilde's homosexuality was distasteful to many at the time.

[17] Wilde does mention Vyvyan by name in *De Profundis*, but ironically it is in the same sentence where he describes how Constance has taken the precaution of appointing a guardian for the two boys: "She has chosen Adrian Hope, a man of high birth and culture and fine character, her own cousin, whom you met once at Tite Street, and with him

Cyril and Vyvyan have a good chance of a beautiful future."
By contrast, see Vyvyan's remarks on pp. 149 and 200.

[18] Gladys Palmer later married the younger brother of the White Rajah of Sarawak and became the Dayang Muda of Sarawak. Her autobiography, *Relations and Complications* (1929), recalls the visits of the Wilde children.

[19] Most of the houses in Tite Street date from the 1870s and 1880s.

[20] The interior of the Wildes' house in Tite Street is also described in some detail by Otho Lloyd, Constance's brother, in *The Soil: A Magazine of Art* 1, no. 4 (April 1917): 149–56.

[21] See illustrations.

[22] G. P. Jacomb Hood, together with Walter Crane, did the illustrations for Oscar Wilde's *The Happy Prince and Other Stories*, which was published in 1888.

[23] A London County Council commemorative "blue plaque" was unveiled on 34 Tite Street by Sir Compton Mackenzie on the day this book was first published, 16 October 1954, the centenary of Wilde's birth. It states very simply: "Oscar Wilde wit and dramatist lived here".

[24] This song is an "aisling", or visionary poem, entitled "Tá mé in mo chodladh agus ná dúisigh mé", and dates from the eighteenth century. It is outspokenly anti-English in parts: "So rise up, my people, and take arms so that those knaves of Sasanaigh can be thrown back into the waves . . .", suggesting that Oscar is more likely to have heard it from his mother.

[25] Cyril's school was Bedales in Sussex, founded by J. H. Badley, with whom Oscar was acquainted. It was not, however, a preparatory school for the Navy.

[26] Wilde's first trial against the Crown ended on 1 May 1895 and he was not released on bail until 7 May. Half of the £5,000 was allowed to Wilde on his own recognizance; the remainder was guaranteed by Alfred Douglas's elder brother, Percy, and an unorthodox socialist Christian, the Rev. Stewart Headlam, who believed that Wilde was in

danger of being prejudged and wanted to help secure his release so he could prepare his case properly.

[27] Constance's loyalty in staying until the end of Wilde's final trial is evidenced by letters of support from her friends still writing to her in London at the end of May (MSS Holland).

[28] Some of the inscribed copies have since resurfaced in American collections. The sale, which realized about £300, included nearly 2,000 books, which were sold for £130.

[29] Constance returned to England on 18 September and visited Oscar in Wandsworth Prison three days later. She wrote about the experience to one of Wilde's friends, Robert Sherard: "It was indeed awful, more so than I had any conception it could be. I could not see him and I could not touch him. I scarcely spoke . . . He has been mad these last three years, and he says that if he saw Alfred Douglas he would kill him."

[30] On 19 February 1896 Constance made the second and last of her visits to Oscar in prison, this time at Reading where he had been moved the previous November.

[31] In fact, Vyvyan had his photograph taken when he was in Lausanne in the winter of 1904/5. It is reproduced here as one of the illustrations.

[32] My father's memory was slightly at fault here, as shown by Constance's letters of the time to her brother. They did spend holidays with the Blacker family but not at this time. Constance had already decided to send Vyvyan to Monaco and, presumably so that she could devote herself entirely to him for the Christmas holidays, she took Cyril to her brother Otho in Neuchâtel, going on with Vyvyan to Verona and hence to Monaco. She settled him in to the Collegio della Visitazione on 2 January 1896 and by 4 January was back in Nervi.

[33] *Intentions* was a collection of four of Wilde's essays published in 1891. Cyril and Vyvyan (as Vivian) appear in "The Decay of Lying".

[34] With characteristic modesty, Vyvyan omits to say that not only did he read Green's *Minuit*, but also translated it for its first publication in English in 1936.

[35] Wilde was released from Reading on the evening of 18 May and taken to Pentonville, from where he was released the following morning. The regulations of the day required prisoners to be released from the same prison in which they had originally been incarcerated and in this case it also helped to avoid the press. He was met by Stewart Headlam and More Adey and the same night was accompanied by Adey across the Channel. Ross and Turner met him off the boat in Dieppe the following day.

[36] Constance's allowance to Oscar of £150 was paid on condition that he did not keep the company of "disreputable persons". When, in September 1897, he decided to set up house again with "Bosie" Douglas in Naples, she stopped it but started it again after Oscar and Bosie parted at the end of the year. The allowance was continued after her death until Oscar's own death in 1900.

[37] The "friend" was Lord Alfred Douglas. Perhaps for similar reasons of discretion and of not wanting to put more emphasis than necessary on Wilde's homosexuality and imprisonment, at the end of the second paragraph of this letter my father suppressed the sentence: "It was an amusing experience as I am hardly more than a month out of gaol". Similarly on pp. 58–9 the reasons for Wilde's arrest and trial are carefully circumlocuted. Homosexuality was still something of a taboo subject in 1954 and it is a sobering thought to realize that it remained a crime until three months before my father's death in 1967.

[38] Constance died on 7 April 1898.

[39] *The Ballad of Reading Gaol* was published on 13 February 1898. Constance wrote to her brother on 19 February saying: "I am frightfully upset by this wonderful poem of Oscar's of which so far I have only seen extracts in the *Daily Chronicle* . . . it is fearfully tragic and makes one cry."

She later wrote to Carlos Blacker saying: "Have you seen his new poem? His publisher lately sent me a copy which I conclude came from him. Can you find this out for me and if you do see him tell him I think the *Ballad* exquisite."

[40] "Son of Oscar Wilde" now appears alongside Cyril's name in the *Radley Register*.

[41] See the letter that Wilde wrote in March 1899 to Robert Ross about this visit (*Letters*, p. 783).

[42] Oscar Wilde died in Paris on 30 November 1900.

[43] Dorothy "Dolly" Wilde was in fact born on 11 July 1895.

[44] The only surviving letter of any length from Oscar to Constance is at the Pierpont Morgan Library in New York. Its text is given in *Letters*, p. 165.

[45] The woman's name was Ruby Deane.

[46] *De Profundis* was published on 23 February 1905 and Vyvyan's diary entry is dated 7 February 1905.

[47] Oscar Wilde's body was moved from Bagneux to Père Lachaise on 20 July 1909.

[48] The 1949 edition of *De Profundis* which my father published from the typescript given to him by Robert Ross was later discovered to be neither complete nor accurate. It was not until the MS was released by the British Museum for public view in 1960 that an accurate transcript could be made. The text is reproduced in *Letters*, pp. 423–511

[49] The fully annotated versions of Wilde's letters to Harding and Ward can be found in *Letters*, pp. 11–53. The Harding letters are now in the Hyde Collection in New Jersey.

[50] There is some mystery surrounding the true provenance of these "Unpublished Poems in Prose" Aimée Lowther published them in a Florentine magazine called *The Mask* between January and October 1912, prefacing each with: "This story was told by Wilde to Miss Aimée Lowther when a child and written out by her. A few copies were privately printed but this is the first time it has been given to the public." The private printing ("five or

six copies") appears to have been done by the theatre historian and collector Mrs Gabrielle Enthoven, who also claimed to have written them down from memory. Both texts are almost word for word the same, suggesting a single origin, but which of the two women was the recorder it is impossible to say. See *Letters*, p. 802 n.

[51] Since the first publication of this book in 1954, Oscar Wilde has been publicly commemorated in several locations both in London and in Dublin. On 3 January 1995, the centenary of the first night of *An Ideal Husband*, an English Heritage plaque was unveiled by Sir John Gielgud at the Haymarket Theatre; on 6 February 1995 a plaque was unveiled by the Irish Minister for Arts, Michael D. Higgins, at 1 Merrion Square; on 15 February 1995, the centenary of the first night of *The Importance of Being Earnest*, a window dedicated to Wilde was unveiled in Westminster Abbey's Poets' Corner; on 28 October 1997 a polychrome statue of Wilde was unveiled in Merrion Square opposite the Wilde family home; and on 30 November 1998 a memorial sculpture, "A Conversation with Oscar Wilde" was unveiled in London's Adelaide Street.

Select Bibliography

Amor, Anne Clark. *Mrs Oscar Wilde: A Woman of Some Importance* (Sidgwick & Jackson, London, 1983).
Careful, well-researched life of Constance Wilde.

Coakley, Davis. *The Importance of Being Irish* (Town House, Dublin, 1994).
Gives Oscar's Irish background the prominence it deserves.

Douglas, Lord Alfred. *Oscar Wilde: A Summing-Up* (Duckworth, London, 1940).
Last and least biased look at Oscar by Bosie.

Ellmann, Richard. *Oscar Wilde* (Hamish Hamilton, London, 1987).
Most comprehensive biography to date but not without errors. See Schroeder, below.

Harris, Frank. *Oscar Wilde: His Life and Confessions* (Constable, London, 1938).
A colourful, often unreliable, occasionally sensational account by a close friend.

Hart-Davis, Rupert, ed. *The Letters of Oscar Wilde* (Hart-Davis, London, 1962).
Oscar in his own words – the correspondence encyclopaedically annotated.

Hart-Davis, Rupert, ed. *More Letters of Oscar Wilde* (John Murray, London, 1985).
Supplement to the above.

Hyde, H. Montgomery. *The Trials of Oscar Wilde* (William Hodge, London, 1948).
Verbatim account of the three trials.

Hyde, H. Montgomery. *Oscar Wilde: The Aftermath* (Methuen, London, 1963).
First detailed account of Wilde's last five years from imprisonment to death.

Kohl, Norbert. *Oscar Wilde: The Works of a Conformist Rebel* (Cambridge University Press, 1989).
In-depth textual criticism by a highly respected scholar.

Mason, Stuart. *Bibliography of Oscar Wilde* (T. Werner Laurie, London, [1914]).
A remarkable work full of biographical and other snippets. Occasional errors but still indispensable for early publications of Wilde's works. Contains valuable information on periodical publications, piracies, etc.

Melville, Joy. *Mother of Oscar* (John Murray, London, 1994).
Meticulously researched life of "Speranza" and her influence on her son.

Mikhail, E. H., (ed.) *Oscar Wilde: Interviews and Recollections* 2 vols (Macmillan, London, 1979).
First-hand recollections of Wilde.

Page, Norman. *An Oscar Wilde Chronology* (Macmillan, London, 1991).
Useful, detailed chronology of Wilde's life in 100 pages.

Pearson, Hesketh. *The Life of Oscar Wilde* (Methuen, London, 1946).
Still one of the best pre-Ellmann biographies.

Raby, Peter. *Oscar Wilde* (Cambridge University Press, 1988).
Concise, very readable insight into the works.

Schroeder, Horst. *Additions and Corrections to Ellmann's Oscar Wilde* (Braunschweig, 1989).
Corrects many slips made by Ellmann.

Sherard, Robert Harborough. *The Life of Oscar Wilde* (T. Werner Laurie, 1906).

Sherard, Robert Harborough. *The Real Oscar Wilde* (T. Werner Laurie, [1917]).
Wilde's first biographer and close friend. Full of first-hand anecdotes.

The Complete Works of Oscar Wilde (HarperCollins, 1994).
Most easily available "complete" Wilde with a selection of journalism, lectures,
etc.

Index